THE CINEMA OF SPAIN AND PORTUGAL

First published in Great Britain in 2005 by
Wallflower Press
4th Floor, 26 Shacklewell Lane, London E8 2EZ
www.wallflowerpress.co.uk

A catalogue for this book is available from the British Library

ISBN 1-904764-44-4 (paperback)
ISBN 1-904764-45-2 (hardback)

Printed by Antony Rowe Ltd., Chippenham, Wiltshire

THE CINEMA OF
SPAIN AND PORTUGAL

EDITED BY

ALBERTO MIRA

 WALLFLOWER PRESS LONDON & NEW YORK

24 FRAMES is a major new series focusing on national and regional cinemas from around the world. Rather than offering a 'best of' selection, the feature films and documentaries selected in each volume serve to highlight the specific elements of that territory's cinema, elucidating the historical and industrial context of production, the key genres and modes of representation, and foregrounding the work of the most important directors and their exemplary films. In taking an explicitly text-centred approach, the titles in this list offer 24 diverse entry-points into each national and regional cinema, and thus contribute to the appreciation of the rich traditions of global cinema.

Series Editors: Yoram Allon & Ian Haydn Smith

OTHER TITLES IN THE **24 FRAMES** SERIES:

THE CINEMA OF LATIN AMERICA *edited by Alberto Elena and Marina Díaz López*

THE CINEMA OF THE LOW COUNTRIES *edited by Ernest Mathijs*

THE CINEMA OF ITALY *edited by Giorgio Bertellini*

THE CINEMA OF JAPAN & KOREA *edited by Justin Bowyer*

THE CINEMA OF CENTRAL EUROPE *edited by Peter Hames*

FORTHCOMING TITLES:

THE CINEMA OF SCANDINAVIA *edited by Tytti Soila*

THE CINEMA OF BRITAIN & IRELAND *edited by Brian McFarlane*

THE CINEMA OF FRANCE *edited by Phil Powrie*

THE CINEMA OF CANADA *edited by Jerry White*

CONTENTS

NOTES ON CONTRIBUTORS

MARK ALLINSON is Professor of Spanish at Leicester University. His principal research interests are in modern and contemporary Spanish culture, particularly cinema, drama and subcultures, as well as other areas in European cinema. He is the author of *A Spanish Labyrinth: The Films of Pedro Almodóvar* (2001) (updated and translated into Spanish as *Un laberinto español: las películas de Pedro Almodóvar*, 2003).

ELENA CARRERA has taught at the universities of Zaragoza, Nottingham, Oxford and Birkbeck College, London and is currently Senior Lecturer at Oxford Brookes University, where she teaches cinema. She has published a number of articles and chapters on critical theory, women's writing and comparative literature. She is author of *Teresa of Avila's Autobiography: Authority, Power and the Self in Mid-Sixteenth-Century Spain* (2005).

PETER WILLIAM EVANS is Professor of Hispanic Studies at Queen Mary College, University of London, and has published extensively on Spanish literature and film. He is the editor of *Spanish Cinema: The Auteurist Tradition* (1999) and the author of a BFI 'Modern Classics' study of Pedro Almodovar's *Women on the Verge of a Nervous Breakdown* as well as a monograph on Buñuel: *The Films of Luis Buñuel: Subjectivity and Desire* (1995) and *Jamon jamon* (2004).

XON DE ROS is Senior Lecturer in Modern Spanish Studies at King's College London, where she teaches Spanish cinema and literature. She has published articles on film and literature in a number of collective volumes and journals. Her most recent publication is as co-editor (with Federico Bonaddio), *Crossing Fields in Modern Spanish Culture* (2003).

RANDAL JOHNSON is Professor of Brazilian Literature and Culture at UCLA. His research interests include Brazilian cinema, modern Brazilian literature, the sociology of literature and culture, and cultural policy. He is co-editor (wih Robert Stam) of *Brazilian Cinema* (1995) and author of *Cinema Novo x 5: Masters of Contemporary Brazilian Film* (1984) and *The Film Industry in Brazil: Culture and the State* (1987).

ANTONIO LÁZARO-REBOLL is Lecturer in Modern Spanish at the University of Kent. His main research interests include cultural studies, film studies and reception studies, and art-horror in Spanish visual culture. He has published on Spanish horror cinema in the 1960s and 1970s, and is co-editor (with Andy Willis) of *Spanish Popular Cinema* (2004) and (with Mark Jancovich, Julian Stringer and Andy Willis) of *Defining Cult Movies: The Cultural Politics of Oppositional Taste* (2003).

ALBERTO MIRA is Reader at Oxford Brookes University and a freelance writer. He teaches film theory and narrative and European cinema, as well as representations of gender in film and literature. He has written articles on Francoist cinema and Spanish film noir, as well as a number of books and articles on gender representation. His most recent publication is *De Sodoma a Chueca. Una historia cultural de la homosexualidad en España* (2004).

LÚCIA NAGIB is Centenary Professor of World Cinema at the Leeds University. Her books include *Werner Herzog: o cinema como realidade* (1991), *Em torno da nouvelle vague japonesa* (1994), *Nascido das cinzas: autor e sujeito nos filmes de Oshima* (1995) and *O cinema da retomada: depoimentos de 90 cineastas dos anos 90* (2002). She is the editor of *Ozu* (1990), *Mestre Mizoguchi* (1990) and *The New Brazilian Cinema* (2003).

CHRIS PERRIAM is Professor of Hispanic Studies at the University of Manchester, where he lectures on European cinema and Spanish cinema and literature. He has published on contemporary Spanish Cinema, especially in relation to Star Studies and queer writing in Spain. Among his most recent publications is *From Banderas to Bardem: Stars and Masculinities in Recent Spanish Cinema* (2003).

RYAN PROUT is Lecturer at the University of Cardiff, after a period as a research lecturer at Oxford University. His current research is focused on Spanish cinema and Cuban exile culture with publications forthcoming on films by Carlos Saura and Pedro Almodóvar. His recent publications includes 'Femme Foetal: The Triple Terror of the Young Basque Woman in Daniel Calparsoro's Pasajes', in *Contemporary Spanish Cultural Studies* (2000).

LISA SHAW is Senior Lecturer at Leeds University. Her teaching interests cover Portuguese language and translation, Brazilian popular culture (especially music and film), twentieth-century

Brazilian literature and Portuguese popular cinema. Among other projects, she has published *Popular Cinema in Brazil* and *Latin American Cinema: Essays on Modernity, Gender and National Identity* (both edited with Stephanie Dennison, 2004).

VICENTE SÁNCHEZ BIOSCA is Lecturer in Film Studies at the University of Valencia and editor of *Archivos de la Filmoteca*. He has worked on many areas of film history and general aesthetics, including avant-garde, postmodernism, theory of editing and German Expressionism. Among his publications are *Teoría del montaje cinematográfico* (1991), *NO-DO. El tiempo y la memoria* (with Rafael R. Tranche, 2000) and *Cine y Vanguardias artísticas* (2004).

AGUSTÍN SÁNCHEZ VIDAL is Professor of Art History and Cinema at the University of Zaragoza. He has published extensively on Spanish cinema, including monographs on Luis Buñuel, Florián Rey, Carlos Saura and José Luis Borau, and a key study of the relationship between Dali, Lorca and Buñuel: *Buñuel, Lorca, y Dalí: el enigma sin fin* (1988).

ISABEL SANTAOLALLA is Reader at Roehampton University, currently lecturing on Hispanic cultures and societies, as well as on Spanish cinema and media. She has published on contemporary Spanish Cinema, postcolonial theory and criticism, racial and ethnic minorities, cultural studies and gender studies. She is the author of *Los "otros": minorías étnicas y raciales en el cine español contemporáneo* (2005).

PAUL JULIAN SMITH is Head of Spanish at Cambridge University and teaches at the University of Stanford, California. He specialises in Hispanic literature and culture from the fifteenth century to the present day, especially Spanish and Mexican cinema. He is the author of *Laws of Desire* (1990) as well as a book on Pedro Almodóvar: *Desire Unlimited* (1995/2000). His most recent publications are *Contemporary Spanish Culture: TV, Fashion, Art and Film* (2003) and a BFI 'Modrn Classics' study of *Amores Perros* (2003).

PREFACE

The variety and originality of Iberian national cinemas is one of the great unexplored areas in European cultural history. Pushed into the southwest corner of the continent, predominantly rural and walled up by the Pyrinees, the evolution and influence of Spanish and Portuguese film traditions have been marginal to the main thrust of European cinemas. In spite of difficulties (competitivity, resources, and so on) Spanish cinema was extremely popular under the Second Spanish Republic (1931–36), helped by the spread of Spanish language on both sides of the Atlantic, and often their box-office returns exceeded those of American films. Also in Spain, militant cinema produced during the Civil War (1936–39) was the first experience of mass propaganda sound cinema, setting the pace for the kind of developments that would be explored elsewhere during the Second World War. In Portugal the *Cinema Novo* belongs in the avant-garde tradition of 'new cinemas' during the 1960s.

No doubt, the Franco and Salazar dictatorships contributed to the isolation of Iberian cultures for several decades, and strict censorship contributed to the restriction of freedom of expression in both countries. This did not keep dissident filmmakers such as Antonio Bardem, Luis García Berlanga, Carlos Saura or Víctor Erice (as well as the two incursions of Luis Buñuel in Spanish production) or the persevering Manoel de Oliveira in Portugal from making the kind of films that contested such limitations and even gained some degree of international prestige. In recent years, younger historians have been reassessing the more popular output in both countries. This volume within the *24 Frames* series, *The Cinema of Spain and Portugal*, balances both the artistically significant traditions and these lesser-known popular genres. Such films have tended to appear conventional or reactionary and have thus been recurrently ignored, but elements of originality or dissidence can be found in between the interstices of their images.

If Iberian cinemas have dealt with cosmopolitan genres, following traditions from Hollywood or Paris, as in other countries, they have also drawn from their specific cultural traditions the expressive force that gives exemplary quality to films such as Florián Rey's *La aldea maldita* (*The Cursed Village*), José Cottinelli Telmo's *A canção de Lisboa* (*Song of Lisbon*) or Benito Perojo's *La verbena de la paloma* (*Fair of the Dove*), all three represented in the present volume. Even the films pejoratively included under the label *españolada* (from the French *espagnolade*) have worked as the bedrock to put forward specific alternatives on national culture and identity. For instance, the frustrated nun of Buñuel's *Viridiana* could be considered as a character displaced from one such *españolada* seeking an alternative fate.

The arrival of democracy in both countries in the late 1970s allowed a rapid normalisation of Spanish and Portuguese film cultures, and in both cases they manifested their transgressive impulse (as in the case of João César Monteiro's *João de Deus* trilogy or Ívan Zulueta's *Arrebato*). The situation also encouraged the incorporation of many women as directors, contributing new approaches to the representation of reality.

Pedro Almodóvar is one of the directors who has best reworked national cultural roots. He took up the traditions of the picaresque novel, the short comic play known as *sainete*, latin melodramas of excess, and that grotesque satiric style called in Spain *esperpento*. The result is that such national distillation has achieved extraordinary international acceptance. Even the films starring the police inspector Torrente, paradigm of the most successful characters in Spanish popular film, constitutes a reflection of the country's identity as it inscribes in a national tradition of 'bad taste' popular theatre and literature (cultivated, for instance by painters like Gutiérrez Solana or some counter-cultural magazines such as *El Víbora*), and trash 'B' comedies of the late 1960s.

Iberian cinema is here thus revealed as a many-faceted prism of singular richness that deserves and rewards, for its diversity and the originality of many of its products, worthy of close study that holds many surprises in store.

Román Gubern

Barcelona

February 2005

INTRODUCTION

Iberian national cinemas show a particular historical evolution which is the result of the specific contexts for the production, reception and assessment of film, but traditional proposals for national canons did not tend, until well into the 1990s, to reflect this evolution. In particular, academic studies were reluctant to deal with cinema as popular entertainment as a result of the emphasis placed on its social and political values by intellectuals brought up in a tradition of anti-dictatorship ideology. This anthology proposes to discuss popular genres (melodramas, comedies, musicals) as well as the conventionally canonical one, represented by well-known directors such as Manoel de Oliveira, Juan Antonio Bardem, Luis García Berlanga and Carlos Saura. Twenty-four films have been selected from both countries' traditions, emphasising evolution and variety rather than quality or aesthetic innovation alone. The focus for this introduction and, indeed, for the selection overall is strongly on the Spanish tradition: this is not a derogatory comment on the richness of Portuguese cinema, just a reflection of the differences in production output. We hope that the issues dealt with in the contributions in this volume trace a historical line that will necessarily be incomplete but is nevertheless a representative entry point to Iberian cinematic traditions.

In the following pages, we will outline the historical contexts in which different strands within such national cinemas developed and subsequently attempt an outline of canon-making ideologies, based on those contexts. In particular, we will single out a number of shaping influences for both cinematographies: the battle with Hollywood products at the box office and the perceived need for protectionist measures, together with the exclusion of the popular from authoritative canons have determined a certain shape to Iberian cinema histories. Politically, both countries seemed to follow parallel evolution from the 1930s onwards: they went through a period of political unrest that ended up in dictatorship (Salazar in Portugal fom 1926 to 1974, Franco in Spain from 1939 to 1975) and then transition into democracy; stabilisation of democratic regimes brought about new challenges (and a new found permisiveness), along with full integration in Europe.

Portuguese authorities did not show any interest in cinema during the silent period; Salazar's regime only introduced substantial legislation to encourage film production in 1948, but it was never applied with any efficiency or produced substantial results. Spain had a pre-dictatorship sound cinema during the Second Republic, between 1931 and 1936, although the Republican government's interest focused mainly on censorship and issues of safety until the 1940s. Republican cinema brought in populism and a certain cosmopolitan outlook (represented especially by the work of Benito Perojo, whose *La verbena de la paloma* [*The Fair of the Dove*, 1935] is analysed in this volume) to replace the traditional silent films in the mould of Florián Rey's *La aldea maldita* (*The Cursed Village*, 1930).

It is the same populist approach that one finds in Portuguese films like José Cotilleni Telmo's *Canção de Lisboa* (*Song of Lisbon*, 1933) and Oliveira's first feature film, *Aniki-Bóbó* (1942). The reduced size of its film industry (an average of about eight films a year until the 1990s – some films are produced but never, or only belatedly, released in cinemas; a crisis in the 1950s that threatened the very existence of commercial cinema) is the key to understanding the way certain traditions have become canonical: until the 1960s, Lisbon comedy and documentaries accounted for the majority of films; otherwise, something resembling a classic golden age came in the late 1930s and the 1940s.

The establishment of a right-wing dictatorship in Spain from 1939 (after a *coup d'etat* and a Civil War) saw the start of a period of political and economic isolation (known as *autarquía*, 'autarky') in which the film industry thrived in spite of periodic crises. The key film production company was the Cifesa studios, which attempted to copy the Hollywood production system on a modest scale. Autarky (which lasted until the early 1950s) also meant that national culture became intensely xenophobic and reactionary (as exemplified with such films as Antonio Román's *Los últimos de Filipinas* [*Last Stand in the Philippines*, 1945]), but soon the need of opening up to foreign markets forced changes in the view of history and international relations (a change that is felt as soon as 1952 in Luis Lucia's *Lola la Piconera* [*Lola the Coalgirl*]). Portuguese institutions also encouraged, in spite of more limited means and a less active industry, the same kind of patriotic cinema (given a distrust of social cinema, based on its potential for political dissidence) in which a heroic version of the country's history was illustrated (as exemplified in such films as Leitão de Barros' *Camões* (1946) or Rafael Gil and Aníbal Contreiras' *Rainha Santa* (*Reina Santa*, 1947).

Clearly, in both countries, the notion of national cinema was being put into practice according to an idealised interpretation of the phrase: the nation was represented 'as it should be' (concealing poverty, political repression and corruption), and such a view was encouraged by both regimes until the very end. It also contributed to a number of ardent, Catholicinflected films such as Ladislao Vajda's *Marcelino Pan y Vino* (*The Miracle of Marcelino*, 1955).

Censorship has been central in influencing the themes and practice of Iberian cinemas, although it has been argued that there were ways in which obstacles could be circumvented. Sometimes, however, state organisms just failed to exercise any right to control. The Portuguese *Estado Novo* ('New State') financed a number of challenging films like Fernando Lopes' *Uma Abelha na Chuva* (*A Bee in the Rain*, 1972). In Spain, films like Luis María Delgado's *Diferente* (*Different*, 1961), which presents a (for the time) neutral portrait of a homosexual, unrelated to official guidelines on the subject, slipped through the censors and even received official awards. Until the early 1950s, censorship criteria were extremely unclear: the Church and several political factions within Francoism, together with censors' personal tastes, all contributed to this confusion. Given that every script had to be submitted to censorship committees, filmmakers never proposed narratives that could be deemed controversial from any point of view, and for a long time such self-censorship seemed to be enough. The first clear guidelines were issued in 1963 (following the disappearance of strict censorship in the US), and even at that point these were disappointingly narrow in terms of what was allowed.

It has to be said that, until the 1955 Conversaciones de Salamanca (a conference of representatives of the film industry aiming to tackle the problems of Spanish cinema) encouraged a new generation of filmmakers in Spain, there were few attempts to make films critical of the regime. Things became more complicated as political dissidence increased in the late 1950s. In Portugal, a number of directors worked on innovative films that questioned, aesthetically and ideologically, the political *status quo*. Critiques of the system were constructed through the use of codes (in terms of subject matter or film technique) that only a few members of the audience, familiarised with these, would be able to understand.

One of the issues to bear in mind is that the censors were, as is often the case, far from insightful readers of film. If these elements were conveniently disguised, they would not be able to interpret them. What this means is that, on the one hand, ambiguity became automatically suspect for the censors, but also that the 'art film' was seldom able to be understood by substantial audiences and consequently the gap between art and commerce widened.

As noted in passing, the mid-1950s became a period of crisis for film production in Portugal: the year television was introduced in the country (1955), no films were produced at all. In Spain, the need to become part of the Western market system ensured a strong influence from Hollywood and made possible a more popular cinema, to be followed from the late fifties by popular comedies and musicals (Juan de Orduña's *El último cuplé* [*The Last Torch Song*, 1957] remains among the most representative hits of the period). Some of these (like Pedro Lazaga's *La ciudad no es para mí* [*City Life is Not For Me*, 1966], starring Paco Martínez Soria) were, until the late 1990s, among the most popular films in Spain. The country was becoming more receptive to international trends. One theme recurrently developed in many of the most popular films was the way progress was eroding the backward but essentially good Spanish character, with roots in rural culture. A satire of this idea can be found in Fernando Fernán Gómez's *El extraño viaje* (*Strange Journey*, 1964). The late 1960s brought in a series of timid issue-led films (a series known as 'Tercera via' [Third Way]), which also dealt with the effects of progress on the habits of the Spanish (particularly regarding sexual behaviour).

At the same time, two parallel traditions (known as *Cinema Novo* and *Nuevo Cine Español*) of political dissent gave rise to a generation of young filmmakers, aware of and sensitive to contemporary trends in European filmmaking; Antonioni and neorealism were the main models in Spain, the *nouvelle vague* in Portugal. The sense of unease reflected in Bardem's *Calle Mayor* (*Main Street*, 1956) is an example of how Spanish cinema began to address social issues.

Similarly, New Portuguese Cinema directors voiced dissent mostly through the documentary. Feature films also subtly questioned the foundations of the Salazar regime and by the early 1960s the influence of avant-garde movements taking inspiration from the *nouvelle vague* can be clearly perceived. Some of these tended to make proficient use of images and metaphorical motives, pregnant with meaning that questioned the truths of the regime and reflected an alternative perspective. The Cunha Telles production company specialised in more radical films. Examples are Fernando Lopes' *Belarmino* (1964), Carlos Vilardebó's *As Ilhas Encantadas* (1964) and António da Cunha Telles' *O cerco* (*The Circle*, 1970).

For decades, the Spanish film canon was made up of instances of such non-mainstream filmmaking, which was unrepresentative of the industry at large. Examples included in this volume are Luis Buñuel's *Viridiana* (1961), Víctor Erice's *El espíritu de la colmena* (*Spirit of the Beehive*, 1974) and Carlos Saura's *Cría Cuervos* (*Raise Ravens*, 1975), often leaning towards social realism. Berlangas *El verdugo* (*The Executioner*, 1963) and Fernán Gómez's *Strange Journey* are often included in this tradition, although their inspiration does not lie primarily in socially-aware conscience or the artistic avant-garde but in earthier popular Spanish traditions with a strong element of humour and irony.

On the other hand, it is worth noting that, for instance, not all cinema made under Franco or Salazar can be easily pigeonholed as 'pro-' or 'anti-'regime. A number of films could be said to be indifferent to the ideological programme of the period and can in fact be read without reference to the political context. Melodramas by Manuel Mur Oti are an example of this. There were indeed pressures that affected plot and the use of certain images, but they had much in common with other instances of the genre being made elsewhere.

In the mid-1970s, both countries underwent a period of political transition bringing freedom of political expression (film censorship was repealed in 1977 in Spain and in 1974 in Portugal), but this freedom also gave rise to audience expectations in the desire to see what had hitherto been forbidden. What had been until then taboo subjects (mostly sex, specific periods of history and politics, as exemplified by Eloy de la Iglesia's *El diputado* [*Confessions of a Congressman*, 1978]) were now given free rein, but this did not necessarily make for substantial filmmaking, although it temporarily made for an increase in production and box-office takings. At the same time, films like Iván Zulueta's *Arrebato* (*Rapture*, 1980) and the early Pedro Almodóvar comedies introduced a sense of pop modernity and experimentalism that moved away from the usual notion of the 'quality film'. In spite of the boom provoked by 'destape' films ('nudies') and a popular strand of cheap genre productions (this was the case of Paul Naschy, star of dozens of films, such as León Klimosky's *La noche de Walpurgis* [*Shadow of the Werewolf*, 1970]), the Spanish film industry remained weak and in need of official support.

In Spain, the introduction of a system to encourage a specific notion of quality film during the mid-1980s (basically 'less but better' films) made up for well-received literary adaptations (like Mario Camus' *Los Santos Inocentes* [*The Holy Innocents*, 1984]) and, as the gloominess of the past was left behind, brighter films that had a historical background (such as Fernando Trueba's *Belle Epoque* [1992]), but did not help to revitalise the industry as a whole. In Portugal, the end of Salazar's dictatorship also brought winds of change to filmmaking along similar lines (intervention in cinema, political films), although audiences were less responsive. João César Monteiro's *João de Deus* trilogy (1989/95/98) is a late example of this tradition.

From the late 1980s onwards, these funding formulas were regarded as inefficient and the emphasis was on encouraging new directors and ensuring Spanish films were exhibited. It was a period in which the art tradition remained strong (exemplified by Julio Medem's *Lucía y el sexo* [*Sex and Lucia*, 2001] in Spain or Oliveira's *Viagem ao Princípio do mundo* [*Journey to the Beginning of the World*, 1997] in Portugal) and box-office hits (such as the *Torrente* films [1998/2002], directed by Santiago Segura, and Pedro Almodóvar's *Todo sobre mi madre* [*All About My Mother*, 1999]) opened up new commercial possibilities, but these are the exception to a situation of chronic crisis that seems to be overcome at certain periods (in a small industry box-office success of single films such as *Torrente 2* have a huge impact on the year's balance).

In terms of competitivity and protection of indigenous film industries, even if Spaniards (and, to a lesser extent, the Portuguese) were traditionally a cinema-going nation, this did not suffice to keep their own film industry afloat. One of the key shaping aspects of Iberian cinemas has been their situation of competition with Hollywood, which has led, directly or indirectly, to weak industrial structures. In spite of high potential numbers for audiences, Iberian film retains a chronic image problem.

As Spanish writer Antonio Muñoz Molina suggests in a text which reminisces on cinema attendance, Spanish (popular) film seemed to be regarded in terms of genre, and an unattractive one at that. There was always a feeling of something missing in Spanish films. Or rather, Spanish audiences had been taught to appreciate elements (technical exhibitionism, specific genres, certain star personae) which were felt to be exclusive to American film. The fact that Spanish films dealt with realities and social types closer to audiences seemed to have little attraction. In consequence, until well into the 1980s, Spanish film did not in general achieve good results, and the very label 'Spanish cinema' seemed to work as box-office poison. Whereas a whole genre of unambitious low-budget comedies (known as 'subproductos') by Pedro Lazaga or Mariano Ozores tended to do very well (mostly because they were cheap to produce), audiences seemed reluctant to confess such tastes. Being told by critics that these films were aesthetically execrable and politically incorrect, and with no effort to recuperate any of their pleasures (or even develop their potentialities), the Ozores formula was something of an embarrassment for anybody with any intellectual credentials. One of the outcomes was that the notion of solid entertainment as a middle point between art and trash had no place in critical discussions. Films, for critics brought up with the left-wing ideas of the 1960s and the 1970s, were either profound or worthless. One could argue that 'New' cinemas attempted to erase genres and attitudes of the past, but also eroded a budding film industry in Spain. On the other hand, the 'social realism' and metaphorical films favoured by critics and the institutions were not exactly popular. For Luis García Berlanga, the Salamanca Conference of 1955, with its emphasis on the social and its rejection of the popular had a negative impact on Spanish film in general: as Antonio Gómez Rufo has written, intellectual cinema, no matter how good or ideologically correct, could never be attractive to audiences large enough to support a stable industry.

Unavoidably, protection of national cinema was regarded as a necessity by the same intellectuals who were reluctant to support popular genre formulas as well as by the authorities who felt the impact of the Hollywood product on audiences and the industry. In order to encourage production of quality films, a number of measures have been adopted throughout Spanish cinema history.

The post-Civil War government was the first to show an interest in the film industry, introducing a number of regulations aimed at encouraging film production and maintaining ideological purity. A number of measures were implemented to reinforce the chances for success of national film, and charging for the exhibition of American films was the most immediate one. Hollywood cinema was what Spanish audiences mostly wanted to see, so at least the government could use a form of indirect taxation to make it less profitable for these films to reap high benefits.

Other such measures were in line with the ideological programme of Francoism and had a detrimental effect, such as the obligation, introduced in 1941, to dub every film to be exhibited in Spain. When this was repealed in 1946, audiences were used to dubbing and it was impossible to revert to the old situation. Portugal did not introduce such legislation and results were not encouraging either: people still preferred Hollywood products and tended to reject films in their own language.

Another set of protection measures aimed to encourage industrial growth, such as the obligation for exhibitors to show a certain number of Spanish films and the support of production in terms of grants and other rewards. In Portugal, with an output too low to keep any exhibition quota, the obligation to show a Portuguese short before every show had a similar effect. The granting of licenses to import foreign films was also linked to film production: the more Spanish films produced, the more foreign films distributors were allowed to import. But this approach to protection had a downside. What producers actually wanted was to achieve those licenses, which meant they did not have to concern themselves with quality. And, in fact, cheap and unambitious production in Spain was being used to support exhibition of Hollywood products, which remained more competitive and attractive to audiences.

A third group of measures for the protection of Spanish cinema introduced a series of rewards and subsidies aimed at improving the quality of films. One way of doing this was to grant extra import licenses for films the regime regarded as favouring the so-called 'national spirit' in early Francoism. This led to the imposition of quality parameters that had nothing to do with aesthetic or cinematic criteria, but political ones and continued during 'the Transition' from the mid-1970s onwards. The Pilar Miró legislation in the 1980s, for instance, tended to favour historical films and literary adaptations as signposts of cinematic respectability. In

Portugal, funding from the Gulbenkian Foundation was similarly used to encourage quality filmmaking.

The consequence of such systems of funding for the protection of cinema has been a link between the ideologies the government in power wished to promote at the time and the ideologies of the films produced under that government. For instance, the winners of the war tried to impose an image of Spain based on reactionary ideologies of political unity (thus stifling expression of nationalism within the country), masculinity (women were relegated to the domestic sphere) and Catholicism (religion became imposed and helped to articulate laws). Filmmakers not following these guidelines could still succeed (Berlanga and Almodóvar are two examples of this under widely different conditions), but only with greater difficulty.

In returning to the films themselves and their place in cinematic histories, given that the notion of the canon is interlinked with notions of the national, it is to be expected that ambiguities and discontinuities attending the notion of Spain are reflected in canon-making processes. Comparison between two representative surveys carried out among professionals to produce a list of the best films of Spanish cinema show how little attitudes changed between 1976 and 1995. Among the five first titles, three appear in both lists: *The Executioner* (first place in 1976 and 1995), *Spirit of the Beehive* (second and third, respectively), and *Viridiana* (fourth and second). The 1976 list in *Reseña* is almost completely made up of titles within the New Spanish Cinema tradition, reflecting the attitudes of intellectuals in the early post-Franco period. No 'popular' films, although some off-beat box-office hits are included (Berlanga's *¡Bienvenido Mister Marshall!* [*Welcome Mr Marshall!*, 1952] comes third). Twenty years later, the general attitude among the voters had hardly changed. No post-1975 film makes it to the top five in the 1995 list, and only two are in the top ten: *The Holy Innocents* and Víctor Erice's *El Sur* (*The South*, 1981) (the latter clearly reproducing stylemes of the New Spanish Cinema). Four other films made after Franco's death make the top\-twenty cut: Almodóvar's *Qué he hecho yo para merecer esto?* (*What Have I Done to Deserve This?*, 1984), José Luis Garci's *El Crack* (*The Crack*, 1981) and *Canción de cuna* (*Cradle Song*, 1994) and *Belle Epoque*. The religious melodrama *The Miracle of Marcelino* (number thirty-one), *Mi tío Jacinto* (*Uncle Hyacynth*, also directed by Ladislao Vajda, 1956) and José María Forqué's comedy *Atraco a las tres* (*Hold-up at Three*, 1962) (number thirty-three) are the only representatives of popular cinema under Franco in the first forty places. This suggests a reluctance to revise the Spanish cinematic canon; in particular, there is a bias against comedy and against popular film in general, especially those made before 1975, supposedly contaminated by the regime.

When anti-Francoism became hegemonic in the late 1970s, it was only a confirmation of the centrality the regime would still keep for a whole decade: until the mid-1980s, the only acceptable Spanish films were the ones made 'against Franco'. A certain version of the Spanish film canon based on New Spanish Cinema was thus almost inescapable for decades, and was systematically reflected, for instance, in critics' choices for programming at festivals, in books aimed at popular readers, in academic research projects, and so on. In other words, film history in Spain until the mid-1990s was written using criteria that ignored approaches that would have been relevant should these films have been made in other traditions; political positioning was the main criterion.

Of course, such selection was problematic. Operating as it was through political criteria, it remained blind to the more than evident pleasures of some films whose only fault was to be made without taking a stance in political clashes. One such film was Mur Oti's *Cielo negro* (*Black Sky*, 1951). In the use of conventions of melodrama, in terms the complexity of *mise-en-scène*, *Black Sky* is the equal to a number of Hollywood classic genre pieces of the period. But the fact that it was not made by a 'dissident' filmmaker means that is has been marginalised from the history of Spanish film.

The list of Spanish films worth seeing was thus reduced to a number of directors, regarded as real 'auteurs', who made films in opposition to or on the margins of the Francoist regime. Buñuel, Berlanga, Bardem, Saura, Erice and José Luis Borau set the standard for Spanish films worth studying and were represented as constituting the backbone of Spanish film history. There is a certain lack of variety in terms of genre and perspective in that list, and many trends in Spanish film (horror, sex comedy, musical) are completely unrepresented. Whole genres and some innovative films were ignored, notwithstanding their originality, inventiveness and substance. There is a fascinating tradition of little-known Spanish cinema that only rarely makes it to textbooks or cinematheque programming. Snappy musicals like *Fair of the Dove* or *Different*, excellent melodramas, such as *Condenados* (*Condemned*) and *Orgullo* (*Pride*) (both directed by Mur Oti in 1953 and 1955 respectively), fairytales such as *The Miracle of Marcelino* or thrillers such as Vajda's *El Cebo* (*It Happened in Broad Daylight*, 1958) together with experimental films such as Lorenzo Llobet Gracia's *Vida en Sombras* (*Life in Shadows*, 1952) or even Zulueta's *Rapture*, to give just a handful of examples, tended to go unnoticed, remaining strictly uncanonical, as if ancillary to the mainstream.

In particular there is a resistance to the popular that has to be counterbalanced in any representative selection of Spanish films. Traditionally, the films starring actors such as Alfredo

Landa, Paco Martínez Soria, Manolo Escobar, Gracita Morales and Lina Morgan were critically maligned as intrinsically reactionary. Of course such accusations can hardly be countered. But it is less clear that this has to prevent them from any consideration as cinema. Fortunately, the situation changed in the late 1990s, and it is maybe such a shift towards the popular that made possible the box-office success of the *Torrente* films, *The Others* (2001), *Historias del Kronen* (*Tales of the Korean*, 1995), *La comunidad* (*Common Wealth*, 2000) and other recent films. This suggests that at last the fact that the 'social realist' frame had at least been recognised as limiting for Spanish film and it was the time to move forward.

A revision of Spanish film history took place during the 1990s under the influence of cultural studies. Spanish commentators seem now to be less reluctant to deal seriously with films not belonging to the dissident tradition. This process has materialised in the United Kingdom in two works of particular interest that are the starting point for the present collection. Peter Evans' *Spanish Cinema: The Auteurist Tradition* revisits the canon of Spanish cinema. To established central figures in the tradition, Evans adds others that introduce different perspectives to the selection, most notably in terms of national identity, gender and influence of the popular traditions: filmmakers such as Julio Medem, Bigas Luna, Pilar Miró and Pedro Almodóvar represent change within the auteurist tradition (let us remember that Almodóvar was only very lately and very reluctantly admitted as an auteur by the Spanish critical establishment) that begins to look at different areas of experience unrelated to anti-Franco dissidence (nationalism, sexuality, feminism and camp). Even more radical is Nuria Triana-Toribio's approach in *Spanish National Cinema*, which revises traditional approaches to the canon by identifying the forces behind canon-making and promoting a comprehensive approach that can include the popular tradition.

A similar reassessment of Portuguese national cinema is still in its beginnings, with investigations that tend to unmask particular myths on the control of cinema under Salazar. Also, as articles in the present volume show, the transgressive potential of Portuguese comedy is being taken into fuller consideration. Unfortunately a comprehensive full-length study of this fascinating cinematography is yet to appear in English.

The present volume gathers both the auteurist and the popular strands and attempts a representative selection of Spanish cinema. On the one hand, while traditionally central figures such as Erice, Saura, Buñuel and Oliveira are represented, revision of such classics as *Spirit of the Beehive*, *Raise Ravens*, *Viridiana* and *Journey to the Beginning of the World* moves away from the emphasis on political dissidence. But it is also important to complete the view with other films such as *Last Stand on the Philippines, Lola the Coalgirl, The Miracle of Marcelino, Werewolf Shadow* and *Song of Lisbon* that have tended to be absent from serious consideration.

Alberto Mira

REFERENCES

Da Costa, João Bénard (1991) *Histórias do Cinema*. Lisbon: Imprensa Nacional – Casa da Moeda.

Evans, Peter William (ed.) (1999) *Spanish Cinema: The Auteurist Tradition*. Oxford: Oxford University Press.

Gómez Rufo, Antonio (1990) *Berlanga contra el poder y la gloria*. Madrid: Temas de Hoy.

Muñoz Molina, Antonio (1995) 'Confesiones', in *Nickelodeon*, 1, Winter, 158–65.

Reseña (1976) 'Diez mejores películas españolas. Votaciones de los críticos', February, 39–41.

Triana-Toribio, Nuria (2003) *Spanish National Cinema*. London: Routledge.

LA ALDEA MALDITA THE CURSED VILLAGE

FLORIÁN REY, SPAIN, 1930/1942

Florián Rey made two films 12 years apart under the title *La aldea maldita* (*The Cursed Village*). For many years, the first film was believed to be from 1929 although now it is commonly agreed that it dates from 1930. The second version, made in 1942, was so affected by the period's ideological upheavals that it reflects badly upon the original. Nevertheless, such shortcomings also entailed the exploration of a particular aesthetic mode (characterised by its tableau-like effect) which, although a failure, remains interesting.

Both plots are, unsurprisingly, similar. One intertitle at the start of the 1930 film helps us to place the action, although there is no indication that the events themselves are to take place in a period which is not contemporary to the film itself. The camera then introduces the main characters of the story: Juan Castile (Pedro Larrañaga), his wife Acacia (Carmen Viance), Martín, the blind grandfather, father of Juan (Víctor Pastor), and the scatterbrained Magdalena, friend of Acacia (Amelia Muñoz). Clearly, these names are symbolic, as is the blindness of the grandfather, with his role of blind transmitter of outdated values, such as honour, which many of the film's commentators described as 'Calderoniano' (that is to say, old-fashioned, as featured in the works of playwright Pedro Calderón de la Barca).

Unlike the second version, the protagonist here is not an affluent landowner but a poor peasant. When a hailstorm ruins the crop despite the prayers of the pious in the church he reacts, as one would expect from a labourer in his position, by blaspheming and cursing the heavens.

In vivid contrast to the state of general misery, the village's usurer Uncle Lucas' (Ramón Meca) well-stocked larder incenses Juan to such an extent that, on the verge of throttling him he is thrown into jail just as the village square fills with the handcarts awaiting the exodus of peasants, unable to make a living out of the land. Acacia's friend, Magdalena, tries to convince her to accompany her to the city, leaving her imprisoned husband and the grandfather. Acacia initially resists but ultimately tells the grandfather of her decision to leave the village and to take the child with her. He warns her sternly, that his main virtue is honour and that he will not let her take his grandson.

The two women join the mass exodus and are seen passing in front of the prison bars by Juan, who cries in vain to his wife, begging her not to leave him. His release will come from the clemency of Uncle Lucas who, feeling guilty, writes a conciliatory letter of repentance in which he asks the authorities to let Juan go free.

The words 'After three years in a workhouse in the capital, Juan Castile, emigrant of the cursed village, has reached a comfortable position' accompany a camera shot which focuses in on a map centred on Segovia. Whilst celebrating his saint's day with labourers in a popular tavern, Juan recognises Magda, who has become a fallen woman. When he thinks she is flirting with him, he hurls her to the ground. In revenge, she pulls aside a curtain revealing Acacia with a man. Beside himself, Juan drags his wife home and, menacingly, advises her that she will stay only until the death of the grandfather so that he may never know of her dishonour. Then he will throw her out.

The dying grandfather stresses the need to preserve honour at all cost, thus sentencing Acacia. This *blind* defence of honour is, through a neat ellipsis, followed by its consequences: after a close-up of a crucifix and the two candles burning at the wake of the dead grandfather Acacia, a small bundle of belongings in her hand, and with slow and grieving step leaves her home for the stormy winter which awaits her outside.

The appearance of two newspaper texts being read by Juan inform us of Acacia's sad fate: 'A few days ago a desperate woman, incapable even of saying her name or from where she came, was saved from the harsh snow. The sorry state in which she found herself made it necessary to admit her to medical care ... Yesterday, taking advantage of the nurses' negligence she fled from the benevolent establishment. The sick woman appears to be obsessed with children.' The camera shows her leaning on an acacia tree and looking towards a village where a suspicious mother moves her children away. Other children, considering her a witch, throw stones at her.

Once again we are presented with the cursed village of Luján, where Juan enters reading a letter which tells us why he has returned there: 'It's vital that you come to the village with the child ... Lucas.' Accompanied by his son, they enter their old house, where a distracted Acacia rocks the cradle and sings a lullaby for an imaginary child. Juan pushes his son towards her saying: 'Give your mother a kiss son.' This the son does, much to the mother's delight, and she promptly recovers her wits and recognises them. Lucas, who in his time forgave Juan, gives his seal of approval to this reunion with the words: 'You do well to forgive her, Juan.'

In Paris in the summer of 1930, Florián Rey added sound to this version of the film which had been made in Spain with silent film equipment. Presenting it to the public of the French capital he chose to stress even more strongly the moment of final absolution, writing in the synopsis of the programme distributed to the public, 'Juan arrives and, understanding the Calvary through which his wife has passed, forgives her … and gives her back her son. And then the three of them leave The Cursed Village in the hope of better days.'

The 1942 version deviates significantly from its 1930 predecessor, which is hardly surprising, with the Spanish Civil War separating the two. Their respective budgets were also substantially different, with Pedro Larrañaga y Florián himself contributing the 22,000 pesetas for the 1930 version while the budget of the 1942 version rose to 1,050,000 pesetas. Naturally there are numerous other differences and the influential role of the censor on the film has recently been confirmed by the publication of the shooting script of this second version. In this original script the story took place in Segovia and began '*1930. Amongst the ruins of Castile.*' Nevertheless, 'Segovia' was crossed out and substituted with 'Salamanca'. And on screen, after finally presenting the film as a 'cinematic poem', the opening read, '*Castile 1900. When the city cut the ties with the countryside which fed it, it left the peasants powerless in their fight against the hostility of the elements. Due to this, ruined villages, emigration and exodus slowly bled the lifeblood from the nation.*'

Thus, Rey had initially intended to underline the continuity of the 1942 version with its 1930 counterpart. But for whatever reason, the events were moved to a more distant past and the geographical location to Salamanca. The gothic lettering accentuated this historical difference. Unlike in the previous version, which dwelled on contemporary problems, as reflected in the newspapers, it was more like an unearthed artefact from an older time.

The division into chapters reinforces this 'poetic' character and the visual translation of an inward looking time. Another intertitle in gothic lettering marks the start of the film: '*Chapter I. On the village's patron saint's day the master serves the servant.*' Orchestral adaptations of popular tunes play as the crane-mounted camera sweeps past those who are riding the old ferris wheel and circles around the villagers who in their turn are dancing around the bonfires where their old furniture is ablaze. A long tracking shot leads us toward the house of Juan de Castile.

The staging and planning of this opening contrasts vividly with that of the 1930 version where there was not a single camera movement. Such narration through static shots had been meticulously planned by Florián Rey, who made reference in a 1943 interview to the 'virulent superstition of dynamism' dominating cinema at the time. His film would be 'unflinchingly static; a cinema of tableaux. The action, as I see it. Sentimental dynamism as opposed to the crazy dynamism of superimpositions, and proliferation of fade outs.' The plot changes also differ significantly. Juan de Castile (Julio Rey de las Heras) is no longer the 'humble *hidalgo*' nor is he the 'poor peasant with the ideas and feelings of a great man', as he was in the original version. He is a successful farmer with numerous labourers at his charge. Another addition worthy of mention is that he has a brother, Justo (Agustín Laguilhoat), who arrives with his two daughters, and with whom he seems to have some hidden conflict. Although it is implied that this is due to Acacia, the Civil War which separated the shooting of the two versions must not be forgotten, so as yet another element, the biblical motive of hate between brothers, lurks beneath.

Justo has come to visit the grandfather, Martín (Delfín Jerez), behind whom we cannot fail to see a crucifix. Lucas (Pablo Hidalgo) is also present, the usurer, to call in an old loan from the old man. Notably he is treated, not only by Juan but also by both the script and the camera, with considerably more respect than in the 1930 version. Here, not only is he not attacked, but he is offered a glass of wine by Juan, which he refuses.

A comparison of the shooting script with the final cut makes one conscious of the censor's role. In the film all salacious details have been neatly stripped away, as, for example the insinuation that the coquettish Luisa (the name which was substituted for the Magdalena of the 1930 version, played in this version by Alicia Romay) has had relationships with her employers during her time in Madrid as a maid. Similarly suppressed were the attempts by the farmhands to seduce Luisa, as are the shots in which Acacia (Florencia Bécquer) should be seen breast-feeding her son, with notes in the script as explicit as: 'While saying these phrases Juan plays with his son, separating him from the breast various times.'

Also notable is the difference in emphasis with which the prayers during the storm are planned in the script and the way in which they appear in the final film. This sequence was already in embryo in the 1930 version of the film, where the women who appear praying in the church allowed the blasphemy of Juan in a medium shot to be 'answered' by a devout woman crossing herself in a shorter shot. In the script of 1942 the planned use of sound made it possible to add to this sequence a more precise rhythm, as the images were intended to develop to the ten chimes of the church clock. After the first, on the steeple, and coinciding with each chime, short shots were contrasted with one another: an image of Saint Bartholomew, a niche on the corner of a street, the Christ-child in a side chapel on a table, a missal open with a hand passing over the pages, offerings to which are added some ears of corn, an old man holding a figure of the crucified Christ, the son of Juan and Acacia in the cradle, some old women making the sign of the cross, and a return to the image of Saint Bartholomew which opened the sequence to show that some more old women have joined in with the prayers.

The film's script preserves these ideas, but the emphasis is not what one might expect. Above all, it is not in proportion with the role that these clock chimes play. Because it will be another ten chimes, at the end, which accompany Acacia's return to the village, and which are accompanied by another series of images, this time superimposing the key episodes from her Calvary. It is as if the film were rewinding itself and the spell broken, to the point where time returns to zero, in order to rewrite the story from before the fateful moment when the curse fell on the whole village and that home in particular.

On the other hand the religious imagery, which appears here dispersed and fragmentary by the rapid succession of intercut shots, finds a response in the closing still shot which ends the film, whose iconographic burden asserts itself over them, silencing them with the final pardon.

The differences between the final cuts of the two versions, are of considerable importance. After the hailstorm which destroys the crops, Juan's blasphemy of the 1930 version has been removed; the role of Acacia is of greater importance and less negative, and after disaster strikes, she shows solidarity with her husband. Now Acacia keeps his spirits up with: 'We're young, strong, we'll start again, but not here; down on the plain where the earth is less ungrateful. Or in the city, Juan, in the city.' Nevertheless Juan wishes to leave alone, and therefore it is he who leaves her and not the opposite as in 1930; nor is there a jail here in which to keep the man as there is no motive. How could there be if he and Uncle Lucas are almost friends, and both well-off? What's more, nobody rebels here.

In the tavern scene (which in 1930 was clearly a brothel) we find a kind of rustic cabaret, described thus in the script: 'One of those absurd provincial places for the entertainment of the lowest class of society,' which is located 'below street level.' There Luisa is at the bar and Acacia in a dressing room and so Juan finds his wife, not in a private room with a man, as in the 1930 version, but alone and about to step on to the stage and sing. The potentially sharp corners of the script have also been smoothed over; where in the script Luisa asks for help and organises a general fight in the film she merely gets up and runs to advise Acacia.

Apart from that, the film retains the same sequences as the 1930 version, when the wife returns home to keep up appearances before the grandfather's death: the same change of clothes which Juan throws over Acacia in the house so that she dresses 'decently', the same close-up of the candles and the crucifix to indicate the death of the grandfather without the necessity of showing his body. And the same bitter farewell of the woman with her small bundle of clothes.

A symbolic aurora ('In Spain the dawn is just beginning', as in the final lines of the Falangist hymn, *Cara al sol*) ushers in a new order, marked by the last sign: '*Chapter IV: Dawn. "Our fields receive God's blessing once again"*'. A rapid montage, Soviet fashion, shows the fevered activity of the farmhands: ploughs pulled by oxen, teams sowing the fields, a procession which moves over them, solemnly, with a priest who blesses them… The harvest could not be more abundant: overflowing ears of corn, the carts of sheaves and the threshing floor covered with sacks of wheat.

'In all these shots one must feel the joy of the Castilian countryside at the sight of a vast harvest', notes the script. And, in fact, the liturgy of the procession allows us to hear perfectly, in Latin: 'Blessed be the fruit of thy womb' which connects female fertility, and honour, with that of the, until that point at least, cursed earth. Set against this background of rebirth and abundance Acacia makes her penitential return.

In the village the church tower chimes out the same ten strokes that accompanied the disaster during the hailstorm. The penitent reaches the church, whose doors are wide open, and enters, prostrating herself on her knees. A halo of light illuminates her face and celestial music sounds. The villagers advise the husband of her presence and advise him to throw her out like a dog. But with firmness Juan says that if the doors to God's house are not closed to her, he will not close his to her. And then only the absolution remains, with the implicit undercurrent of the evangelical episode of the exoneration of the adulterous woman, the parable of the prodigal son and the lost sheep returning to the flock. Juan orders his workers to stop work and dress up, to sacrifice and roast all the lambs which were being saved for the day of the Virgin.

Acacia advances across the village square to the quiet murmurings of the locals. The script says that Juan receives her sitting in his father's chair, wearing his best suit and cloak but in the film he carries her home, sitting her in the chair next to her son, and washes her feet in a basin brought by their two nieces. The frozen image becomes an altarpiece in the style of the Catholic Kings and the word 'end' appear in the keystone of an arch.

A folkloric patina gleams on the surface of the 1942 version, reinforced by the use (and the abuse) of studio facilities. Its 1930 predecessor chose location shooting, which suggested fresh air, authenticity, immediacy and credibility. In the earlier version the people went about in their daily clothes and Juan was seen working with the hoe, the hens sheltered from the storm, the cat got caught in the cat flap. In the second, the village appears to be overrun by the women's folkloric dances and the main characters, wooden and inexpressive, give off more than a mere whiff of mothballs which is difficult to bear.

Thus *La aldea maldita* of 1942 remains profoundly troubled at its very centre, for not being able to face up with sufficient frankness to the two faces of the rural drama: the hunger *in situ* and the prostitution in the city. It is reduced to a numb allegory, with no contemporary relevance whatsoever. If the first version was up to date thanks to the adaptation of some of the best ideas from Russian and German cinema to the Spanish situation, how could a film which had already been shown to need this neorealist breath of life possibly be expected to work without it? Even a critical Falangist like José Antonio Nieves Conde was still nine years away from dealing effectively, after numerous trials and tribulations, with the problem of rural depopulation in his film *Surcos* (*Furrows*, 1951).

To gauge the conditions which Florián Rey had to face, the synopsis offered of the film when it was shown at the Venice Film Festival in 1942 is particularly eloquent: 'It tells the story that the heavens, *justly* wished to punish the inhabitants of Luján, a Castilian village, destroying their crops over successive years' (the italics are mine). In as much as the new fertility of the earth after the exodus, it emphasises the efforts of Juan, but above all the redeeming Calvary of Acacia: 'As the prize for this sacrifice, those Castilian lands proudly boast the richness and abundance of their golden ears and we witness the harvest, the threshing…' All of which culminates in the return of this woman who strayed from the path: 'And we see her arrive dressed in rags with shoeless, bleeding feet, the living incarnation of the repentant sinner… Two maids, with *ritual* bearing, bring a bowl which they place on the floor on front of Acacia. Juan kneels at her feet and, doing a duty only seen in *biblical passages*, begins to wash her wounds, a symbol of the forgiveness which he offers her, before the emotion of the people.'

At this point one may conjecture that the film was being presented as a parable of the history of Spain in the light of contemporary events. And, as if there were room for doubt, the allegory was clarified in a text by the Falangist Ernesto Giménez Caballero, 'El significado nacional de *La aldea maldita*', which appeared in the 18 April 1943 issue of *Primer Plano*. This is a manifesto that one could call 'programmatic'. His thoughts referred, at least in principle, to the 1942 version but even without mentioning the shift, they seem to be referring to the 1930 version as well. It would appear that the title answers that of an article 'La conciencia social de *La aldea maldita*' by the communist Juan Piqueras, executed during the war, and who Giménez Caballero must have known well as he had been the literary editor of *La Gaceta Literaria* where Piqueras' text had appeared in September 1930.

The static or 'tableaux' cinema, which Florián Rey deliberately postulated in this film of 1942 and which provoked so many misunderstandings, is a less obvious matter. It is in this area that we find ourselves faced with considerable differences between the two versions. What in 1930 was a road full of possibilities – a crossroads – in 1942 was a dead end. Before the Civil War the *tableau*, as a cultural *mould*, had benefited from its immersion in vivid and dynamic territory where the sacred and hallowed could collide with the profanity of fairs, parties and carnivals. Thus was proposed an anti-hierarchical no-man's-land (or maybe *every*-man's-land), full of uncertainties, fears, anomalies and innovation capable even of patronising the transition toward modernity and the process of osmosis from Tradition to Vanguard. The literary works of Ramón Valle-Inclán and Ramón Gómez de la Serna and the paintings of Julio Romero de Torres, José Gutiérrez Solana and Maruja Mallo can all be considered good examples of this.

Florián Rey attempted something similar in the cinematic field thanks to the laying down of a popular audiovisual iconography on which a substantial proportion of Spain's cinematic industry was then based. The main problem which he had to face was the creation of a system which could compete with cinema already as evolved as that of America, France or Germany but without breaking from the complex cultural heritage of Spain. The Spanish audience might have been illiterate but they possessed, by way of compensation, a vastly rich mental stock of audio and visual references.

It may in fact be in these two versions of *La aldea maldita* where this system sits most comfortably. After the premiere of the first version Juan Piqueras was not slow to perceive this particular use of religious iconography: 'The sense of honour of the main character and of his father; some images, namely that of the Virgin and Christ, deftly placed; and the exemplary punishment meted out on the wife who forgets her duties affirm that *La aldea maldita* is a purely Spanish film.'

Effectively, the 1930 version of *La aldea maldita* turns to religious situations and images, both explicit and subliminal, or which have been turned on their heads. There is the stoning of the adulterous woman at the hands of the young children, the temptation in the desert at the hands of the coquettish Magdalena, and the 'son, here is your mother' of the end. But perhaps the best devised is the visual sequence, which we might define as the 'crucifixion of the Spanish peasant', when we see one of the locals grasping on to one a cart with his arms spread open.

The key problem therefore of the 1942 version is that all of this happens in close-up, imposing itself in such a way that the supporting cast do not support but seem to carry the film's real message and ideology. In so doing, what could have been a fruitful investigation ended up stifling the critical perceptions of the first *La aldea maldita* under the dense weight of its sodden vestments.

Agustín Sánchez Vidal

REFERENCES

Caballero, Ernesto Giménez (1943) 'El significado nacional de *La aldea maldita*', *Primer Plano*, 18 April.

Piqueras, Juan (1930) 'La conciencia social de *La aldea maldita*', *La Gaceta Literaria*, September, 89.

Rey, Florián (2003) *La aldea maldita. Guión original 1942*. Asociación Cultural 'Florián Rey', La Almunia de Doña Godina.

A CANÇÃO DE LISBOA SONG OF LISBON

JOSÉ COTTINELLI TELMO, PORTUGAL, 1933

Portugal's *Estado Novo* or New State (1933–74) came into being in the same year as the premiere of *A canção de Lisboa* (*Song of Lisbon*), the first Portuguese sound film produced entirely within the country's borders. *Song of Lisbon* premiered at the São Luís cinema in Lisbon on 7 November 1933 in an atmosphere of enthusiasm and expectation. It proved to be the first in a long line of popular comedies, generically referred to as the *comédia à portuguesa*, such as *O pai tirano* (*The Tyrannical Father*, 1941), *O pátio das cantigas* (*The Courtyard of Songs*, 1942) and *O Costa do Castelo* (*Costa from Castelo*, 1943). Many of these early sound films starred well-known comic actors trained in the *teatro de revista*, Portugal's version of music hall, such as Vasco Santana, Beatriz Costa and António Silva, all three of whom gave memorable performances in *Song of Lisbon*. This was the only feature-length film directed by José Cottinelli Telmo, an architect by profession, who participated in the building of the Tobis Portuguesa studio in 1932, where *Song of Lisbon* was made the following year.

The creative possibilities and excitement generated by the nascent film industry in Portugal are reflected in the impressive roll call of those who collaborated on this production. They included the painter Carlos Botelho (who acted as production assistant), a young Manoel de Oliveira (who played the role of the *galã* or heartthrob, Carlos), and the acclaimed artist, Almada Negreiros, who designed two stunning posters to advertise the film. The women who played the parts of the seamstresses who work alongside the character, Alice, in the film were cast by means of a competition, which generated a great deal of publicity in cinema magazines such as *Cinéfilo*, *Animatógrafo* and *Imagem*.

Vasco, or Vasquinho Leitão (Vasco Santana), fails his examination to qualify as a doctor just as he finds out that his two aunts, Dona Efigénia and Dona Perpétua, who have supported him through his studies and unwittingly through his rather libertine existence, are making their way from rural Portugal to Lisbon for the first time to check up on his progress. The flirtatious Vasco is the suitor of a fellow inhabitant of the *bairro*, or district, of Castelo, a seamstress by the name of Alice (Beatriz Costa). Her father, Caetano (António Silva), a tailor, enlists the help of his neighbour, the local cobbler, in convincing the two provincial ladies that Vasco is, in fact, a dutiful medic and worthy of his future inheritance. When the aunts discover the truth, Vasco is forced to earn his living as a singer of *fado*, Portugal's national folk music, becoming something of a celebrity. This does not deter him, however, from pursuing a career in medicine, and he finally passes his final examination with flying colours, regaining the favour of his dowager aunts and winning the hand of Alice in marriage.

Song of Lisbon has remained a classic of Portuguese cinema and established the paradigms for the *comédia* tradition, not least via its ideological dimensions. António Salazar's authoritarian *Estado Novo* found a welcome ally in the fledgling film industry and in the *comédia à portuguesa* in particular. As early as 1933 the city council of Lisbon contributed capital towards the creation of the Tobis Portuguesa film studio, and the State always maintained an important position within this company. However, the regime never utilised cinema as a propaganda tool in a systematic way. The industry's precarious position in Portugal, with its relatively low number of cinema theatres and thus restricted audience, was such that there was little incentive for the State to invest heavily in it. (It has been estimated that in the 1930s less than a third of the population of Portugal had access to the cinema.)

Song of Lisbon, and the musical comedies that followed in its wake, were optimistic, innocent and good-humoured, serving as a reflection of an orderly and respectful society. The realities of life in Salazar's Portugal were ignored, in keeping with the policy of obscurantism pursued by the New State, and in favour of a utopian vision of life in the capital city, where the traditions and value system of rural society were incongruously preserved. These films provided momentary excuses to poke light-hearted fun at the ruling elite, but ultimately the status quo remained unchallenged and gratefully accepted by the *povo*, ordinary folk, represented on screen. As leading film critic Luís de Pina has said, Portuguese filmmakers in the 1930s and early 1940s went in search of real people, of a national style, and of a brand of humour that was considered truly Portuguese. The official censors ensured that filmmakers were fearful of tackling controversial issues, preferring instead to deal with superficial themes and conventional story lines, or to make pro-establishment documentaries.

Though set in Lisbon, the action in *Song of Lisbon* focuses on the homely *bairro* of the capital city, Castelo. Community spirit and a surprisingly bucolic atmosphere reign in this traditional enclave, which remains untainted by the modernity of the capital, glimpsed only momentarily in establishing shots of the city centre and in the form of modern modes of transport, such as motor cars, taxis, lorries and electric trams. The action of the *comédias* typically unfolds in a very limited number of confined spaces, located within a particular *bairro* of Lisbon, such as that of Estrela in *A menina da rádio* (*The Radio Girl*, 1944) and *O leão da Estrela* (*The Lion from Estrela*, 1947), and that of Chiado in *O pai tirano* (1941). The impersonal city streets are rarely shown in these films. In *Song of Lisbon* everyone knows each other in Castelo, and neighbours lean out of their windows and over their flower-strewn balconies to exchange pleasantries. As Paulo Jorge Granja writes, in relation to the *comédias* as a whole: 'The neighbourhood or the courtyard thus function as a small village where everybody knows one another and the old ways of relating to each other are preserved, based on values that are passed on and honoured from one generation to the next and on respect for order that is, of necessity, deemed to be fair and natural – an order that continues to exist in the routine calm of rural life.'

The city and the countryside do, nonetheless, come into direct opposition in *Song of Lisbon* when Vasco's two matronly aunts from the backward northern region of Trás-os-Montes arrive in Lisbon for the first time, dressed inappropriately in straw hats laden with flowers. On alighting at Rossio railway station, their rural sensibilities are shocked by the theft of one of their bags, causing them both to faint in shock. Later a donkey passes by in the street, and the traditional *varinas* (fish-sellers) of Lisbon are seen carrying their wares on their heads, juxtaposed with fast-moving cars and the general bustle of the capital. The inhabitants of the provinces are portrayed as naïve hicks, a stereotype that is endorsed by Caetano who says that it will be easy to dupe Vasco's two aunts into believing that Vasco is a qualified doctor.

All the inhabitants of the *bairro* are courteous and respectful citizens, upholding the myth of Portugal's *brandos costumes* or peaceful way of life. During the local celebrations for the *festa de São João* couples dance happily together. The harmony is only briefly interrupted by a punch-up between Vasco and a handsome resident who has taken a shine to Alice. The customary fireworks then light up the Lisbon sky, transforming the rambunctious melée into wide-eyed children, who look on transfixed. The carnivalesque atmosphere is restored as a hot-air balloon ascends into the sky and everyone applauds. This is the cue for a musical interlude, in which Alice and Vasco take turns to sing about the annual festivities and lead two processions that unite the whole community. Neighbourhood associations often provided a setting for the *comédias*. Again, as Granja writes, 'When a proper family environment is lacking, both the boarding house and the recreational club provide a surrogate "family".' In *Song of Lisbon* a competition to crown the annual 'Miss Castelinhos' is held in the local *sociedade recreativa* (recreational club). All the inhabitants of the neighbourhood attend, in spite of the tedious solemnity and rather laborious rhetoric of the patriarchal jury, with their pseudo-aristocratic, bristling *bigodes* (moustaches). The pretentiousness of the elite is made fun of and this film, in keeping with the *comédia* tradition as a whole, promotes a rigid social hierarchy in which paternal figures enjoy a certain power. Paulo Jorge Granja has argued that the various older male characters, like Caetano in *Song of Lisbon*, who happen to be widowers or confirmed bachelors, can be interpreted as an allusion to Salazar himself. These characters often share the legendary puritanical, self-sacrificing ways of Portugal's head of state, and, like Caetano, their social responsibilities frequently extend beyond their families to encompass small businesses, their employees and recreational groups. The message is clear: the need for an authoritarian, paternalistic leader is paramount. Although at first sight these characters come across as domineering and verging on the tyrannical, they are ultimately shown to have the best interests of their charges at heart.

Fado music is a recurrent presence in *Song of Lisbon*, both in the extra-diegetic soundtrack and when performed by actors on screen. Songs were especially written for the film by Raul Ferrão and Raul Portela, and went on to become ingrained in popular consciousness. When Vasco becomes an acclaimed *fado* singer, he is billed on posters as 'Vasco da anatomia' (Vasco of anatomy), and performs to rapturous applause, accompanied by the typical *guitarra* (Portuguese guitar) and *viola* (classical guitar). Like many other *comédias*, such as *The Courtyard of Songs* in which a comic contrast is drawn between the musical tastes of the snobbish elite (imported opera) and those of ordinary folk (home-grown *fado*), *Song of Lisbon* celebrates popular traditions, popular religious practices and popular music.

Many of the earliest Portuguese talkies were vehicles for the performance of *fado*. *A Severa* (1931), a sound film shot partially in Portugal and in the studios of Tobis Francesa in Paris, depicted the life story of the eponymous legendary *fadista* or *fado* singer. Countless Portuguese filmmakers would go on to use the nation's folk music and its glamorous performers as the point of departure for their productions. *Fado* reached the whole of the nation via the radio in the 1930s and 1940s, and its popularity was reflected on screen in films such as *Capas negras* (*Black Capes*) that premiered in 1947 and starred the great *fadista* Amália Rodrigues. During his directorship of the Secretariado da Propaganda Nacional (Secretariat of National Propaganda) and later the Secretariado Nacional da Informação, Cultura Popular e Turismo (National Secretariat of Information, Popular Culture and Tourism), António Ferro promoted films that centred on *fado*, inspired by the Spanish musicals of the Franco era known as *españoladas*.

Mockery of the bourgeoisie characterised the *comédia à portuguesa*, and *Song of Lisbon* is no exception. The pompous academics that submit Vasco to his final examination in medicine are implicitly made fun of. The impenetrable language of the educated elite is derided when Vasco answers one of their questions perfectly, and the ordinary folk in the audience then repeat the phrase: 'He even knows what the "estenocleidomastodeu" is!' The age-old conflict between the aristocracy and ordinary folk is explored in many other films belonging to the *comédia* tradition, for example, in *Costa from Castelo*. The false, devious and egotistical nature of the rich is contrasted with the simple and joyful life of the poor. Nobility and its concomitant riches are depicted as a burden and poverty as the key to happiness, in keeping with the ideology of a political regime that bestowed a moral significance on the material sacrifices made by the poor.

In *Song of Lisbon* a playful visual joke directed at the Salazar regime features in one memorable scene in the tailor's workshop; a tailor's dummy wearing a second-hand coat displays a sign saying: 'Ocasião / 95:00 / Estado Novo' (Second-hand / 95:00 / New State). Vasco hangs the sign around his own neck as part of his disguise, when hiding from his future father-in-law, but when he is discovered he childishly attaches it to the posterior of a matronly customer. Similarly, the fact that Caetano single-handedly decides on the outcome of the competition to crown 'Miss Castelinhos' so that his daughter, Alice, can win is a tongue-in-cheek comment on rigged elections. As one disgruntled mother of another candidate says: 'Celestina, let's go. This was all one big fix!'

There are fleeting instances of deviance in *Song of Lisbon*, not least in Vasco's drunkenness at the *fado* house 'O Retiro do Alexandrino', when he curses *fado* and its performers in a moment of uncharacteristic bitterness: 'Fado is the poison of the people. Death to the audience and the guitarists. I'm a doctor. It's my duty to cure social ills. Let's promote an Anti-*Fado* week!' Granja cogently argues that all the action in the *comédia à portuguesa* stems from minor transgressions or deviations from the established order on the part of certain characters, and that the tension that these situations create is only defused when normality is re-established.

Ultimately, obedience to the State is advocated in the *comédia à portuguesa*. In *Song of Lisbon* policemen appear on screen at two key intervals; first, when Caetano and his neighbour, the cobbler, break into a spontaneous *fado* in order to literally sing the praises of Vasco for the benefit of his aunts. A crowd gathers to enjoy the moment, but a policeman breaks up the frivolity by asking if they have a licence to perform in the street. Later, when Vasco is down on his luck and sleeping on a park bench, another policeman moves him on, telling him that such behaviour is forbidden. Luís de Pina points out that it is no coincidence to find in many Portuguese *comédias* from the 1930s and 1940s one or more policemen appearing on screen to assert the authority of the State.

The humour of *Song of Lisbon* owes much to the comic traditions of the *teatro de revista*, ('revues') where the three stars of the film had earned their stripes, and it centres on visual slapstick and verbal punning. A typical example of word play is when one of Vasco's fellow medical students answers the register to the name 'Sr Claro' (literally, 'Mr Pale'), and the camera then focuses on his black face. Physical clowning takes the form of a sash-window falling on Vasco's head like a guillotine, a mouse crawling on his head when he disguises himself as a tailor's dummy, and several fight sequences, one of which involves Vasco and Alice throwing food at each other and smashing crockery.

Much of the film's humour stems from Vasco Santana himself, whose ample physique and podgy child-like face serve to enhance his comic timing. (There are numerous jokes at the expense of his physical size, not least the fact that his character's surname is Leitão, literally 'sucking pig', and such as when Alice says that the full moon reminds her of him.) He is the quintessential, at times rather camp, buffoon who embraces his potential father-in-law and says, 'You are my second mother'. Mistaken identity constitutes another comic device, when Vasco takes his aunts to Lisbon zoo and a zookeeper confuses him with the official veterinary surgeon, to whom he bares a striking resemblance. Feigning technical knowledge (and thus again taking a comic swipe at the learned classes), Vasco describes a pair of otters (*lontras* in Portuguese) as a '*bilontra*' (literally, a rogue or scoundrel).

Song of Lisbon occasionally engages directly with Hollywood cinema, introducing an element of self-deprecation and parody in relation to First-World film. When Vasco chats up one of his attractive neighbours, Maria da Graça, he calls her the local Greta Garbo. Later, his real sweetheart, Alice, sings for her fellow seamstresses: 'I'm going to be happy/ To live in castles in the air/ To live a fake ideal/ A chimera'. The film simultaneously employs a classic Hollywood dream sequence, in which she imagines herself and Vasco, just married and gambolling through the hills of Sintra, a small town outside Lisbon with a romantic, fairytale quality. With his portly physique and inane grin, he cuts a ridiculous figure, comically undermining this borrowing from the Hollywood musical. This fantasy interlude is rudely interrupted when Alice burns a large hole in a pair of Vasco's trousers that she is ironing, abruptly bringing her back to reality, and drawing an ironic contrast with the utopian aspirations of the US musical comedy, so different from this homely Portuguese equivalent, rooted in 'reality'.

As well as receiving overwhelming critical praise and enthusiastic responses from the general public in Portugal on its release in 1933, *Song of Lisbon* was a big hit among the Portuguese community in Brazil, and played up to expatriates' rose-tinted views of their native land. As

Heloísa Paulo says, 'The most popular films were those that tuned into the community's memory and reminded emigrants of their birthplace, while also incorporating the new tastes they developed after setting foot on Brazilian soil.' She goes on to explain that the New State cultivated, through Salazarist ideas and official and unofficial propaganda, a special 'gaze' for the benefit of its emigrant communities, designed to obtain more support for the regime by creating a vision of a peaceful, wholesome homeland. This approach was adopted throughout the *comédia* tradition, and many other examples, such as *Costa from Castelo*, were equally successful in Brazil.

Song of Lisbon remains an integral part of popular consciousness in Portugal, as was evidenced by the use of a famous line from the film, repeatedly uttered by Vasco ('Idiot, there are lots more hats'), in Mário Soares' televised presidential campaign in February 1986. Since its initial release, the film has been regularly screened in national cinemas and more recently on television. As Luis de Pina writes: 'Cottinelli's film, the freshness of the dialogue, the vivacity of the actors, the cheerfulness and spontaneity, the pace that even today is difficult to match, the authentic local colour of characters and settings, all this makes *Song of Lisbon* an exemplary comedy, whose scenes, songs and dialogue the Portuguese people know off by heart, passed from one generation to the next, from grandparents to children and grandchildren.'

Song of Lisbon, in spite of its understandable technical weaknesses and indebtedness to the comic traditions and dialogues of popular theatre, is a landmark in Portuguese cinematic history. Not only was it the first sound feature film to be made exclusively by Portuguese nationals in their homeland, but more importantly it has continued to strike a chord with domestic audiences. Thanks to its dehistoricised optimism and innocent playfulness, this film has become a part of popular consciousness. Again, to quote de Pina, writing in 1994, 'Today, like 61 years ago, *Song of Lisbon* continues to be contemporary.'

Lisa Shaw

REFERENCES

Granja, Paulo Jorge (2000) 'A comédia à portuguesa, ou a máquina de sonhos a preto e branco do Estado Novo', in Luís Reis Torgal (ed.) *O cinema sob o olhar de Salazar*. Coimbra: Círculo de Leitores.

Paulo, Heloísa (2000) 'A colónia portuguesa do Brasil e o cinema no Estado Novo', in L. R. Torgal *O cinema sob o olhar de Salazar*. Coimbra: Círculo de Leitores, 2000.

Pina, Luis de (1994) *A comédia clásica portuguesa*. A Corunha: Xunta de Galicia.

LA VERBENA DE LA PALOMA FAIR OF THE DOVE

BENITO PEROJO, SPAIN, 1935

The proclamation of the Second Republic in Spain on 14 April 1931 almost exactly coincided with the first talkies made in the country. Naturally, the use of music was fully explored during the early 1930s, which also sent out suggestions of the populist spirit of the new government. Out of 101 films made in the years leading up to the Civil War in 1936, 45 included songs or could be considered musicals. Among these, no less than thirteen made during the Republican period were adaptations of a specific brand of operetta known as *zarzuela*, with some elements that looked forward to the integrated Broadway musicals of the 1940s.

La verbena de la Paloma (*Fair of the Dove*, 1935) has been regarded not only as the best adaptation of a *zarzuela* but also the jewel in the crown of popular Republican cinema and one of the best examples of the Republican version of populism. Well-established traditions were recycled into the new medium and the product was meant for working-class audiences; there was no attempt to impose old fashioned catholic morality (as in such films as *La aldea maldita* [*The Cursed Village*], 1930 and *Nobleza baturra* [which could be translated as 'Aragonese Nobility' or 'Rustic Chivalry'], 1935, both directed by Florián Rey), no redemption through prayer, no divine intervention; working-class characters could be funny without becoming ridiculous caricatures, their appeal made identification easier. There was a celebration of the small events in their lives, rather than the use of grand gestures and heightened plots.

Fair of the Dove opened to unanimous praise on 23 December 1935 and went on to attract an international audience. Reviewers recognised it as the first masterpiece of Spanish cinema. It also constituted the most original and imaginative blending of music and cinematic resources in the history of the Spanish musical, practically unsurpassed in its ambition until Carlos Saura's work over the last two decades. To find an equivalent in the merging of popular and high cultural traditions we have to think of original early film musicals like Rouben Mamoulian's *Love Me Tonight* (1932) or daring popular operas such as Kurt Weil's *Street Scene* or George Gershwin's *Porgy and Bess*.

Benito Perojo (1894–1974) had a controversial career that started with the dawn of the Spanish film industry. He began as an actor and director of short features in 1913. A few years later he founded a production company, Patria Films. He then worked as an actor in France and Italy. Back in Spain, he founded another production company with Nobel Prize-winning playwright Jacinto Benavente, Films Benavente SL, and worked continuously throughtout the 1920s and the early 1930s to produce a series of films that included the box-office successes *Boy* (1925), *Malvaloca* (1926) and *El negro que tenía el alma blanca* (*A Black Man with a White Soul*, 1927). It is interesting that even though locations for these films were in Spain, the studio work for Perojo's films before the mid-1930s was carried out in France. In this way, he could take advantage of technicians and innovations, thus effectively introducing them into the Spanish film industry. In the early 1930s, he directed Spanish versions of foreign films in France and Hollywood. Ultimately, he was the most prolific Spanish director in the Republican years, directing eight films between 1931 and 1936.

He also had strong detractors amongst critics. In part, the objections had to do with the fact that he had become the best-known Spanish director abroad (in France he was widely regarded as a French filmmaker during the late 1920s). His exuberant use of film technique also worked against him: Spanish reactionary nationalism had always mistrusted technological prowess in detriment of what were regarded as 'essential' values of the motherland. A recurrent element in the condemnation of his work was, therefore, chauvinistic: Perojo was 'too cosmopolitan'. According to such critics, he was not making the kind of films Spanish audiences (and the country itself) *really* needed. He was therefore disfavourably compared with Rey, who was regarded as someone more in touch with Spanish folklore and tradition, something that films such as *La aldea maldita* (*The Cursed Village*, 1930), *La hermana San Sulpicio* (*Sister Saint Sulpice*, 1934) and *Morena Clara* (1936) made evident.

Perojo had, so far, tended to avoid themes and motives that were identified with the national project (Spanish folklore, the theme of honour, the hardships of rural life). His comedies were reminscent of classical Hollywood, and his work in the 1930s, where he was assisted by technicians fleeing the Nazi regime, gave his films a distinctly international look, so different from the rural infernos of Benavente, Arniches and the Alvarez Quintero brothers.

The decision to turn his attention to a *zarzuela* was therefore surprising and strategically apt in terms of critical reputation. With its popular flavour, its setting in a popular Madrid quarter and its focus on idiosyncracies of behaviour and speech, Perojo was indeed moving away from his usual cosmopolitan sophistication and engaging with more traditional notions of 'the national'. Such efforts can be compared to Federico García Lorca's use of popular theatre in his 'puppet plays'. But, as was also the case with the playwright, the appearance of working class spontaneity was deceitful: under all the undeniable local colour, sophistication and wit were more prominent than ever (not to mention the fact that the film received international funding).

The film is the second acknowledged screen version of one of the most popular *zarzuelas* (the earlier version was directed by José Buchs in 1921). The play, which opened at the Madrid Apolo theatre in 1894 is widely acknowledged as the most successful piece of Spanish musical theatre. Such was the popularity of the genre that many Spanish films since the days of the silent cinema consisted of *zarzuelas* with live players providing the music, sometimes arranged by the original composers. With the arrival of sound *zarzuelas* came back in fashion. Some of the genre's key titles were remade in the years 1930–36, although most of the adaptations are unremarkable, mainly filmed stage musicals with few cinematic devices at work.

Tomás Bretón and Ricardo de la Vega's *La verbena de la Paloma* is the epitome of Madrid-set *zarzuela*. It takes place on the eve of the festivity of the Virgin of the Dove, 14 August, celebrated with street parties in certain popular areas of the Spanish capital. The sense of fun of the working classes during their day off is perfectly captured in the music and lyrics, creating a vivid picture of a joyful evening in which love is confirmed and any threats are erased. The plot centres on the efforts of a young man (typesetter Julián [Roberto Rey]) to take the girl he loves (seamstress Susana [Raquel Rodrigo]) to the street carnival. (In this, as well as in the presence of an undesirable lover competing for the girl's attentions and in its celebration of community rites, *Fair of the Dove* resembles another milestone of musical theatre: Rodgers and Hammerstein's groundbreaking *Oklahoma!* [1943].) But cheeky, flirtatious Susana has decided to make him jealous by accepting the invitation of chemist Don Hilarión (Miguel Ligero), a fatuous wealthy older man. Don Hilarión is a traditional stereotype (the randy old goat), who invites ridicule, and his interference with the love of simple people will be punished at the end. He has also invited Susana's sister Casta, through the mediation of the girls' vulgar aunt Antonia (Dolores Cortés). In the end, the lovers reconcile and Don Hilarión is chased away. In the context of the Republic, this has been read in terms of class struggle which reflected intellectual concerns of the times, although it is a motive with a rich tradition in popular culture.

Zarzuela combines spoken and sung sections. Songs tend to move the action forward or pointedly express the feelings of the character in a popular idiom, rather than the polished language of nineteenth-century Viennese operetta; there is a consistent attempt to have characters use slang and working-class dialects. The main principle of dramatic organisation consists of developing a libretto with both a sentimental love plot and a comic one, in which additional dialogue are interspersed with musical numbers. These are used for the expression of love, character (normally through comic songs) and description of background. *La verbena de la Paloma* includes the three kinds of numbers. Don Hilarión, a stock character in popular theatre, is introduced in the opening number and in his 'Tiene razón Don Sebastián' ('Don Sebastián is right'); two choruses describe the anticipation of the Madrid people as they head for the street carnival, Julián's feelings are expressed in an operetta-like aria, 'También la gente del pueblo tiene su corazoncito' ('Working-class people also have a heart'), and his jealousy is the theme of a duo with his friend and confidant Señá Rita (Sélica Pérez Carpio). But in terms of musical scoring, the most outstanding element in the best *zarzuelas* is the use of the musicalised scene, which allows for the interweaving of musical themes and genres in order to provide detailed pictures of character, situation and background. In one particular instance, the three separate types of numbers mentioned above cohere into a musical unit, the whole cast is brought together in a similar fashion to *West Side Story*'s 'Quintet', made fifteen years later. The solutions adopted by Perojo to reflect such complex unities on screen won instant acclaim and constitute one of the film's highlights.

Even though there are no consistent attempts to promote *zarzuela* as a 'national art' (Francoism would favour other musical genres such as the Andalusian-inflected *copla*) it is justified to think of the genre exactly in these terms, given its consistent popular success since the mid-nineteenth century and the prominence of working-class types and motives. Intellectuals and the bourgeoisie looked down on the genre, regarding it as lacking in sophistication (or even plainly reactionary in providing old-fashioned stereotypes of the working classes).

As in the Broadway musical, the best *zarzuelas* show an awareness of the mechanisms of popular melody with some techniques adopted from classical musical traditions. For the lovers' arias and duets, the musical conventions tended to remain close to operetta: elegant melodies that soar gently, moving and easy on the ear. The comic characters express themselves in popular song styles and rhythms, borrowed in each case from the geographic regions in which the play is set. Although the repertoire of song situations is recognisably that of the operetta (for example we find the same settings, celebrations, drinking songs, banter songs, and so on), the music itself is not. Many *zarzuelas* were set in rural backgrounds, which was an excuse to use the popular musical tradition of those places: *Fair of the Dove* is a clear distillation of Madrid culture (the same distinction between 'rural' and 'urban' can be found in the popular theatrical tradition of *sainete*). The details of Madrid daily life as experienced by the working classes are all present. Advisor Pedro de Répide took responsibility for faithful reproduction of settings and rituals, and helped to introduce elements not present in the original play. The types and situations as well as idiolects are typical of late nineteenth-century Madrid, just on the verge of becoming a bustling metropolis.

If there is one recurring word in contemporary reviews of *Fair of the Dove*, it is 'dynamism'. This is articulated not just in terms of camera movements (and Perojo's camera is undeniably dynamic) but also through editing, that swiftly takes us from one place to another, linking them in narrative terms.

The conventional way to shoot a *zarzuela* song is through a three-quarter shot that keeps the singer centre-frame; the equivalent to a spotlight focusing attention on an actor's centre-stage position. At the same time, a static camera gives the audience the oportunity to let the attention wander into the diegetic world, offering the chance to identify more subtle details. A mobile camera, on the other hand, draws attention to relationships and narrative. In adapting *La verbena de la Paloma* to the screen, Perojo expressed an awareness of the difference between film and theatre: he warned his audiences that he would move the drama as far from the original as possible. He intended to make something as removed from theatrical performance as was possible; as stated in the volume by Román Gubern: 'I am not making a film in three acts and two scenes. I don't intend to photograph *La verbena de la Paloma* just as audiences see it on stage. It is my intention to achieve a work that is absolutely and eminently cinematic. In order to make it less theatrical and fit the songs I will make use of cinematic techniques.'

In *Fair of the Dove*, camera movements are clear signifiers of an authorial voice dominating the action. In other words, for Perojo it is not enough to shoot the character as a singer surrounded by objects that recalled the local world as a setting. Indeed, Perojo's camera actively invites connections between different sections of the plot and the setting.

Even if the spirit of the original and the plot remain unchanged, Perojo was not interested in following the stage play structure too closely. The changes introduced all help to open up plot. The outcome of the changes was to provide the film with a more developed intrigue. In terms of narrative, he introduced several changes that contributed to a fuller cinematic treatment of time. Perojo's script employs a longer time-span than in the original, so to broaden the scope of the action. Whereas the play adheres more closely to real time, starting more or less at 8pm, as the characters prepare to leave for the party, and finishing before midnight, the film spreads the action throughout the whole day, starting at 7am, with guests gathering for the wedding of Julián's boss, and following the characters as they have breakfast and go to work. This is a bold step that adds a sense of symmetry to the whole structure: the narrative opens with two newlyweds and closes with a couple who, we assume, will soon get married.

The expansion of narrative span allows Perojo to fill the narrative with action and comic scenes and aid character development taking place in front of the audience. In the original, some of the background action happens before the play starts and is related by the characters. For instance, Julián tells Rita of the moment when he saw Casta and Susana with an unknown man earlier in the day. Now we get to see how Julián glimpses Casta and Susana in a coach ride with Don Hilarión, which will intensify his jealousy (in the play this is an episode related to his confidant Señá Rita) but it is also an occasion for comedy as it features a street accident caused by Julián trying to board the coach. This scene contributes to evolution of character, which, again is shown to happen in front of the eyes of the audience and becomes better motivated narratively. The script also adds a scene, later in the day, when Julián visits Susana's flat just after Don Hilarión has stopped by for a quick visit. The girls and aunt Antonia hide the chemist in the closet 'with all the junk', which is an occasion for intrigue and a first humiliation of the character.

With the exception of the short opening number and a few minor cuts, the score from the stage work is transferred in its entirety, but numbers have been changed to fit the plot structure. The communal number in which Madrid folk look forward to the street carnival has been moved to an earlier spot, and Julián's aria is now sung as he is at work, with Rita appearing not as an actual interlocutor, but as a voice within his conscience, while the chorus is provided by his fellow workers.

In terms of technique, Perojo seems to have decided to make language visible by the use of a number of spectacular devices. Pictorialism in *zarzuela* tended to underplay plot by foregrounding elements from the backgound (settings, costumes, local colour). In creating connections between the different locations and characters through editing and *mise-en-scène*, the plot becomes more important. At the same time, technique in *Fair of the Dove* becomes so visible as to deny any idea of a realistic reproduction of reality. The world of *Fair of the Dove* is acknowledged as fictitious. To a large extent it is created by the camera and editing.

Several such techniques are used to underline the progress of the narrative and the relations between its parts. Editing between different locations is on many ocasions motivated by a sentence of the script. For instance, when Julián tells Rita of his woes, the film cuts to Susana and Casta in their flat on the sentence 'they have a bad counseller', which refers to the way Aunt Antonia is influencing the girls to go out with the chemist. Both scenes are linked through a quick pan that moves first to the right (in order to show the girls' flat) then to the left (bringing us back to the café where Julián and Rita continue with their breakfast). The effect of such juxtaposition of spaces is to underline the relationship between Julián and Susana, to the point that their spaces are closely related to each other. As the film progresses, the third protagonist, Don Hilarión, is introduced in a similar fashion, and his activities will be intercut with those of the other two. The result underlines the 'universal' structural motive of love threatened by an antagonist. The device also helps to reinforce the chronological dimension of the film: events will be presented throughout the day as parallel narrative lines that will coincide on two occasions before the closing scene: during Julián's visit to Aunt Antonia's flat and on the way to the street carnival. Following the characters through the day may contribute to reinforcing identification: we know more of the characters and they are thus brought closer to the audience. In this way, both Julián and Susana are presented in their workplace, each character is presented as they talk to their confidants about the other.

But the most interesting aspect of the film is Perojo's handling of the musical numbers, in which he seeks an integration of music, narrative and image. In ordinary operetta or *zarzuela*-oriented musicals, the bursting into song rarely produces a change in the film's style. At most, we get a long take, with the character performing, alternated with close-ups and medium shots of devoted audiences, as in the Angelillo musicals for Filmófono (such as *La hija de Juan Simón* [*Juan Simón's Daughter*], 1935). Perojo integrates the language of music into his editing and *mise-en-scène* and even if musical numbers are perceived as something different to book scenes they propel the action forward instead of stopping it. This is clear from the first number, 'Por ser la Virgen de la Paloma' ('Today's the Virgin of the Dove'), which makes use of rhythmic editing, closely organised to reflect musical phrasing. Perojo presents his characters on a horse-drawn tram as they head for the wedding breakfast. In the original, neighbours came on stage singing in anticipation, here the motivation is more natural. The first stanza involves straightforward editing that helps the audience to place the characters in the moving vehicle, but as we hear the second stanza, the contagious rhythms of the melody dominate the editing and framing, all gaining tempo as the song progresses. Towards the end of the song, musical phrases are mirrored in the increasingly fast editing, from the horses to the singing guests to the conductor or shots of the carriage. This view of the director as an intervening factor in the story is also apparent in Perojo's editing of the play's most famous number, 'Dónde vas con mantón de manila' ('Where are you going in that Manila shawl?'). Although it starts by emphasizing Julián, who is the initiator of the song, it seems to move gradually to focus on Susana, who is putting up resistance. Given that in the end it is her decision to leave with Don Hilarión, it is logical that her personality should be shown to be the stronger.

Such devices establish a close relationship between music and *mise-en-scène*, but the way this is manifested is different for each number. Perojo is the consummate technician, seeking different ways to express the exact values for every song. As already mentioned, Julián's romantic aria is in the original play, sung to his confidant Señá Rita. The song says that working-class people also have a heart and tells audiences of his suffering for Susana. The typical approach to such a number would be very straightforward: Julián sings his song in close-up, intercut with reaction shots of Señá Rita who performs the second verse. In the Perojo film it takes place in the typesetting workshop. This is, in itself, an interesting decision. In order to avoid sameness, Perojo has set the numbers in locations as widely different as possible. Then, as Julián goes about his daily chores, another self splits from him suggesting his attention is elsewhere. It is this superimposed image who sings the aria. At one moment, a projection of Rita appears, as if her voice was inside Julián's head. The number ends with a chorus in which other workers join in. The effect is extraordinary, as if Julián's inner feelings had somehow transformed to his surroundings and that now the whole world was commenting on his dilemma.

Narrative editing that mimes melody and the interweaving of musical themes is also the organisational device used to articulate the scene with Julián at the girls' door, who descend the stairs accompanied by Hilarión. The distinction between the musical themes is reflected in camera movement: inside the building, we watch Don Hilarión descending the staircase with the girls, outside, Julián sings of his woes tightly framed by a static camera. As in the first number, *mise-en-scène* is 'reflecting' on the music, rather than 'commenting' on the song (as in Julián's earlier aria).

This emphasis in community is also shown through cinematic devices instead of just through objects represented. The sequence known as 'Nocturno' is a musical number without protagonists, organised around editing of different parts of town that seem to participate in the festive spirit. It starts quietly as the nightwatch light up the street lamps, and swiftly we are taken to the street carnival and even a high-society ball. The ferris wheel and the carousel in the carnival contribute with movement to the feeling of joy shared by Madrilenos.

But the most remarkable scene in this sense is the *Seguidilla*. The camera tracks into a popular café where a folkloric singer performs a song completely unrelated to the plot. Then the camera leaves the place through the window and moves along rooftops and house fronts to show how the tune is picked up by different characters who add their own lyric. We see people leaning out of the window as they prepare for the party, and especially we hear Aunt Antonia's version, totally in character. Again, the effect is that of the community joining in to a common theme. In the same way as neighbours have a say in Susana's decisions, the feeling of a whole community joining in the same theme is astounding. Each character sings individual words that express their own attitudes, but the total effect goes beyond individuals.

In the treatment of musical numbers and in the creation of a whimsical world made out of music in which love triumphs, Perojo was bringing the best traditions of popular cinema to one of the key pieces of national art. Technique foregrounds the vivacity and joy of the popular classes and evidences new directions for Spanish cinema which would, sadly, be thwarted by the Civil War.

Alberto Mira

REFERENCE

Gubern, Román (1994) *Benito Perojo: Pionerismo y Supervivencia*. Madrid: Ediciones de la Filmoteca.

ANIKI-BÓBÓ

MANOEL DE OLIVEIRA, PORTUGAL, 1942

In 1942, when Manoel de Oliveira released his first feature-length film, *Aniki-Bóbó*, war was raging in much of Europe, and Portugal was entering the second decade of António Salazar's moralistic and repressive dictatorship, the *Estado Novo*. Censorship was harsh and dissent not tolerated. The notorious political police, the PIDE, was created to silence malcontents. Not unexpectedly, Portuguese films of the period were conformist. As Alves Costa has written, in the 1930s and 1940s the country's cinema functioned perfectly well within the regime's political objectives, 'mirroring the image and manners that it wants us to believe are those of the good Portuguese people – poor but joyful, sentimental and seductive, with eight centuries of history and an empire (to be respected), conformist and happy with their simplicity, their daily ration of bread, bullfights, *fado* and the sun shining on the Tejo'.

National cinematic production had averaged fewer than three feature-length films per year since the advent of sound in 1931. They generally fell into one of a limited number of genres: urban comedies (*A Canção de Lisboa* [*Song of Lisbon*], José Cottinelli Telmo, 1933; *O Pai Tirano*, António Lopes Ribeiro, 1940), historical dramas or literary adaptations set in the past (*As Pupilas do Senhor Reitor*, Leitão de Barros, 1935; *Bocage – As Três Graças*, Leitão de Barros, 1936), or films with rural settings or that deal with rural characters 'displaced' in the city (*Maria Papoila*, Leitão de Barros, 1937; *A Canção da Terra*, Jorge Brum do Canto, 1938). None of the films produced during the period openly contradicted the State's ideological designs, although some, such as *Song of Lisbon*, poked good-natured fun at the regime. Others were explicitly aligned with it. In 1937, for example, António Lopes Ribeiro, a director and producer closely associated with – and supported by – the Estado Novo, released the propagandistic *A Revolução de Maio*, which was produced by the regime's Secretariado da Propaganda Nacional (Secretariat of National Propaganda).

On one level, *Aniki-Bóbó* is no exception to this general situation. Produced by Lopes Ribeiro, its narrative unfolds into a rather conservative stance of reconciliation and moral rectitude. On other levels, however, it stands apart from mainstream Portuguese cinema of the period. It is a film about children, but its central narrative conflict – a love triangle – and its major themes are traditionally associated with adults. Oliveira has said that when it was released, the film was criticised for representing children who disobey, lie and steal. In other words, they act like adults, who sometimes act like children. The film casts authority, and hence authoritarianism, in a rather sinister light throughout much of the narrative, and it explores, in deceptively simple fashion, such issues as desire, transgression, guilt and punishment. The film is much darker or 'nocturnal' than it appears to be on first glance. (Critic João Bénard da Costa has described Oliveira's cinema, at least until 1981, as a 'cinema of fear'.) *AnikiBobó* deals with children's fears in a world in which they appear to be free, but where they are in reality inhibited and constrained by social institutions and expectations.

Aniki-Bóbó can be understood in multiple ways. Given the historical context of its production, the film can clearly be read in political or sociological terms as a somewhat contradictory exploration of repression and freedom, transgression and punishment. Oliveira himself has said that his film, shot during the war and the dictatorship, 'has a pacifist spirit, even though that was not a direct intention. It spoke against oppression. I only included a policeman because of the film's symbolic aspect as an attack against the dictatorship.' Aesthetically, a political or sociological interpretation finds resonance in the location shooting along the banks of the Douro river and the use of non-professional actors, which have led numerous critics to see the film as a precursor of neorealism. At the same time, its exploration of desire, guilt and fear lends itself to a psychoanalytical reading, which is bolstered aesthetically by the film's oneiric, expressionist sequences. Either reading by itself would inevitably be reductive and would not account for the film's complexity or for the privileged place it occupies in Portuguese film history.

Aniki-Bóbó is based loosely on Rodrigo de Freitas' short story 'Meninos Milionários', which first appeared in 1930 in the Portuguese modernist review *Presença*. The story focuses on a group of boys within the oppressive space of the classroom, a space they enter only after leaving their freedom and their souls at the door. It thus contrasts restriction and liberty, confinement between four fly-stained walls and the freedom of the streets, tedium and excitement. The boys are 'millionaires' because of the richness of their imaginations and their lives outside of the classroom. Inside, they have to deal with a stern teacher who pulls their ears when they get out of line, provoking nightmarish visions of war and black machines pulling thousands of train carriages and rushing toward them. Their attention is frequently drawn to a high window with its narrow ledge, which represents an opening to the outside world, yet they have an underlying fear of what awaits them there. Despite the greater freedom they have outside, there they are afraid of the police and the gardeners who tend to the trees where they like to steal fruit. The story does not individualise its characters; indeed, none of them have names. It focuses, rather, on their collective experience

Oliveira's *Aniki-Bóbó* takes the core idea of Freitas' story and expands its dramatic elements. The film deals with a group of boys – and one girl – who play along the banks of the Douro river in the city of Porto in northern Portugal. Its narrative focuses on two boys, Carlitos (Horácio Silva) and Eduardinho (António Santos), who compete for the attention of Teresinha (Fernanda Matos). Carlitos is shy, distracted, innocent and naïve, whereas Eduardinho, the group's leader, is outgoing, rude and a bully. After several confrontations with Eduardinho, and in order to win Teresinha's favor, Carlitos steals a doll that she had admired in the window of a store called the 'Loja das Tentações' ('Shop of Temptations'). He gives it to her that night by crawling across rooftops to her window. As the competition between the two boys intensifies, Eduardinho slips and falls down an embankment toward an on-rushing train below. Suspecting that Carlitos had pushed Eduardinho, the other boys – and Teresinha – turn their back on him. Abandoned by his friends, Carlitos attempts unsuccessfully to stowaway on a boat leaving Porto. Finally, the shopkeeper, who had witnessed the accident, clears the air by declaring Carlitos innocent, resulting in his friends' return. Carlitos attempts to return the stolen doll, but the shopkeeper wants him to have it. He again gives it to Teresinha, and the final narrative shot shows the two of them climbing a stairway side by side, each holding one of the doll's hands, while Eduardinho recovers in the hospital.

As in Freitas' short story, in *Aniki-Bóbó* the boys' drama takes place in inter-connected spaces of freedom and repression. On the one hand, the river, the streets and the nearby hillside overlooking the train tracks represent spaces of freedom where the children swim or play after school. Their freedom in these spaces is only relative, however, since even there they are always under the watchful eye of authority, particularly of the ubiquitous but largely ineffectual policeman – who, along with the schoolteacher, is the most explicit representative of the state in *Aniki-Bóbó* – and the shopkeeper, who frequently watches them as they walk to school. Perhaps paradoxically, these natural settings give the film a certain level of abstraction and indefinition. The film makes no attempt to reproduce daily life in the city, as a neorealist work might do. The streets are normally empty except for the children and their antagonists.

In sharp contrast to the streets and the river are the school and the home. The school is an institutionalised space of constraint, boredom and even cruelty. The teacher is stern, humourless and rigid, and he is given to humiliating his pupils, either by mocking their academic frailties (for example, Eduardinho's inability to read fluently) or by sending them to the dunce's corner. It is therefore not surprising that students daydream or allow their attention to wander to the open window, which, as in Freitas' story, represents an outlet to the world of freedom.

The home appears infrequently in *Aniki-Bóbó*, and when it does it generally represents a space where children are confined or chastised. It is far from representing a nurturing environment. In the first post-credits sequence, for example, Carlitos' mother helps him dress for school. As she does so, Carlitos plays with a ceramic clown on the dresser and says the words of the children's rhyme 'Aniki-Bóbó'. His mother twice tells him to be quiet, and she accidentally knocks his arm into the clown, which falls onto the floor and breaks into many pieces. She slaps him on the forehead, complaining about the mess he had made, but that she had caused.

It is significant that the few adults in the film do not have names, and none of the children's fathers appear; they have been symbolically replaced by representatives of the state and the economy. The mothers who appear are not identified as such. Indeed, the spectator does not even see the face of Carlitos' mother, the only woman to have more than one appearance in the film. The programme notes for a 1981 screening of the film at the Cinemateca Portuguesa in Lisbon suggest that 'it's as if growing up were an irreparable loss of identity, an inevitable passage to anonymity. If the passage to the adult world means the loss of a name, and if names say what each thing is, then passage to the adult world also represents a loss of being.'

The contrast between the streets, the school and the home becomes even more explicit in an early sequence when the boys leave school and hear music in the streets. They gather around a man singing the words: 'Open your window and life will become more beautiful … Open the school door, let the sparrow out of its cage.' Looking on from above are a woman and her son in a window. When the music stops, the boy wants to hear more, but she reprimands him and slams the window shut. Again, the home and the family mirror the role of the school in its function as a space of repression.

As its very name suggests, the Loja das Tentações, a kind of a dry goods store, represents a space of desire and interdiction because of its possession of items – such as the doll – that are out of the economic reach of the poor children. In many ways, it is the narrative's central focal point, where its conflicts intensify and are resolved. It is a space of both transgression and forgiveness. Its window, dominated by the figure of the doll, allows for a double gaze, as the children look in and the shopkeeper and the doll – the film includes shots from the doll's perspective – look out. Unlike the dour schoolteacher, the shopkeeper is characterised as wise and understanding. He is also the only adult with a sense of humour. He is the one who clarifies the circumstances of Eduardinho's accident, leading to the group's reconciliation with Carlitos, and who provides the film's final explicit message about the futility of anger and conflict. In short, the Loja das Tentações is a space of both sin and redemption.

The love triangle between Eduardinho, Carlitos and Teresinha plays itself out against this backdrop through a recurring structure of transgression and punishment. Even the film's title refers implicitly to this structure. 'Aniki-Bóbó' is part of a children's rhyme used to determine who will play cops and robbers. As João Lopes suggests, the children's games are forms of initiation into the adult world, a world of law, order and regimentation.

As indicated above, the first instance of transgression and punishment involves Carlitos and his mother as she is dressing him for school. The fact that he is saying the words to 'Aniki-Bóbó' when the clown falls and breaks implicitly introduces the question of good and evil. After his mother slaps him on the head, Carlitos runs out of the room, and an exterior shot shows him coming out of the door and looking up at the sky. He starts to run off to school, but his mother calls him back. He returns hesitantly, fearful of being hit again. In fact, she calls him because he has forgotten a book. She puts it in his book bag, which then becomes the camera's focus. On the bag are written the words 'Always follow the right path', indicative of the moral strictures presumably guiding society. The words might also be seen as cautionary advice about how to get along under a repressive authoritarian regime.

It is not always easy to follow the right path, however, since human nature can take wrong turns and multiple barriers, temptations and desires get in the way. As Carlitos runs off distractedly, for example, he is almost hit by a truck. He stands in the street looking at it, and he is nearly run over by a car. As he walks along the sidewalk, apparently looking backwards at the car, he runs into a policeman. He continues walking, now looking backwards at the policeman, and he runs into a lamppost. In this comic sequence, the truck, the car, the policeman and the lamppost all represent obstacles to the 'right path'. In a broader, more abstract, and perhaps more paradoxical sense, with the exception of the policeman, who is an obvious symbol of authority and potential repression, Carlitos' brief obstacle course is constituted by symbols of modernity: the truck, the car and the pole of an electric street light. Rather than offering a critique of modernisation, the sequence suggests a recognition of the difficulties the process sometimes entails.

Carlitos meets up with his friends, and as the boys walk to school, they pass Teresinha's house. She comes out on her balcony and waves at Eduardinho. Carlitos also looks up at Teresinha, provoking jealousy in Eduardo. As they walk on, Eduardo pushes Carlitos down, his face in a puddle of muddy water near a construction site. Teresinha reacts with shock, but the other boys, and eventually Teresinha herself, laugh at him. Again we see, albeit on another level, the structure of transgression and punishment. Carlitos unknowingly steps onto Eduardinho's turf and is punished for doing so.

When they arrive at school the boys hang their hats on pegs on the wall, rendering concrete a more abstract element of the story 'Meninos Milionários', where they leave their souls at the door. One boy, Pistarim (António Moraes Soares), is late. As he runs to school, he repeatedly falls down, apparently because his shoes are too large, thus constituting a physical sign of his modest economic means. He finally makes it to school, hangs his hat on the last free peg, quietly enters the classroom and tries to make it to his seat without being noticed by the teacher. As he sits down, the teacher tells him to sit in the dunce's corner, with a paper hat with tall ears on his head. Punishment again follows transgression.

An unsympathetic, old-fashioned teacher, whose authoritarian methods only cause the boys to be easily distracted and to daydream, rules the school. While a student is reading a story in a high-pitched voice, Carlitos' eyes wander to a crack in the wall, a world map, a blackboard, and finally to a cat sitting on the window sill. The window obviously represents a passageway to the freedom of the outside world, while the cat stands in contrast to the teacher in its level of interest. While Carlitos admires the cat, Eduardinho shoots one of the paper 'ears' of Pistarim's dunce cap with a slingshot. Other boys pay attention to the cat. The teacher strikes Pistarim's other 'ear' with his rod, frightening the cat, which runs off, much to the boys' disappointment. Although seemingly inconsequential acts, the fact that both the teacher and Eduardinho destroy one of Pistarim's 'ears' draws a parallel between the two of them, and the film also reinforces the conflict between Carlitos and Eduardinho, since Carlitos and Pistarim are close friends.

The dramatic conflict that had begun while the boys were on the way to school continues later that day, as Teresinha comes down some steps carrying a basket and meets Carlitos in the street. He asks her if she wants to play with him, then looks down to get an apple out of a bag and polish it on his shirt. When he looks back up, she is gone. She has walked off to meet Eduardinho by the river, as Carlitos watches from afar. As Teresinha leaves, Eduardinho looks up and is displeased to see Carlitos gazing at Teresinha. Eduardinho then changes clothes alongside a boat by the river. Carlitos does the same, and he and the other boys swim, while Eduardinho climbs to the top of a crane, dives into water and swims toward other boys (the shot of Eduardinho diving beautifully into the Douro can be seen as an autobiographical reference: in his youth, Manoel de Oliveira was a diving champion). Eduardinho tries to force Pistarim to swim as well, but he is afraid to do so. Carlitos defends Pistarim, and he and Eduardinho fight. Although Carlitos' defense of Pistarim is the immediate cause, in reality the scuffle represents a displacement of the dispute over Teresinha.

After the fight is broken up and the boys flee from the policeman, Carlitos and Pistarim come across Teresinha looking at the doll in the window of the Loja das Tentações. Teresinha notices that he has a black eye, which she gently touches. She walks to a nearby fountain and wets the hem of her dress to soothe Carlitos' pain. He asks her if she likes the doll, and the three of them stand in front of the shop-window sighing. The camera then pans up to the store sign, which has angels on either side. The sequence ends with a lap dissolve to the sky, as if to suggest the providential nature of their encounter.

The conflict between Eduardinho and Carlitos intensifies in the following sequences. In school, Carlitos draws a stick figure of a girl – obviously Teresinha – on a small blackboard. Eduardinho hits him with an ink-stained spitball. The day after Carlitos gives Teresinha the doll, the boys play hooky from school. Eduardinho makes a kite, while Carlitos sits by himself. Eduardinho goes to the store to buy some paper for his kite, telling the shopkeeper that the teacher had sent him to buy it. The boy is extremely rude to the shopkeeper, telling him that he will go to the shopkeeper's funeral when he dies. The storeowner, perhaps suspecting Eduardinho of having stolen the doll, leaves his store and follows him down to the river where the boys are playing. They see him and run away, but he finds Carlitos' bag under a boat and runs after them. They run to a hilltop and across a bridge over the train tracks to escape the pursuing shopkeeper.

The following sequence shows the group of children, including Teresinha, on a hillside marching in quasi-military formation to the sounds of 'Aniki-Bobó'. The rivalry between Eduardinho and Carlitos breaks out again when Carlitos attempts to join Eduardinho and Teresinha at the head of the group. They fight again, but the other boys break them up. The group hears a train coming, and they run over to the hillside. Eduardinho trips and falls off the hill. After the fall, the camera shows him lying beside the tracks below. Teresinha screams and the group looks accusingly at Carlitos, pointing fingers at him as the shopkeeper arrives.

Several things can be said about this sequence. On one level, transgression and punishment are collective, since the entire group is playing hooky from school, a fact emphasised by a shot of their empty desks in the classroom. On another, both Eduardinho and Carlitos suffer the consequences of their actions, the former through a potentially fatal accident, and the latter through banishment from the group. At the same time, one cannot help but notice that the increased regimentation of the boys' lives corresponds to an increase in the level of conflict that exists between them.

That night, in what has become known as the film's 'philosophical sequence', most of the boys sit outside, look up at the stars and discuss the meaning of life and death. Carlitos is not among them. He is home in bed, trying to sleep, but he has a guilt-ridden nightmare, which the film depicts expressionistically through the superimposition of rapidly changing, recurring images: a swirling vortex, an on-rushing train, the doll, the shopkeeper as an ogre, the policeman, Eduardinho, fire, the teacher, Teresinha screaming, the Loja das Tentações, Teresinha beckoning to him with a balloon in hand. His mother awakens him. He had slept in his clothes, and when he gets up and washes, his image is reflected in a broken mirror, his identity shattered. When he goes to school, the boys must write 'I will not skip school again', and while the teacher lectures about doing bad deeds, all of the other boys look at Carlitos. It is after this series of events that he attempts unsuccessfully to leave Porto as a stowaway on a boat, while the other boys visit Eduardinho in the hospital.

As indicated in the brief narrative summary provided above, the shopkeeper clears the air by telling Teresinha that he had seen Eduardinho's fall and that it was in fact an accident. Carlitos had nothing to do with it. This leads to reconciliation among the group and to Carlitos' attempt to return the doll. It is when the shopkeeper tells Carlitos that he can keep it that he provides the film's moral message against anger and violence. The film's final shot shows that Carlitos finally manages to take Eduardinho's place beside Teresinha. As Carlitos and Teresinha walk up the stairs holding the doll between them, the camera again providentially pans to the sky.

Nevertheless, can one say that everything is truly resolved in *Aniki-Bóbó*? Carlitos gets Teresinha; Teresinha gets the doll; and Eduardinho gets medical treatment. The naïve and innocent boy wins out over the unsympathetic bully. After all, as the shopkeeper says, Carlitos had 'cleared his conscience' by confessing to his sin, and it seems that he will henceforth 'follow the right path'. Seen in this way, *Aniki-Bóbó* might, in the final analysis, appear to cede to a form of Christian morality, with obvious conservative political implications. Such an interpretation, however, might be somewhat precipitous. What about Eduardinho, who is not blessed with the same good fortune and redemption as Carlitos? He had been very rude to the shopkeeper, telling him that one day he would gladly go to the man's funeral, but he did not steal from him. The answer to the question perhaps lies in the associations made almost from the beginning between Eduardinho and the more sinister figures that appear in the film, particularly the teacher and the policeman. He can therefore be seen to represent an authoritarian posture, whereas Carlitos is associated ultimately with the generous, benevolent and paternalistic shop-keeper. It is perhaps in this sense that Manoel de Oliveira can correctly assert that, among other things, *Aniki-Bóbó* offers a critique of Salazar's dictatorship.

Randal Johnson

REFERENCES

Costa, Alves (1978) *Breve história do cinema português: 1896–1962*. Lisboa: Instituto de Cultura Portuguesa.

Da Costa, João Bénard (1981) 'O cinema é um vício', in *Manoel de Oliveira*. Lisboa: Cinemateca Portuguesa, 5–12.

Lopes, João (n.d.) *Aniki-Bobó*. Lisboa: Secretaria de Estado da Reforma Educativa.

63.

LOS ÚLTIMOS DE FILIPINAS LAST STAND IN THE PHILIPPINES

ANTONIO ROMÁN, SPAIN, 1945

Few films express the official spirit of early Francoist Spain and the priorities of its film industry in the 1940s better than *Los últimos de Filipinas* (*Last Stand in the Philippines*, Antonio Román, 1945). This fictionalisation of the incident where a group of Spanish soldiers put up desperate resistance for their last stand in the Philippines in 1898, made at the height of the regime's autarkist period (1939–51), remains a landmark in the history of Spanish cinema. The director, Antonio Román, was one of Spain's most respected filmmakers at the time, having made a name for himself first with his epic film *Escuadrilla* (*Squadron*, 1941) and then with *Boda en el infierno* (*Marriage in Hell*, 1942). The film was given strong official backing from the start: it was branded *de interés nacional* (of national interest), and received a pre-production subsidy from the National Syndicate of Spectacle. The press of the time, in particular *Primer Plano*, the official film magazine, gave the production process ample coverage, with regular features on its planning and shooting stages months before its release on 28 December 1945. Upon public screening, the film enjoyed tremendous box-office success and enthusiastic critical reception, and was given two major awards, by the National Syndicate of Spectacle and by the Cinema Writers Circle.

Given that, in the 1940s, Spain had the highest rate of film-attendance in Europe, it is no wonder that the State should view cinema as a privileged means of indoctrination, and a useful way of legitimising a political structure born of a military rebellion. *Last Stand in the Philippines* belonged to an industry pressed into the service of illustrating and upholding the nobility of the Spanish 'race', a concept that, in the Francoist imagination, did not refer to physical or somatic characteristics, but, as the official rhetoric proclaimed, to ingrained attributes. In the words of critic Antonio Fraguas Saavedra: 'Our personality in the cinema has to be gained by showing to the world those cultural and temperamental features that characterise a race that had the whole planet under its control. A race of bloody births, of gigantic adventures, of immense virtues and sins, of brilliant saints and captains … a race which God always saw as a dam against great blasphemies and heresies. This constitutes the Spanishness of our cinema: the fidelity to those features that endow our race with an eternal and unmistakable profile.'

Through tight control of education, culture and the media, the State worked hard to re-create its historical and ideological foundations or, to use Pierre Sorlin's phrase, the Nation's 'historical capital' – the series of dates, events and figures known to the members of a community and viewed by them as their common historical heritage. Such a monolithic project was matched by careful policing of an industry that was, on the one hand, limited by strict censor-ship laws and on the other, actively supportive of filmmaking, as long as the products fell within clear generic patterns: *cine de cruzada* (civil war cinema), historical cinema, religious cinema and folkloric musicals. In more or less explicit ways, films in these categories sought to vindi-cate the newly established order, often by appealing to national characteristics which, traceable – it was argued – throughout the country's long history, could be appropriately adopted as myths and symbols for the 'new' Spain.

From the regime's point of view the most apposite notion was that of Spain's historically-sanctioned imperial grandeur. But given the impoverished, depleted state of the divided Spain of the 1940s, it was necessary to resort to past glories in order to revive the myth of national supremacy. Not surprisingly, these stories – and among them those set in Spain's former over-seas colonies – were often seasoned with nostalgia, and designed to sublimate what, after all, were narratives of defeat and loss. This was the case, for instance, of *Héroes del 95* (*Heroes of '95*, Raúl Alfonso, 1946) and *Bambú* (*Bamboo*, José Luis Sáenz de Heredia, 1945), both set in the final years of Spanish rule in Cuba, and also, clearly, of *Last Stand in the Philippines*.

The genealogy of *Last Stand in the Philippines* is long and complex. Its screenplay, writ-ten by Antonio Román and Pedro de Juan, was based on two literary scripts, *El fuerte de Baler* (*The Siege of Baler*), by Enrique Alonso Barcones and Rafael Sánchez Campoy, and *Los héroes de Baler* (*The Heroes of Baler*), by Enrique Llovet. These, in turn, had been based on a chroni-cle entitled *El sitio de Baler* (*The Siege of Baler*), written upon return from the Philippines by Lieutenant Saturnino Martín Cerezo, and published in 1904. The storyline of *Last Stand in the Philippines*, then, emerges from a combination of historical truth and the mythologizing effects of years of oral and literary re-creation.

Román's filmed version runs as follows: in the church of Baler, a small village on one of the many islands in the Philippine Archipelago, a Spanish garrison formed by fifty soldiers, a doctor and a priest, all commanded by Captain de las Moreras (José Nieto), defend a military position at a time when Tagalog rebels are escalating their attacks on Spain's colonial strong-holds. At first, the film shows brief vignettes of canteen relaxation and banter, including the competition between soldiers Chamizo (Fernando Rey) and Santamaría (Carlos Muñoz) for the love of Tala (Nani Fernández), a Tagalog woman. As expected, the insurgents attack the garrison, which finds refuge in the church, where it braces itself for a long siege. As the days pass rations run scarce, sickness rages, and more and more men die, including Captain de las Moreras, leaving Lieutenant Martín Cerezo (Armando Calvo) in command of the post. The men remain under siege for eleven months and one day, initially not knowing, and later not believing, the news that on 10 December 1898 Spain had signed the Treaty of Paris handing over the control of the Philippines to the USA. After months of suffering, Martín Cerezo reads a news item about a friend in one of the papers given to him by a Spanish military envoy sent to convince him of the end of Spanish rule in the Philippines. Finally accepting the new order, he agrees to leave the church, and on their way out the 33 remaining men are accorded due military respect by the Tagalogs.

Last Stand in the Philippines was praised for its acting, formal and technical virtuosity, apt repertoire of popular songs (*alegrías, soleares, villancicos, habaneras*), blend of drama and humour, and above all, its flattering portrayal of Spain's noble, heroic stance at a fateful hour. Following the release of the film, Antonio Román drew attention, in an interview with critic Alfonso Sánchez published in June 1945, to the recurrence of the last stand motif in Spanish history, even going so far as to identify it as a defining element of Spanishness: 'This race of ours is magnificent … Yesterday it was the names of Sagunto and Numancia. Baler is worthy of them. Still fresh in the memory are those of the Toledan Alcazar and Santa María de la Cabeza.'

Comments like these call to mind Pierre Sorlin's claim that 'the historical tradition defended by each group and class is of course only an instrument for talking about the present'. As has been argued convincingly by Antoni Rigol and Jordi Sebastian, the film's eulogy of stubborn resistance in the face of isolation acted as a convenient metaphor for Spain's situation in 1944, after the imposition of sanctions by the Second World War victors on the Franco regime. The combination of historical fact and legendary rhetoric attached to the motif of the last stand delivered a message to its audience that despite the hardships of the moment, their proud resilience would eventually earn the plaudits of history.

Even though reviewer Alfonso Sánchez, later in August 1945, remarked that 'those who demand fidelity to History will find it abundantly', and the director himself insisted that he had 'respected the history of the heroic incident', the film nevertheless took liberties with historical fact. Román himself admitted, in the interview quoted above, that 'naturally, I have had to give the narrative the necessary filmic coherence, and that means certain sacrifices that do not alter the reality of events'. Later assessments of the film would be less forgiving. According to

Malén Aznárez, the film displays a 'remarkable lack of historical rigour, an ingenuity bordering on naïveté'. It is unlikely, though, that the film's departure from historical fact would have been prompted by naïveté. After all, in the words of Leger Grindon, 'what is left out of a historical fiction can suggest almost as much about its politics as what is emphasised'. Thus, when Román's film is set against Martín Cerezo's account following his return from the Philippines (itself a version undoubtedly shaped by personal interests), and against historical data on the period in question, significant absences become apparent. Those include censorship of the summary execution of two potential deserters, the hierarchical tensions between members of the regiment, the power-driven rivalries of Church and Army in the Philippines, the Lieutenant's criticism, in the chronicle, of the Spanish authorities for failing to send help, and his mention of unspecified forms of 'perverse' behaviour by some soldiers. Clearly, the cinema of the time could not serve as a platform for the expression of cowardice, military insubordination, criticism of authority, or sexual deviance. If *Last Stand in the Philippines* was to contribute to the regime's project of national reunification, it had to display unflinching heroism in the service of the common good, and avoid anything that might hint at fissures in the body of the collective hero.

In view of its tendency towards propaganda, the Spanish film industry of the early Francoist period has often been compared to the cinema of Fascist Italy or Germany. But, in addition to these overlaps, Spanish films of the time bear striking resemblances to some Hollywood films made during the Second World War, when, as Ralph Willet points out, 'the alliance between the American film industry and the American government became complete, with the authorities even suggesting particular themes that Hollywood should exploit'. As noted by Robert Ray, US wartime films adhered to an ideologically and emotionally simplistic pattern that relied on a series of fixed motifs, including the focus on an isolated male group involved in a life-and-death task, and the portrayal of that group, composed of distinct types, that depends on both teamwork and individual exploits, and displays professionalism and stoicism in the face of danger and death. Of particular interest here are the so-called 'last stand' films, a sort of sub-genre that, as Willet explains, focused on survival, 'depicting glorious American defeats in the Pacific in the cause of freedom [which] masochistically expose complacency and counsel unity'.

The parallels are self-evident, even uncanny, particularly when *Last Stand in the Philippines* is compared to films like *Bataan* (Tay Garnett, 1943), released at a time when the Second World War was not yet over. Like Román's film, also set in the Philippines, it focuses on a group of soldiers desperately defending a position that is ultimately lost (in this case to the invading Japanese army). But the similarities between both films reach beyond plot and setting to form, particularly in relation to *mise-en-scène* and camerawork. Both rely heavily on creating a feeling of claustrophobia through shots with little depth of field, often cluttered up with tropical vegetation or various forms of barrier in both foreground and background, as if to imprison the characters in the frame. There are also numerous night shots that further contribute to the feeling of entrapment, and the occasional low-angle or long shot of a building that becomes identified with their resistance: in *Last Stand in the Philippines* the church that protects the Spaniards from the advances of the Tagalogs, in *Bataan* the bridge that the Americans must keep on destroying to prevent the advance of the Japanese. Even the shot, towards the end, of Martín Cerezo staring at the crosses of all the soldiers who have been buried in the churchyard is very similar to the one in which the only survivor of the American group, Sergeant Bill Dane (Robert Taylor) – like Martín Cerezo forced to take command of the group following the death of his superior – is seen against the backdrop of a line of crosses crowned with the rifles and helmets of the fallen men. In both films, too, an authoritative voice-over provides reassuring closure by endowing with heroic value what are, after all, stories of loss and defeat.

Where *Last Stand in the Philippines* departs from *Bataan* is in its depiction of the group as a much more uniform, compact entity. To a certain extent out of line with the dominant tendency of Spanish historical war films of the time, where the individual hero, as outlined by Casimiro Torreiro, was the undisputed protagonist, *Last Stand in the Philippines* goes a long way towards emphasising the collective heroism of the group. Through manipulation of the narrative voice and point of view, character construction and *mise-en-scène*, the film attempts to create a unified heroic group, guided by a single, firm will. The film deviates from the pattern of the memoirs by avoiding the subjective point of view of Martín Cerezo, and opts, instead, for the external, omniscient point of view of an unseen narrator. An authoritative voice-over opens and closes the film, and inserts further commentary half-way, relying on phrases like 'a handful of men', 'the characters in this story', or 'that handful of brave men', thereby prioritising group over individual acts of courage. Despite awareness of the hierarchical nature of the army, where the commander-in-chief is necessarily superior to the rest of the soldiers, the film avoids attributing all merit to Martín Cerezo and depicts the rest of the garrison as equally brave, patriotic and resilient. Whereas in *Bataan* the men's various ethnic, social and psychological idiosyncrasies are given prominence, *Last Stand in the Philippines* avoids reference even to regional distinctiveness, and to suggestions that individual differences are potential causes of disruption. In this, *Last Stand in the Philippines* is also unlike, say, *Agustina de Aragón* (*Agustina of Aragon*, Juan de Orduña, 1950), where the disagreements between the Aragonese and the Catalan characters are raised superficially at the beginning, as a prelude to reconciliation and ideological endorsement of the notion that no differences of substance divide the regions of Spain.

The *mise-en-scène* in *Last Stand in the Philippines* also contributes to the sense of compactness and unity, as the soldiers are frequently seen engaged in group activities. The camera often dwells in medium or long shots on ensembles of men: drinking in the canteen, falling in line on the village square, fighting the Tagalogs, saluting the flag, singing or praying. Shots of single characters are rare, and individual close-ups also kept to a minimum, being almost exclusively reserved for the expression of Martín Cerezo's anguish at a few climactic moments.

Against this background of group activity, two couplings, Tala and Juan, and, later, Lieutenant Martín Cerezo and Doctor Vigil, are given narrative prominence. Tala is the only woman in the story and, to all intents and purposes, the only Philippino character of any real significance. For Chamizo and Santamaría, as well as for the rest of the garrison, Tala embodies a longed-for femininity. Furthermore, in making herself available every day to the men in the canteen, singing songs for a few coins, she also becomes a metaphor for the colony's submission to Spain. In the same way as the voice-over at the start of the film defines the setting for the action as 'the delicate but terrible land of the Philippine Islands', Tala is shown to be simultaneously seductive and perilous. As in so many other contemporary stories of interracial love, the relationship between the native female and the Spanish male remains inconclusive. In this *Last Stand in the Philippines* aligns itself with contemporary practices, in Spain, as well as in Hollywood, which demand the eventual separation (often by death) of the interracial couple, as in, say, *Legión de héroes* (*Legion of Heroes*, Armando Seville y Juan Fortuny, 1942), *Bamboo,* or *La dama del armiño* (*Lady in Ermine*, Eusebio Fernández Ardavín, 1947). An interesting exception is *La manigua sin Dios* (Arturo Ruiz Castillo, 1947) in which Panambí, a naïve indigenous Guarani girl (again played by Nani Fernández), falls in love and eventually marries the Spanish Javier (Antonio Casas). In *Last Stand in the Philippines* neither member of the interracial couple dies, but, though briefly seen together in the last scene, their union is undermined by Juan's previous warning to Tala that their lives must follow separate paths. The metaphorical significance of the difficult relations between Tala and Juan points to the ultimately impossible union between Spain and the Philippines.

The two scenes in which Tala sings the *habanera* 'Yo te diré' ('Let Me Tell You') bring the action to a halt, and replace the heroic mode with nostalgia, as if, through these tableaux, the film were attempting to slow down the dénouement of events that would inevitably lead to the loss of imperial control. In the first, longer, scene, Tala is sitting on the bar top, her arm sensuously raised, shoulder and legs exposed, as she sings to an audience of attentive soldiers. The *mise-en-scène*, the camerawork and the lighting all construct the native woman as beautiful and desirable. But although she is portrayed as essentially innocent and wholesome, the ideologised narrative demands her conversion into a source of division, danger and sadness: Chamizo and Santamaría vie jealously for Tala, and she herself recounts that, after only his first view of her, Juan became involved in an argument with her boss Moisés (José Miguel Rupert); later, her distracting presence leads to Chamizo's dereliction of duty in an important military mission; and finally, when she is tricked by the Philippinos into singing her 'Yo te diré' again, the song stirs feelings of longing and sadness in Spanish soldiers who have been deprived of female company for months, even leading to the death of a soldier who is ordered to rise to this provocation by answering her with another song.

In direct opposition to the tensions and divisions caused by desire for the female native, male comradeship within the group is depicted as a noble source of emotional fulfilment. The film thus dramatises various types of libidinal exchange, attaching different value to each of them. In an analysis of group dynamics, Freud argues that the same libidinal drive the individual may direct towards him/herself (self-preservation), could be directed towards others. This non-narcissistic emotional expenditure can take the form not only of sexual love, but also of friendship, comradeship, or love for humanity or for any abstract idea, such as patriotism. According to Freud, 'these impulses [can] force their way towards sexual union, but in other circumstances they are diverted from this aim or are prevented from reaching it, though always preserving enough of their original nature to keep their identity recognisable (as in such features as the longing for proximity, and self-sacrifice)'.

In *Last Stand in the Philippines*, libidinal energy is deflected from male/female romantic or sexual ties towards strengthening the bonds between men. The contrast between the potentially treacherous waters of heterosexual love and the safer environment of male friendship is expressed most vividly through the parallelism established between two important scenes: first Chamizo and Tala's romantic encounter in the *manigua* (woods), and second, Martín Cerezo's visit to Doctor Vigil on his sick bed, where their feelings for each other are also laid bare. Dialogue, *mise-en-scène* and camerawork all establish subtle connections between both scenes, in each of which the couple occupies the same frame in medium shot for most of the time, and words and characters acquire clearly allegorical meanings: in the former, the lovers stand for their respective homelands, their sentiments an amalgam of duty and desire; in the latter, the men represent the military and scientific professions, their initially dissimilar outlooks on life eventually proving no barrier to mutual affection and respect. In the scene between the Lieutenant and the Doctor, the *locus amoenus* is, though not the jungle itself, nevertheless – since the Doctor's sick bay is full of plants – its miniature equivalent. Here Martín Cerezo, as earlier Tala, declares that he has derived strength and knowledge from their relationship. Echoing Tala's feelings in the earlier scene with Juan, Martín Cerezo pleads with Doctor Vigil not to be left alone, thus reiterating sentiments previously conveyed indirectly in the lyrics of the *habanera*. When Martín Cerezo tells the sickly Doctor Vigil 'you can't leave me now! … I need you!', the scene, though less explicitly homoerotic than its famous precursor involving Alfredo Mayo and Luis Peña in *Harka!* (Carlos Arévalo, 1941), is nevertheless intense enough to be seen as a contrast to the moment when Tala asks Juan never to abandon her.

Eventually, whereas Tala's love for Juan cannot be reciprocated, Doctor Vigil's for Martín Cerezo, since it does not violate duty, is condoned by the narrative. Furthermore, as Tala/the Philippines must ultimately be surrendered, the object of desire can only be constructed, melancholically, as regretfully expendable: in fact both Roland B. Tolentino and José F. Colmeiro rightly argue that nostalgia is the dominant tone of the narrative. For this reason Tala, both as a female and as a native, is aligned with everything that contradicts Spanishness in the series of binaries marking the differences between Self and Other: metropolis vs. colony, handful of heroic Spaniards vs. many anonymous Philippinos, bravery vs. cunning, male vs. female, endurance vs. temptation.

Last Stand in the Philippines thus preaches surrender of sexual desire to purer, less physical, forms of love: male comradeship and patriotism. In this it falls into line with other similar all-male, Hollywood as well as Spanish, adventure/war films. Primo de Rivera (the founder of the Falange) and Franco are known to have admired the genre, particularly *Lives of a Bengal Lancer* (Henry Hathaway, 1935) and *Beau Geste* (William Wellman, 1939), stories that also privilege male friendship over heterosexual love. *Beau Geste* is even prefaced by an Arabic proverb that reads: 'The love of a man for a woman/ waxes and wanes like the moon/ but the love of brother for brother is as steadfast as the stars.' The heroes in *Beau Geste* and *Lives of a Bengal Lancer*, like those in comparable Spanish films such as *Harka!* (1942) and *Legión de heroes* (*Legion of Heroes*, 1942), end up dying, sacrificing themselves for a higher cause. This is the type of hero of which early Francoism approved: a male ready for martyrdom, driven by honour and duty, willing to sacrifice his own life for others.

In its celebration of male friendship and scepticism of heterosexual love *Last Stand in the Philippines* is of course partly a response to generic demands of the war or military adventure film and partly a reflection of the dominant ideology of the day. For all its compromises, however, the film is rescued from its reactionary agenda through its vibrant form and compelling narrative, which have guaranteed its reputation as one of the key films of 1940s Spanish cinema.

Isabel Santaollala

REFERENCES

Aznárez, Malén (1999) 'Héroes a la fuerza', *El país*, June, 52–60.

Colmeiro, José F. (2000) 'Nostalgia colonial y la construcción del Nuevo orden en *Los últimos de Filipinas*', in Florencio Sevilla and Carlos Alvar (eds) *Actas del XIII Congreso de la Asociación Internacional de Hispanistas*. Madrid: Castalia, 294–302.

Fraguas Saavedra, Antonio (1944) 'Personalidad española del cine español', *Primer plano*, 5, 168, January 2.

Freud, Sigmund (1985 [1915]) 'Thoughts for the Times on War and Death', in *Civilization, Society and Religion: The Pelican Freud Library*, vol. 12. Harmondsworth: Penguin Books, 57–89.

Grindon, Leger (1994) *Shadows on the Past: Studies in the Historical Fiction Film*. Philadelphia: Temple University Press.

Ray, Robert B. (1985) *A Certain Tendency of the Hollywood Cinema, 1930–1980*. Princeton: Princeton University Press.

Rigol, Antoni and Jordi Sebastián (1991) 'España aislada: *Los últimos de Filipinas* (1945) de Antonio Román', *Film-Historia*, 1, 3, 171–84.

Sánchez, Alfonso (1945a) 'Valor heróico de Los últimos de Filipinas', *Primer plano*, 6, 243, June 10.

_____ (1945b) 'En busca del paisaje de *Los últimos de Filipinas*', *Primer plano*, 6, 253, August 19.

Sorlin, Pierre (1980) *The Film in History: Restaging the Past*. Oxford: Basil Blackwell.

Tolentino, Roland B. (1997) 'Nations, Nationalisms, and *Los últimos de Filipinas*: An Imperialist Desire for Colonialist Nostalia', in Marsha Kinder (ed.) *Refiguring Spain: Cinema/Media/Representation*. Durham and London: Duke University Press, 133–53.

Torreiro, Casimiro (1999) 'Por el Imperio hacia Dios. El cine histórico de la autarquía', in José Enrique Monterde (ed.) *Ficciones históricas. Cuadernos de la Academia 6*. Madrid: Academia de las Artes y las Ciencias Cinematográficas de España, 53–65.

Willett, Ralph (1981) 'The Nation in Crisis: Hollywood's Response to the 1940s', in Philip Davies and Brian Neve (eds) *Cinema, Politics and Society in America*. Manchester: Manchester University Press, 59–75.

LOLA LA PICONERA LOLA THE COALGIRL

LUIS LUCIA, SPAIN, 1951

Lola la Piconera (*Lola the Coalgirl*, 1951) tends to be passed over in accounts of early Francoist cinema in spite of belonging to the two most typical genres of the period: the historical epic and the folkloric musical. As the last in the Cifesa series of historical films, it is felt to be somewhat marginal to the cycle. Still, the film clearly shares many of the features that made *Locura de amor* (*The Mad Queen*, 1948) or *Agustina de Aragón* (*Agustina of Aragon*, a.k.a. *The Siege*, 1950) distinctive box-office hits: an intense central performance by a popular star, lavish settings, melodrama, action sequences (hyped as 'The most exciting ever' in the publicity materials), intrigue, comic elements and a strong supporting cast. Songs and dances introduce a sense of joy and escapism that is at odds with the earnestness displayed by Aurora Bautista in previous films. Featuring a singer as a central character also had an impact on the way audiences engaged with the performance and the film as a whole.

Lola the Coalgirl sought new ways to replay the patriotic formula as outlined by Cifesa head Vicente Casanova. In particular, such innovations are in tune with new attitudes of the regime: at the beginning of the 1950s Spain was trying to find a place in the international community after the long period of post-war isolationism (known as *autarquía*, 'autarky'). Although the first results would come towards the end of the decade (and required a thorough redesign of policies) it was by then clear that the country could not survive in isolation. If films like *Last Stand in the Philippines* (1945) and earlier Cifesa epics such as *Agustina of Aragon* are apologies for isolationism, for unyielding resistance against the enemies of the nation, in *Lola the Coalgirl* we find how such attitudes are beginning to change: the French are viewed more generously, and the real enemy turns out to be within Spain; the paradigm is slowly moving towards reconciliation and integration of the defeated.

Cifesa had been founded in 1932 as a small-scale American-style production and distribution company and, after producing a number of hits before the Civil War, it became the leading light in early Francoism's ailing film industry. In the aftermath of the Second World War, the Cifesa company experienced a severe financial crisis and was badly in need of new paths to lure audiences back into cinemas. It was the idea of Casanova to start producing a new series of lavish historical epics that could help to bring the company back into the black. The series was, then, an example of formula filmmaking which is typical of the classical studio system: it is a shrewd producer, rather than an *auteur*, who comes up with an idea that will generate a series; directors might introduce their own personal trademark (as Juan de Orduña and Luis Lucia would in the Cifesa series), but basically their role is that of a craftsman. In 1947, Casanova proposed that what an impoverished country needed at that point was escapism, and what better way to achieve it than in films that turned away from iconic representation of reality, and even from the present tense. Besides, there was nothing to detract spectacle from a certain degree of ideological indoctrination. Casanova had clearly identified his films with the interests of the new government and tended to be on good terms with the authorities throughout the 1940s (although in practical terms this did not keep him from frequent clashes with different groups within Francoism). Political support was indeed necessary for the formula to become financially sound. Even for a consolidated studio with contracted technicians and stars, these were expensive films to produce and therefore needed huge returns at the box office, which could only be achieved through government support and, not coincidentially, a new system of grants for film had been introduced in the early 1940s. As long as Casanova could convince government officials of the effectiveness of the fomula in terms of the strengthening of national spirit, these films earned awards, tax breaks and publicity.

Even if the stories told were situated in the distant past, it was impossible to miss the connection with the present: the emotions experienced by the characters were placed at historical junctures that recalled the one Spanish people were actually going through (international isolation, rationing, poverty); through this obvious connection, the suffering and grand gestures of a central character could be processed into a particular brand of populist patriotism.

The films were lavish illustrations of well-known historical episodes, moments in which 'the nation' is in crisis, often brought upon by the threat of foreign forces (normally represented by the French) or foreign customs (such as capitalism or liberalism, alien to authentic Spanish traditions). The preferred periods were also defining moments in the creation of an essential national spirit. No matter that some of the narratives were set in a period when 'Spain' had not even been born as a national state with a unified political identity: the idea of Spain as promoted by Francoist historiography was essential and eternal, placed beyond specific historical avatars. The critical situation thus sketched out required a strong sense of national identity and a deployment of the virtues of the race, and it was normally an exceptional individual who has to save the endangered nation (which, in abstract terms, brought to mind the idea of Franco as a saviour of the nation in times of trouble): at one point in the narrative, the protagonist usually had to face a dilemma, and a deep sense of patriotism always had some weight in the decisions made by the characters; it is the character's action that brings a solution. Such actions may not always lead to success, but they are clearly exemplary, intended as strong gestures that present resistance against foreign influence as heroism.

In most cases, the central characters were women (*Alba de América* [*Dawn of America*, 1951] is the exception in the series), ideal vehicles to focus emotional energies that could then be turned into patriotic feelings. Actually, heroic women seemed to be a central ingredient, as conventional stereotypes around masculinity made it difficult for male characters to show such emotion. The plots were rich in melodrama and intrigue. The demand for excess in the formula made for hysterical performances by central characters, and actresses like Aurora Bautista (who starred in both *The Mad Queen* and *Agustina of Aragon*) owed their later careers to their role in Cifesa epics. *Lola the Coalgirl* is, in this sense, a perfect example of the genre.

For this film Casanova counted on the luminous presence of singing star Juanita Reina. Born in Seville in 1925 she was the daughter of a middle-class businessman. As a child, she started singing at wedding ceremonies and other celebrations and in her teens the stage beckoned. The father was at first reluctant (performing was hardly regarded as a respectable career for a young lady at the time) but finally came around, although he became his daughter's agent to prevent anything untoward happening to her. In a very short time she became one of the most successful performers of the 1940s, threatening to outshine the reigning queen of the genre, Concha Piquer. Reina's repertoire consisted mainly of *coplas*, Andalucian-inflected popular songs, in which the deep expressiveness of flamenco was somewhat trivialised and combined with narrative elements belonging to café singing, popular in Spain since the 1910s. The key lyricist of the genre was Rafael de León, whose repertoire would feature prominently in Reina's programmes. *Lola the Coalgirl* recycles some of his hits (most notably 'Callejuela sin salida' ['Street with no issue']) and introduces some new ones with music by Quiroga.

Reina had made her film debut in 1942 with two popular comedies, very close in spirit to those starring another singer actress of the period, Estrellita Castro. But Reina had one advantage over other *copla* singers, and this lay in her ability to portray credible romantic heroines: other singers' performances were hindered by acting that was wooden or limited. It was in this ability that lay the key to her screen persona. Reina had what was known as a 'racial' beauty (oval face, dark hair, large black eyes framed by strong eyebrows), both intense and serene, and her countenance possessed a dignity that seemed to confirm the intimations of royalty suggested by her name.

She reached stardom by playing another woman named Lola in an adaptation of the Machado brothers play *La Lola se va a los puertos* (*Lola Leaves for the Ports*, 1947), directed by Juan de Orduña, who specialised in drawing strong performances from actresses (as the cases of Aurora Bautista and, later, Sara Montiel, would amply prove). In this film, set in the mid-nineteenth century, she plays a singer of *coplas* who is described as the essence of the poetry emanating from the people and expressed in popular song. Lola is well-known everywhere and there is something bewitching in her singing that captures the imagination of everyone listening to her. In this, she comes close to La Piconera. Orduña's Lola is solicited by a number of men, but she will finally choose José Luis, the son of a landowner who will eventually become a bullfighter. Still, her gift seems to demand that she keep away from love, and when she is about to accept her feelings for the young man, tragedy threatens. She promises the Virgin to devote herself to her singing in exchange for saving José Luis from death. Although the film was a betrayal of the Machados' liberal views (for instance, closure is achieved through what seems to be a miracle of the Holy Virgin, and the playwrights' subtle feminism is definitely underplayed), it is still among the finest musicals of the period in terms of integration between theme, songs and plot, and some of the lyricism of the original play remains intact. Such elements are also prominent in Reina's second 'Lola' character.

In *Lola the Coalgirl* we can see how the conventions of the Cifesa historical epic (more precisely, the demands of history as propaganda), affect character development. In the earlier Reina film, the protagonist's dilemma is between love and singing, here the character has to choose between her love for the French officer and her patriotic duty. Both of the 'Lola' characters illustrate the limits and the possibilities of a folkloric singer to stir the soul. In each case, their passionate nature will lead them into romance, but both will have to give it up for a higher reason. If the Machados' Lola becomes a legend by giving up what she loves most, in the case of La Piconera the plot will have her die for Cádiz and for Spain. The highest form of romanticism in the Cifesa series is thus patriotic martyrdom.

Lola the Coalgirl was certainly a 'big' film (the credits declare this is a 'superproducción') with detailed, expensive sets and large numbers of extras, which followed the example of *Agustina of Aragon* (something made explicit in the publicity). It opened on 3 March 1952 and was a moderate hit. The box-office results help illustrate some of the intrinsic problems of the cycle. The film had cost over seven million pesetas (the average cost at the time being under three million), and by 1956 had only recovered around six million, including income generated by licences for import. Compared to other films of the period (such as the Cifesa melodrama *De mujer a mujer* [*Woman to Woman*, 1950]), these were good returns, but not in relation to the film's cost. By then, the formula was revealing itself as economically unsound: *Dawn of America* had trouble making a profit, even though it was one of the hits of the post-war years.

Luis Lucia's film was, as in other instances, a prestige project, this time based on a famous play by José Maria Pemán, one of Francoism's leading playwrights, which had recently been turned into an opera (with music by Conrado del Campo and libretto by José Maria Pemán; this opened at the Barcelona Liceu Theatre on 14 November 1950). The play was written before the Civil War and was intended as an indictment of Republican liberalism that reinforced a vision of the Spanish people as close to their traditions and heroically resistant to change. The winds of liberalism were regarded as some kind of national illness. The plot was drastically changed between the stage and the screen, the love affair between Lola and Gustavo being the most remarkable addition. The original was not interested in portraying the French: Pemán's reactionary critique was not directed against foreigners, but against liberalism eroding Spain from within. The two men competing for Lola's affections were young patriot Juan de Otero and devious politician Don Luis de Acuña. Both remain as characters in the film, although the latter does not seem to be in love with Lola and is clearly only using her to advance his political career. The Cifesa convention strengthens patriotism through representation of the French invader. In the film version, Lola has to choose between Spanish officer Juan and French officer Gustavo, both equally desirable and noble. In a melodramatic coup, a clash is introduced between Lola's feelings and her patriotism (in the play she was a heroine because she accepted a dangerous mission to save the city): she loves Gustavo more, but in the end she will leave him in order to carry out her mission. This shift in the emotional choices contributes to the ideological project of the film: in placing at the centre of the plot Lola's feelings for a Frenchman, it shows, on the one hand, awareness of the foreign, but also the need to overcome differences based on nationality.

Earlier Cifesa epics had shown foreigners desperate to break into the motherland and the brave Spanish trying to resist at a time when autarky meant complete political isolation. In *Dawn of America* it is Jewish bankers and Portuguese schemers; in *The Mad Queen* it is the court of the foreign monarch Felipe who brings new habits. But more to the point, many films represent the siege more directly: in *Agustina of Aragon*, Zaragoza, another city resisting the advance of Napoleon's troops, is surrounded by the French army. In *Lola the Coalgirl*, the last bastion of Spanish values is Cádiz, where the first Spanish Constitution was prepared in 1812.

The portrayal of the French that opens the film is typical of the manicheism and stereotyping one can find elsewhere in the series. In terms of plot, such stereotyping was unnecessary (the French are threatening Cádiz, but in narrative terms they are not the main villains of the story). In order to make the essential distinction between the Spanish and the foreign clear, the opening scene constructs a cartoonish image of the French: some of them are in drag, others are shown playing children's games or just plain drunk; Spaniards in the film will be portrayed as having an easy disposition, wit and goodness. In a way, the patriotic imperative means the victory of the French has to be somehow tarnished. Technology and organisation may be on the side of foreigner (a situation all too familiar to Spaniards in the early 1950s), but God is definitely on the side of the Spanish people (a far less obvious point).

Still, manicheism in the film is tempered with the portrayal of officers, which reveal a more positive image of the French. The French Field Marshall (Manuel de Luna) is portrayed as a man of principle. It is his duty to conquer Cádiz, and a good officer cannot help but carry out orders. His demeanor is dignified and his regret at the end of the film will contribute to the sanctification of the protagonist: as he sentences Lola to her end, for the first time in his life, he feels disgust for a war that has forced him to do such a thing. In spite of the jingoistic approach to the French in the first scene, both the Field Marshall and Gustavo are shown fairly. Even if they are unequivocally the invaders of the nation, there are worse villains.

In the portrayal of one such villain, the film remains closer to the spirit of the original play. To the first distinction between 'the French' and 'the Spanish', another one will be super-imposed between the military and the politicians. The former always behave according to impeccable codes of conduct, the latter are either weak, incompetent or deceitful. The film's real contempt is reserved for democratic populist politicians. Don Luis de Acuña is a 'liberal' member of the Cádiz parliament who is secretly planning to boycott the city's defence so that he can become a high authority under a French government in Cádiz. On the one hand, Don Luis is an echo of the Republican politicians who used the name of the people for their own purposes. Even at the Cádiz parliament, politics are shown in the film in terms of overblown rhetoric, which may seem fancy, even flashy, but is never fully understood by the people. Not that they are really deceived (we see two representatives of the popular classes joking about one of Don Luis' speeches), but their naïveté means they end up admiring his ability to speak so forcefully.

The character is used to develop another theme of contemporary relevance, that of the enemy within. Of course this is a motive of long standing in Spanish history: legend has it that it was a Spaniard, Count Don Julián, who actually let the Islamic armies into the peninsula. In making Don Juan the most despicable character in the film, there is a stress on personal behaviour rather than just on questions of nationality. Don Juan is despised even by the French, and it will be his two-faced behaviour that will send Lola to her death.

Populist historical epics normally give a simple image of the people as children with big hearts. In this case, the people of Cádiz are represented as a patriotic mass in several scenes. They are also characterised by their devotion to Lola. The central character's presentation is articulated precisely in terms of the adoration of the people and the way they are enthused by her singing. In her first appearance on screen, singing a song about herself, we see Lola chastising one of them for his cowardice. When she starts singing again, they will all be moved by the patriotic message of the song, encouraging them to face the foreign enemy, forgetting despair. Even more significant is the scene in which Lola cheerfully leads them into a rousing song in order to mock Gustavo who has come within the city walls to negotiate with the authorities. They ask Lola to be their voice in singing about the French:

> With the bombs
> Those frogs throw
> Cádiz women make
> Their spitcurls

If the main politician is presented as a pompous character who, in posing as a representative of the people, is only thinking in his own interests, the actual citizens are down to earth, unconcerned by questions of politics and fascinated by the heroine's singing.

Lola is also a reflection of the people to which she belongs. As in other Cifesa epics the central female character, is in some ways the 'Spanish woman' but, more generally, represents Spanish virtues. Whereas in other films protagonists were bourgeois or aristocratic women, here the protagonist is a woman of the people and a singer to boot. This constitutes a change of direction in Franco's cinema, allowing for inter-class love stories, but also is a result of the demands of the folkloric musical. The stereotype of the folkloric singer demanded she was of low extraction, maybe with some gypsy blood (which Lola has, as she acknowledges explicitly). Her gentle leading of the masses arises out of identification with them, not from any kind of imposition, and song is a metaphor for the spirit she shares with them.

The use of musical numbers seems to reinforce the ideological programme of the film. The first few songs are quite well integrated into the plot. 'Lola la Piconera', sung at the café, introduces the protagonist. A reprise of the song later on interestingly changes the lyric to describe Lola's dangerous journey outside the city's walls: the singer in this way becomes a legendary character through the song. The second is the mocking march about the Cádiz women which is actually a reworking of a popular ditty whereas the third, an adaptation of the 1943 classic 'Callejuela sin salida' explains the emotional situation of the singer, who feels trapped by feelings without a clear issue: she despises the French and therefore cannot show her feelings for an officer of the invading army, on the other hand, she is becoming progressively weaker to withstand such feelings (in the original version, the protagonist is in love with a married man). In this scene, the personal and the political are conflated. Love is consistently presented as something that can bridge the differences between nations. Lola is at this point torn between two lovers: one of them is an officer in the Cádiz army, the other in the French army. When in previous instances of the series the woman fell in love with (or even married) a foreigner, disaster would ensue for the nation (as in *The Mad Queen* or *Agustina of Aragon*). The visit of Gustavo, wounded by a Spanish soldier as he slipped into the town in disguise, rekindles the love she felt for him in her youth. Although they fight for different armies (eventually, the character will have to decide between love or political ideas) such opposition is qualified and, to a certain extent, overcome narratively.

This leads to a remarkable sequence that reveals the strength and the weakness of the conventions of the musical when integrated in the patriotic film. The politicians in Cádiz need the assistance of General Ballesteros, and someone has to deliver a message to him. Lola is chosen for the dangerous mission. In fact, Don Pedro has given her a blank piece of paper and has warned the French that she will be undertaking the mission. She is first arrested, then freed by the French, and Gustavo is asked by the Field Marshall to escort her to her destination in order to find out who her contacts behind the lines are. On the road, they meet a troupe of travelling gypsies. Gustavo and Lola dream of a world beyond differences. This is expressed in terms of a dream ballet with no narrative connection with the plot. But it contributes to the creation of a utopic space beyond politics at one central point of the film. Of course, such a shift threatens to bring into question the ideological discourse articulated so far: are the audiences supposed to identify with the yearning to become travelling gypsies and therefore place themselves beyond politics, or are they meant to acquire warring spirit to face all the threats facing the country? There is a contradiction between both sets of demands that the narrative does not seem to be too interested in resolving.

In any case, such a utopian space can only be precarious. One important difference between this film and others of the Cifesa cycle has to do with closure. Decisions must be made in the real world and the next morning Lola will escape, intent on fulfilling her patriotic mission. She will be arrested again, and shot by the French army. In terms of the film's ideological project it is the right decision (the Spanish nation always has to come first), but her sacrifice will move the hearts of everybody, including the Field Marshall. The final sequence shows the moment in which Lola's corpse is returned to Cádiz where she belongs. Gustavo makes sure the corpse is taken to the gates of Cádiz, and there is a truce. The opposing armies both regret the evil of war in a final scene reminiscent of *Romeo and Juliet*. At the end of *Lola the Coalgirl*, the starting situation is not resolved. Cádiz is still under siege, the traitor has not been discovered. What the film was leading to was not victory (which would have been against historical truth) but a new understanding, a reconciliation with the foreigners typical of the post-isolationist period. The utopian aims of the musical temper the earnestness of other historical epics. Ideologically, the Cifesa cycle had adopted a compact rhetoric to become the expression of a specific political programme, shown again, as if back from the dead. As we can see, *Lola the Coalgirl* articulates a yearning to go beyond political differences, although it eventually retracts from the notion. The only image that lingers is Lola, walking along the beach, an incarnation of the national spirit that seems to reach out beyond any intimation of politics.

Alberto Mira

MARCELINO PAN Y VINO THE MIRACLE OF MARCELINO

07

LADISLAO VAJDA, SPAIN, 1955

Based on a short story by José-María Sánchez-Silva (1911–2002) and made with a subsidy of two-and-a-half million pesetas from the Spanish state in 1955 by émigré Hungarian director Ladislao Vajda (1906–65), *Marcelino Pan y Vino* (*The Miracle of Marcelino*, 1955) was a success at home and abroad, winning critical acclaim at the Cannes and Berlin film festivals. The film's popularity has lasted into the twenty-first century. Not only is it regularly shown on Spanish television at Easter but Univision, a US Spanish language broadcaster, also uses the film to mark the Christian holiday. Its international appeal also continues with both subtitled and dubbed versions of the film readily available in the English-speaking world. Opinions about the worth of the narrative represented by the film have become more divided over the years, however. In the 1960s José García Nieto said of Sánchez-Silva's story that it was 'A little piece of eternity … an epic of childhood carried to the level of the divine by the most tender and extraordinary passages of faith.' It was successful enough to spawn two sequels by the author, about Marcelino's adventures in heaven. Forty years on, an anonymous internet reviewer would be as quick to condemn the film inspired by Sánchez-Silva's story as García Nieto was to ascribe to it mystic properties: '[The film] is an atrocious piece of religious manipulation and propaganda … but then again, any one that thinks that priests can "in fact" convert cheap hock and a cracker into the blood and body of Christ will believe everything in this film and not look at the fact that … Jesus Christ murders a child.' What kind of a film could produce responses so diametrically opposed?

Fernando Rey plays a Franciscan monk in the 1950s who is sent to comfort a sick young girl and does so by retelling her the tale of 'Marcelino Pan y Vino', which takes place in the mid-nineteenth century and becomes the film's narrative thread. Rey's priest only returns towards the end. His introduction takes the viewer to a point where twelve Franciscans have assumed control – under an ambiguous and tenuous arrangement with the local council – of a ruined house which their order had rebuilt and made fit for use after it had been ravaged by conflicts in Castile during the nineteenth-century War of Independence. The orderly lives of these twelve contemplatives are placed in turmoil when a baby is discovered at the monastery's gates. The friars are torn between forming an attachment with the baby, and finding him a home with a family from among the neighboring communities. Each brother is charged with reconnoitering the adoption possibilities in a segment of the local area and each returns with the news that no suitable parents can be found. The film shows us that, since the brothers are keen to keep the baby at the monastery, they go out of their way to find fault with prospective parents; it also shows would-be foster carers advancing real arguments to explain why they cannot take on an extra child: 'In my household there are already many mouths to feed and not enough bread.' The brothers are also charged with finding out what may have happened to the baby's biological parents. Here they hit a blank wherever they ask for information. The baby seems to have been delivered as a result of some kind of rustic parthenogenesis. This divine aspect of the baby's birth is more evident in the film than in the book which, by contrast, suggests that the child was left at the gates of the monastery by 'Outsiders passing through who, unable to raise a child, had left the baby there in the hope that the monks would find it in their hearts to bring him up.'

The monks decide to name the baby after Saint Marcelino, on whose feast day he was left at their door. In Sánchez-Silva's story the baby's wet nurse is a goat. In the film, Marcelino's surrogate mother is instead Fray Tomás, the brother best-versed in the ways of domesticity since he is already the one charged with household and kitchen duties. Despite having a baritone voice, Tomás, later renamed Fray Papilla (Brother Porridge) by Marcelino, is also the monk with the most feminine, or most rounded, figure. To an international audience familiar with Robin Hood and the *Cage aux folles* trilogy, he comes over as a cross between Friar Tuck and Albin. The baby and the surrogate mother quickly take to each other and, with the domestic energies of Fray Papilla taken up by a newborn, the other monks are initially at a loss to find their cutlery or set their dinner table. However, the minor domestic god quickly gets to grips with simultaneous parenting and housekeeping and even devises a way of attaching Marcelino's cradle to his kitchen implements so that he can rock the baby and peel potatoes simultaneously. Pablito Calvo as the five-year-old Marcelino is credited with much of the film's success yet Juan Calvo's endearing performance as a comely matron and patron rolled into one must also be credited with some of the film's appeal.

Marcelino grows from a baby to a five-year-old during a montage sequence focused mainly on his innocent yet mischievous games and activities, like floating a paper boat in the holy water or filling Fray Papilla's cooking pots with frogs. By now, the parenting of the child is more dispersed among the community. The bedridden Fray Malo (Brother Baddie) takes charge of teaching Marcelino to read and write, for example. Despite the company of the twelve monks, Marcelino is isolated from other children. In the story he briefly meets Manuel, another boy his own age, but in the film, Manuel is only ever an imaginary friend. With only a goat and a cat for friends, Marcelino becomes a junior mystic and is further isolated when the monks feel some resentment towards him after the picaresque chaos he causes when momentarily left to his own devices at a local fair. A long-standing enemy of the monastery uses the damage caused by Marcelino as an excuse to revoke the community's entitlement to the construction it had rebuilt as a holy order.

Whilst playing outside, Marcelino is stung by a scorpion and the brothers nurse him back to health through fever and delirium. He begins to articulate his sense of having lacked a mother. In the story his psychological change is described more explicitly than in the film. Sánchez-Silva writes that the boy's head began to be filled with 'the most mysterious ideas' and that he went about 'in a happy daydream and drunk on his own thoughts'.

Inside the monastery, only one area – the attic – is out of bounds to the boy. He has been told there is a very tall man in the rafters who will catch him and take him away forever if he dares to ascend the staircase. The prohibition only creates more interest in what the attic conceals and so Marcelino begins venturing up the stairs until he finds a life-size effigy of the Christ on the cross stored in the farthest reaches of the attic space. The effigy looks cold and hungry to him and he begins taking it bread and wine filched from the kitchen. The creaky staircase becomes a Jacob's ladder, a pathway to religious conviction, and the effigy takes on real life for Marcelino, reaching out to take the bread and eventually coming down from the cross to sit and talk with the young mystic. Marcelino's new companion gives the orphaned child a family name in recognition of his gifts of bread and wine in a scene which enacts the Christ's reported injunction to 'Let the little children come to me, and do not hinder them, for the kingdom of heaven belongs to such as these.' The film only shows such transfigurations from behind so that we see just a disembodied hand and arm reaching out of nowhere towards Marcelino, a visual formula which leads one critic to compare these scenes with those in the vampire horror genre when the hungry bloodsucker consumes his prey. Both the film and the story struggle to resolve the paradox of a boy who is smart enough to outwit twelve friars also being credulous enough to believe that the replica is the Christ. In the story, Sánchez-Silva's narrator observes that 'Marcelino's schooling wasn't very good; he knew how to pray, of course, and he was somewhat versed in the Catechism, but, on the advice of the Father Superior, the brothers had not wanted to push him too far.' However, the story glosses over the fact that the same boy who can be rational enough to worry that his friend in the attic will go hungry between fortnightly rations of bread is also sufficiently unthinking to believe that his reclusive friend is in all other respects a normal man. Although Marcelino was familiar with the crucifix as *image*, the story tells us, he had never seen one 'for real' before. Where the writing skates round reality with apostrophes, the film cuts between Marcelino's gaze and the Christ's disembodied yet living limbs. Neither the story nor the film actually shows us the process of wood or wax becoming flesh which, believers would argue, presumably, is the whole point. Such transformations are not open to empirical inquiry. The film depends on a wilful engagement of belief, in much the same way as the 'Dream of the Rood' asks us to believe that a wooden cross can articulate the story of the divine and human sacrifice it bore.

Concerned about Marcelino's change of habits and about the disappearance of victuals from their larder, the friars follow him to his encounters with 'The Friend in the attic' until witnessing him answer the Christ's inquiry about his fondest wish. His reply is that he would like nothing more than to see his mother in heaven and the Christ grants his wish by telling him to sleep. Marcelino says he is not sleepy and the Christ replies that he will bring sleep to him. The friars discover the boy dead between the arms of a chair. 'Miracle!' they cry out in unison, in the story. In the film their order is saved by this preternatural event which also brings closure to the narrative as the conclusion of Fernando Rey's retelling of the story to the sick girl coincides with the celebration of the annual pilgrimage to the monastery to remember the child's death.

Sánchez-Silva supposedly based the original story on a tale that had been recounted to him by his mother. The film picks up on this element of oral history by describing fable in the opening credits as a 'Story passed on from father to son.' The attempt to lend the story some element of orality may have been intended to reinforce its evangelical purpose, something clearly evident in its incorporation of biblical reference points such as the twelve disciples, the Last Supper and Jacob's ladder. Alongside these intended religious parabolic values, the film also possesses a political and social nature.

In a recent article by Juan Miguel Company the film is described as 'a perfect example of the sterile and masochistic official spirituality of the Spain of the [1950s]' and despite the fact that the film is set in a more remote history, it is not difficult to see how it can be read as a parable of the virtues of Franco's centralising use of expedient Catholicism, or *nacional-catolicismo*. The War of Independence is easily translated into the Civil War, for example, so that the supposed contributions of the Church to the reconstruction of the country – represented by this remote Franciscan order's restoration of a derelict house – can be seen in a positive light. Some of the film's early scenes of intense building activity, threshing and corn harvests, look almost indistinguishable from the propagandistic rebuilding narratives of the Soviet Union and Nazi Germany. Furthermore, both the film and Sánchez-Silva's original story put a positive gloss on the pact between the Church and State in 1950s Spain. Such are the good works of the Church, say both narratives, that the Holy Orders deserve a prominent place in society and special exemptions on land and property ownership. The film adds a more clearly defined political dimension to this parable of *nacional-catolicismo* by inserting in the narrative a bad character who can be identified with communists and industrial workers. A novelty in the film is this extra character, a vengeful industrious man who is scorned as an adoptive parent when, in view of a monk, he strikes one of his own children. Swearing eternal revenge on the monks, when he later becomes the local mayor, he revokes the order's rights to the refurbished holy property. It takes nothing less than a miracle and the death of a child to undo the mischief caused by him, a parable in itself for the cause and outcome of the Civil War as seen from a Francoist perspective.

Although the film makes Marcelino's male surrogate mother a likable figure, it also casts him as a man unable to rescue the boy from the arms of the devouring Christ. The maternal Fray Papilla simply swoons and is rendered helpless when he glimpses what is happening in the attic with the 'Friend from On High'. This lends the film a voice in the discussion of gender values and roles. In this, it is very much in tune with the Falangist values of the 1950s which raised motherhood to the state of a cult and presented parenting as the ultimate occupation for a woman. *The Miracle of Marcelino* reinforces this value system by showing that without a mother who is biologically female, a child is destined to die. Men cannot be mothers or raise children alone, however well-intentioned they may be, the film says. It also warns viewers that orphaned children not socialised in a family environment are doomed and will die prematurely. In another addition to the story, the film creates a warning figure in Fray Papilla: men who overlook these injunctions risk becoming effeminate, domesticated and possibly homosexual. The internet reviewer mentioned at the beginning of this chapter would be wrong in assuming that such propaganda was the exclusive preserve of Francoist Catholic Spain, however. American films of the 1980s and 1990s such as *Mr. Mom* (Stan Dragoti, 1983) and *Three Men and a Baby* (Leonard Nimoy, 1987) convey essentially the same message and one that is reinforced in *Mrs. Doubtfire* (Chris Columbus, 1993), in which a father must don an elaborate disguise as a biological female before being allowed by social services to parent his own children. The use of a child actor to articulate the vision of a mirage of divine flesh is not something exclusive to Spain either. Bryan Forbes' *Whistle Down the Wind* (1961), in which Hayley Mills discovers Alan Bates as Christ in the family barn, has many points in common with *The Miracle of Marcelino*. Unlike Hayley Mills, however, after *The Miracle of Marcelino* and a handful of other films, Pablito Calvo did not become a successful adult actor. He retired from film at 16 and became an engineer, though not before starting something of a craze for child-centered films in Spanish cinema. He was followed by Joselito and Marisol, among others, and to this day films which follow the basic format of the Pablito Calvo films, such as *Manolito Gafotas* (Miguel Albaladejo, 1999) and *El Bola* (Achero Mañas, 2000), continue to be popular with Spanish audiences. There is an important distinction between the child-centered films of the 1950s and those of later decades, however. As noted by Carlos Heredero, the Joselito and Marisol films spawned by Pablito Calvo's success 'unravel in an idealised context for which neither civil society nor the State has any commitment or responsibility. The child protagonists thus become angelic beings divorced from all social context and disabled as sources of internal dramatic or psychological conflict, their acting and presence quickly becoming more of a circus act and a pretext for spectacle.' Despite the film's narrative shortcomings, some critics have pointed to a level of technical accomplishment in films like *The Miracle of Marcelino* which was unusual for the time in Spanish cinema. Perhaps in deference to the difficult visual transmogrification it had to pull off (or evade through technical bravado) *The Miracle of Marcelino* makes more proficient use of dolly and crane shots and of deep focus than other Spanish films from this era.

If *The Miracle ofMarcelino* still appeals to Spanish audiences, this is not a question of its technical superiority alone. It would seem that its pro-Catholic image still finds approval as is evident from the contrasting critical opprobrium thrown at works which take a diametrically opposed view of the value of Catholicism in children's lives. Like Sánchez-Silva, Iñigo Ramírez de Haro believes that the Catholic belief system can destroy a child, but in a catastrophic rather than a miraculous way. *Me cago en dios*, his play of 2004, in which an adult educated by Jesuits sits on stage on a toilet surrounded by lavatory paper trying to overcome the constipation of a modern Catholic education, was lambasted by critics, vilified by Spain's bishops, and performers were physically attacked by enraged audience members during a performance of the show in Madrid. Reactions such as these to a critique of Catholicism's role in Spanish education suggest that if Spanish audiences are ready to regard the film as old-fashioned and dated, they may not be ready to see its deeper ideological convictions as redundant or past their sell-by date. The importance and centrality of issues touched on by *The Miracle of Marcelino* for twenty-first century Spanish audiences is also evident from the content and reception of Pedro Almodóvar's 2004 film, *La mala educación* (*Bad Education*) which, like *Me cago en dios*, investigates the legacy of a Catholic education. The passage of *The Miracle of Marcelino*, the boy, to an eternal paradise may be a matter of belief. The film, however, can be judged through empirical methods to have been extremely successful, albeit with some stiff competition from more recent explorations in theatre and cinema, of the interface between children, God and the Spanish Catholic Church.

Ryan Prout

REFERENCES

Anon. (2004) 'Sick, Sick, and More Sick' [review of *Marcelino Pan y Vino*] Internet Movie Database: http://uk.imdb.com/title/tt0047216/ [accessed 24 May].

Company, Juan Miguel (1997) '*Marcelino Pan y Vino*', in Julio Pérez Perucha (ed.) *Antología crítica del cine español 1906–1995*. Madrid: Cátedra/Filmoteca española.

García Nieto, José (1969) 'Prefacio', in José-María Sánchez-Silva, *Marcelino Pan y Vino y otras narraciones*. Madrid: Biblioteca Básica Salvat.

Heredero, Carlos F. (1993) *Las huellas del tiempo. Cine español 1951–1961*. Valencia: Ediciones de la filmoteca.

CALLE MAYOR **MAIN STREET**

JUAN ANTONIO BARDEM, SPAIN, 1956

The mid-1950s was a decisive period for Spanish cinema. Some fifteen years after the Civil War, the country was still subject to the authoritarian rule of the Franco dictatorship, and cinema was strictly controlled by censorship. After more than a decade of films designed to meet the entertainment needs of an uncritical public, whilst simultaneously promoting the values of Franco's fascist state (or at least not offending those values), there was the beginnings of a more socially- or politically-engaged cinema in Spain. The first generation of filmmakers from the Madrid film school had begun to have an impact on the kinds of films being made. They looked outside Spain for models of politically-committed filmmaking, and most especially to Italian neorealism. In 1951 a series of neorealist film screenings was permitted in Madrid and, two years later, the independent film journal *Objetivo* began publication. Before this, the only film journal in existence had been *Primer Plano*, a mouthpiece for the State. After years of isolation, Spanish cinema was beginning to re-emerge onto the world stage. A tiny number of Spanish films were deemed appropriate for submission to European film festivals, though these films were not at all representative of the home market. Spanish audiences in the 1950s continued to prefer Hollywood movies even above the most popular home-grown genres (folkloric musicals, military and historical epics, priest dramas, comedies). But even within the arch-conservative Hollywood industry, some filmmakers were beginning subtly to introduce, from the 1950s, more social commentary into films. In particular, the period saw a recuperation of melodrama as a means of working through social issues, especially with regard to the role of women. For committed young filmmakers like Juan Antonio Bardem, the period presented opportunities and limitations both of which would shape his films.

Bardem was born in Madrid in 1922 into a family of actors. After spending the Civil War years in both Republican and Nationalist zones, he returned to the capital and eventually joined the first intake of the newly-formed film school. Already identified with left-wing opposition ideas, his final degree was denied 'for technical reasons', though he teamed up with classmate Luis G. Berlanga to make *Esa pareja feliz* (*The Happy Couple*, 1951) and *¡Bienvenido Mr Marshall!* (*Welcome Mr Marshall!*, 1952), before going on to make *Cómicos* (*Comedians*,

1954) and *Felices pascuas* (*Happy Christmas*, 1954) as sole director. He was confirmed as a key figure – admired by film-lovers abroad but considered politically suspect by the Spanish authorities – with the release of *Muerte de un ciclista* (*Death of a Cyclist*, 1955), a savage indictment of the complacent Spanish middle classes. Bardem was no less outspoken on the politics of film. In May 1955 he participated in a conference organised by the film club of the University of Salamanca, denouncing Spanish film as 'politically ineffective, socially false, intellectually abject, aesthetically nonexistent and commercially crippled'. Such provocative criticism was sufficient proof of Bardem's dangerous politics for the Franco regime and, when violence broke out at Madrid University in February 1956, he was arrested for a 'crime of opinion'. He was released two weeks later, partly due to the efforts of French co-producers and the French cinema workers' union, and partly to the protestations of filmmakers worldwide, among them Charlie Chaplin. Henceforth he would be hailed by foreign filmmakers and critics as a representative cultural focus of opposition to Franco. The Italian journal *Cinema Nuovo* dedicated an entire issue to Bardem and the publicity for *Death of a Cyclist* and his subsequent fame was assured.

Bardem's brief imprisonment in February 1956 had interrupted the filming of what would prove to be his most acclaimed film, *Calle Mayor* (*Main Street*, 1956). An adaptation of a play, *La señorita de Trevélez* (*The Young Lady of Trevélez*, Carlos Arniches, 1916), it tells the story of a group of provincial young men who play a cruel joke on a local 35-year-old spinster they consider to be unmarriageable. They convince outsider Juan to pretend to court the impressionable Isabel in order eventually to reveal the joke in public, and laugh at her expense. As Isabel falls helplessly in love with him, Juan struggles with his conscience, being advised to tell the truth both by his friend Federico, a Madrid intellectual, and by Tonia, a warm-hearted prostitute who also loves him. In the end, Juan cannot face telling Isabel the truth and flees, leaving Federico to break the news to her. Less rhetorically provocative than *Death of a Cyclist*, in many ways *Main Street* embodies all the currents and contradictions of its time. It combines the ethics and aesthetics of Italian neorealism (a style of filmmaking at times uncompromising in its most radical forms), with the more veiled, less confrontational vehicle of melodrama. It balances the imperatives of socially- and politically-engaged filmmaking against the need to avoid confrontation with a dictatorial regime. And, as we shall see, it reconciles the urge to comment on the specificities of Spain with an acknowledgement of the international context of its production and reception.

The film was a co-production with French producer Serge Silberman who had worked with Luis Buñuel and Akira Kurosawa – international associations Bardem would have welcomed. Though the technical crew was Spanish, only one of the four principal roles was played by a Spanish actor (José Suárez in the role of Juan). Bardem had chosen American actress Betsy Blair for the lead role when he met her at Cannes the year before. Together with French actors Dora Doll and Yves Massard, they would form an international cast clearly designed to appeal to audiences (and festival juries) beyond Spain. The Spanish government did not want the film to represent Spain at the Venice Film Festival of 1956, but threatened with the alternative of it appearing as a French entry (it was a Spanish-French co-production), they acquiesced. In the event, it won the International Critics' Award and Betsy Blair was given a special mention by a jury including John Grierson, Luchino Visconti and André Bazin. Critical reception, both positive and negative, stressed the film's international influences. Some accused Bardem of tagging along behind Italian cinematic fashion (as if Italy were a poor model in the early 1950s), and of copying Federico Fellini. It is true, however, that there are some striking similarities between *Main Street* and Fellini's *I Vitelloni* (1953). There are examples of both *mise-en-scène* and dialogue overlaps. In both films the antisocial group of men stand around in a circle and play football with street debris. And Federico's reaction to Juan's threat of suicide – that he is too much of a coward to kill himself – is almost an exact copy of similar dialogue between Moraldo and Fausto in *I Vitelloni*. Yet Stephen Roberts stresses the differences between the two, and in particular distinguishes between the respectable cads in *Main Street* and the socially outcast cads in Fellini's film. He also contests the internationalising focus of critical opinion on the film, suggesting that critics missed the point in stressing its debt to Hollywood melodrama and Italian neorealism. Roberts argues that such a reaction to what he regards as a film that is 'essentially Spanish in nature' is an injustice based on the erroneous assumption that 'Spanish cinema, perhaps because of the tragic history and circumstances of the country, was fundamentally and necessarily derivative'. All cinema is of course derivative. Certain formulas are recycled and adapted. For a 1950s filmmaker anxious to differentiate his films from the standard fare of Spanish cinema, inspiration would naturally come from abroad. The question of 'Spanishness' in *Main Street* must, therefore, be set against the major international influences on the film: melodrama (Hollywood) and realism (Italy).

Spanish references are, paradoxically, as omnipresent as they are meticulously expunged from the text. The Spanish authorities – in the light of problems with the previous *Death of a Cyclist* – saw the script before filming and imposed some cuts. Scenes cut from Bardem's original script include references to the town's working-class area, the separation of boys and girls in public places, and prohibited books. Juan Francisco Cerón Gómez adds that Don Tomás' name should have been Miguel or José (as in Unamuno and Ortega y Gasset, two philosophers with Republican connections) but the censors objected. Cerón Gómez also mentions that references to the clergy and on-screen kisses were cut at the editing stage. The censors demanded that the camera avoid the names of shops or bars which would reveal the identity of the town; other cuts included references to the town's working-class area, the separation of boys and girls in public places, prohibited books and the censorship of literary journals, as well as references to the clergy, and sexual promiscuity (judged to include on-screen kisses). To dilute the references to any one setting, location filming took place in three cities – Palencia, Logroño and Cuenca. Perhaps the most heavy-handed of the censors' impositions was a narrator's introduction which affirms that the action could be 'in any city, of any province, of any country'. This rather forced addition, which Rob Stone refers to as 'protesting too much', is part of a game Bardem (and others) constantly had to play to outwit the censors. Politically subversive directors saw to it that any doctoring of the film by censors was made as obvious as possible, thus drawing attention to the destructive practice of political censorship itself.

Despite all this, there are references to Spain and even some quite audacious details which the censors failed to pick up, or decided to let pass. José Enrique Monterde points out that Bardem gave all his male protagonists around this time the name Juan ('Juan Español' represents a mythical, national 'Mr Average'). Isabel mentions the Civil War at one point and even the practice of censorship (though the context relates to the presence of double beds – hardly a politically sensitive point in the mid-1950s). Bardem relates how the name of the Spanish national railways, RENFE, appears in one scene, much to the chagrin of the censors who spotted it only after approving the film. Perhaps more than any of these details, the defining presence of the Spanish language (including a non-Castilian accent in the figure of the Andalusian mother), and the setting of the film in recognisably Spanish urban locations, removes any doubt about geographical location. This predilection for real locations also reflects the film's realist aspirations.

A number of formal features contribute to the perceived realism of *Main Street*. The lengthy establishing panning shot which opens the pre-title sequence, along with the narrator's introduction, lend an objective, documentary feel to the film. Reportage-style photography – one frequent feature of neorealist films – is used on a number of occasions (for parts of the procession sequence, and in the long travelling shot following Juan and Isabel along the Main Street). Deep-focus photography is also associated with objectivity and realism in cinema because it offers the audience both foreground and background in clear focus, so that viewers, and not the director, choose where to look in the frame. A good example in *Main Street* occurs when Federico is talking with don Tomás in the library. At the same time, we see Juan and his infantile friends on the street behind, and further in the background, children playing. Viewers can focus on any of these planes, as well as linking them and thus contrasting behaviour. But realism depends on the chosen subject matter as much as on choices about technique and aesthetics. Rob Stone writes of Bardem's 'attempt to inject a conscience and relevance into Spanish cinema … in films that dealt with ordinary people and pressing social themes'. *Main Street* not only meets this objective, but also presents us with characters who can be read – in an almost Lukácsian manner – as typical, and thus as potentially representing a general problem of society (Spanish society, but also, possibly, others). Two social issues are foregrounded in this film: the discussion about the respective values of urban and provincial or rural living, and the differing roles of men and women in society.

The debate around the virtues of city living as opposed to provincial or rural life in Spain stretches from the sixteenth century to the contemporary films of Pedro Almodóvar. After the Civil War, the promotion of a healthy, decent, rural class and the disapproval of the corrupt influences of the city was a priority for Franco's regime. Spain's first truly neorealist film (and arguably its best), *Surcos* (*Furrows*, José Antonio Nieves Conde, 1951) confirmed this reactionary demonisation of the metropolis, despite its more progressive, realist aesthetic. *Main Street* reverses this discourse, portraying the provinces as backward and cruel, and Madrid as a source of reason and civilisation. Juan's friend (and a voice of conscience throughout the film) is the Madrid-based Federico. He sees the boredom of provincial life and how it turns Juan's group of friends into infantile yobs. Juan, also from Madrid, but living in the unnamed provincial town, keeps asking Federico if he is bored. The town's representative intellectual, don Tomás (whose resignation contrasts with Federico's idealism), tells Federico on two occasions that the young are bored, as a means of justifying their bad behaviour. That the retired intellectual and the town cads are confined to the same building – the *Círculo creativo, artístico y cultural* combining library and billiard hall – is a sign of the limitations of provincial life. Another sign is the Main Street itself, a metaphor for a life lived under the gaze of the whole town (Juan and Isabel are constantly interrupted as they walk along the busy street). As if aware of their function in this filmic critique of the provinces, some of the characters fight back, articulating the opposite side of the argument. The juvenile Luis goads Juan telling him 'He *would* be from Madrid, wouldn't he?' when Juan initially refuses to play along with their joke. And the rather rude priest complains to Federico that city people are 'depraved night-owls'.

The urban/provincial dichotomy runs parallel to another, less prominent, but nonetheless significant, set of contrasts: between the modern world, associated with cities and with the USA, and the traditionalist provinces which look to the past. Isabel likes romantic American films with 'wonderful white kitchens', though she acknowledges they may be false. Contrast that image (of US consumerism in the 'never-had-it-so-good' 1950s) with the drab, outmoded interiors of *Main Street*. At one point, the editing of the film clearly juxtaposes these two opposing worlds. In the scene where Juan falsely proposes to Isabel, she is marching in a religious procession, accompanied by an army escort and a military band. The chorus of women, all dressed in black and shot from below making them look almost nightmarish, is cut to the warm, bright interior of the (significantly named) Bar Moderno where a 1950s pop tune is playing.

Editing and locations also contribute to the construction of clearly demarcated spaces designated masculine or feminine according to the social laws of provincial life. The bars and the brothel are male spaces. Whenever we see the men, they are engaged in leisure activities (playing billiards or cards, drinking, dancing with the women in the brothel). Double standards apply to the sexes. While even married men can behave badly whilst claiming to be at work, and have the comfort of the girls of the Bar Moderno, Isabel has only the consolation of the Church to fill her empty days, as it is deemed inappropriate by her society for an unmarried Colonel's daughter to work. The repeated scenes of men misbehaving contrast with scenes showing women fulfilling social obligations – to the Church, to domestic matters or servicing the requirements of men. Isabel, considered an old maid at the age of 35, is innocent, protected from the world by her mother and maid. Until she begins to see Juan, we only see her tending to the birds or her duties in the Church. This film portrays two very different types of women: the girls in the Bar Moderno are of different order; they belong to a modern age (note the American 1950s music as opposed to religious music for other females), and they inhabit a parallel social world, away from respectable wives and daughters. There is a prostitute waiting on the corner outside the Bar Moderno, who looks longingly at Juan as she smokes her cigarette. Despite these differences, the worldly Tonia – whose love for Juan links her with the virginal Isabel – remarks on what they have in common: 'Waiting,' she says, 'is all women can do.'

While Tonia's social function – to provide an alternative gender role to that of Isabel – is not at odds with any aspiration to realism, it also forms part of a world which has as much to do with Hollywood melodrama as with the lives of real women. Indeed, the melodramas of the 1950s (perfected in Hollywood by the likes of Douglas Sirk, himself of European birth) were among the most subtle interrogations of female social roles in all cinema.

Among the features commonly identified in film melodrama are the predominance of female characters, often as victims, a social (and not metaphysical) focus, moral conflicts, twists and reversals, omniscient narration and perhaps most important, music. In *Main Street*, the opening, non-diegetic music strongly suggests melodrama. And the melodramatic orchestral music is very much associated with Isabel, often being heard while she is in her room. The moral conflict involves the male character. Juan has to decide whether to follow his errant friends in their cruel joke or to prevent their victim, Isabel, from suffering any further. The harsh reversal for Isabel is the discovery that her new-found happiness is based on a grotesque lie. The story is told by means of an omniscient narrative structure (following each of the main characters). Another feature which this film has in common with melodrama is its depiction of the secondary characters in a more humorous manner than the principal characters. Here, the mother and the maid characters are types, portrayed with some humour.

Mise-en-scène plays an important role in melodrama, and *Main Street* is no exception. The choice for the opening titles – a black-and-white drawing of the street – emphasises artifice rather than reality, in contrast to the pre-title establishing shot mentioned above. Moreover, many of the choices made within the *mise-en-scène* are carefully staged, encouraging an interpretation of the use of space as metaphoric rather than naturalistic. Isabel, for example, is frequently shot in close-up, giving us an intimate view into her world. The men, on the other hand, are shot mainly in long shots, as we see their behaviour in the context of the bar, the street and the brothel. The camera treats them as a group rather than as individuals. Cross-cutting powerfully displays the different spaces that Isabel and Juan inhabit, spaces which are internal and psychological as much as physical. While Juan wrestles with his conscience in his room, unable to keep still, Isabel lies on her bed, rapturously rehearsing Juan's name to herself. Juan's room is narrow, dark and oppressive, the non-diegetic music which accompanies him, ominous. Isabel is shown in close-up, in plenty of light, and with a delicate, almost whimsical musical score. Another spatial metaphor is the block of flats under construction that Isabel and Juan visit. While Isabel envisages a future home, Juan knows their prospects are as empty as the shell of the building in which they stand. As Isabel leans over an empty lift shaft, Juan appears to contemplate letting her fall, wondering if her death would be a welcome release for both of them. He later throws the floorplan he had been sketching into a puddle, a metaphor for unrealisable plans casually discarded. The divergent paths of our two protagonists are confirmed towards the end of the film. Juan's mental state is indicated by a vertiginous shot looking up towards a high bridge, followed by the reverse-angle shot of his point of view on the river below, indicating, perhaps, that he is contemplating suicide. Isabel, meanwhile, blissfully unaware of what is to come, skates across the polished floor of the empty ballroom, dancing around her dream of what the evening will bring. But this is the setting for her discovery of the unbearable truth. When Federico tells Isabel of the deception, the notes from the piano tuner become discordant, the ubiquitous mood-music of melodrama taking on a new and disturbing eloquence.

The co-existence of melodramatic and realistic elements in *Main Street* is not an uncomfortable one. The examples of camerawork and *mise-en-scène* suggest that Bardem saw the role of the men more in social terms. Frequent long shots emphasise the social group rather than the psychological individual and therefore distance us from the characters, allowing us to judge them, and the social problem they represent, more objectively. The predicament of Isabel, on the other hand, is conceived of in melodramatic terms, and thus the techniques include close-ups (encouraging empathy), domestic interior spaces and emotionally manipulative music. Such mixing of realism and melodrama, far from unconventional, was the key to Italian neorealism, witness the strongly manipulative melodrama of any of the classic neorealist films. At the other extreme, Hollywood melodrama, though primarily an uncritical entertainment genre, nevertheless touched upon social themes, some of them quite contentious. At its best, Hollywood melodrama was able to overcome the strictures of bourgeois realism (and the capitalist, patriarchal values it served), by suggesting – especially through *mise-en-scène* – what it could not communicate directly. In this, it has much in common with progressive filmmakers working in Franco's Spain. It is probably *Main Street*'s successful balancing of realism and melodrama, permitting it to be read 'correctly' by intelligent viewers whilst remaining elusive to the censors, that has assured its place among the great films made under (and against) Franco.

Mark Allinson

REFERENCES

Bardem, Juan Antonio (1993) *Calle Mayor* (facsimile script). Madrid: Alma-Plot.

Cerón Gómez, Juan Francisco (1998) *El cine de Juan Antonio Bardem*. Murcia: Universidad de Murcia.

Monterde, José Enrique (1997) '*Calle Mayor*', in Juliio Pérez Perucha (ed.) *Antologia Crítica de cine español 1906–1995*. Madrid: Cátedra, 401–3.

Roberts, Stephen (1999) 'In Search of a New Spanish Realism: Bardem's *Calle Mayor*', in Peter William Evans (ed.) *Spanish Cinema: The Auteurist Tradition.* Oxford: Oxford University Press, 19–37.

Stone, Rob (2002) *Spanish Cinema.* Harlow: Longman.

EL ÚLTIMO CUPLÉ THE LAST TORCH SONG

JUAN DE ORDUÑA, SPAIN, 1957

When it was released in 1957, the musical drama *El último cuplé* (*The Last Torch Song*) was a surprise hit in Spain, a 'miracle' which forced a re-jigging of programming in Madrid's Rialto cinema, saw queues at Barcelona's Cine Montecarlo (which had reluctantly given it a one-week slot), and sustained a year's run in both cities as well as becoming a huge success in Latin America and, according to its star Sara Montiel, in the USA as well. From an initial invest-ment of five-and-a-half million pesetas the film returned 300 million pesetas within four years. However, its material and its structure did initially seem unlikely to score a hit with Spanish audiences variously or simultaneously attuned by then to the modern look of Hollywood, to glimpses of a new European social realism and, where musicals were concerned, to the distinc-tively 1940s and 1950s and Andalusian-flavoured genre of the folkloric musical and the rising stars associated with it. Enthusiasts of director Juan de Orduña's earlier work – notably the patriotic historical epic *Alba de América* (*Dawn of America*, 1951) – were thought unlikely to be interested in seeing *The Last Torch Song*. Within a strongly melodramatic and sentimentally tragic frame it centres on the performance of 24 musical numbers in the thematically varied but essentially old-fashioned song form of the *cuplé*, the Spanish version of the music-hall song. A cognate of *cuplé* is 'couplet': though never that short, and not always structured around paired lines, the songs are short in line-length and in duration, straddling the areas of popular poetry and song and, as the film's own script suggests in the words of the character Juan Contreras, able pithily to present 'the best of opera and theatre in just two minutes'. It was the success on radio of the young singer Lilian de Celis, who was busy looking back two generations and rediscovering, among other forms, the *cuplé* which made Orduña believe that his project might have modest resonance. The potency of the star image of the form's most famous champion on the radio, Conchita Piquer, might also have been expected to have a beneficial effect on the project. The outline of the story, its timescale (broadly speaking), and several of its musi-cal numbers, are meant as a homage also to another great Spanish (and international) artiste of previous generations, Raquel Meller (1888–1964). The film, helped by such associations, effectively relaunched the film career of the soon-to-be-international-Hispanic superstar Sara

Montiel, and it launched her musical career, with the record album of the show (produced by Columbia/BMG Latin) earning 'two or three million pesetas in old money' (i.e., before the 1959 devaluation) in four months. Subsequent deals with Hispavox rewarded her with substantial worldwide sales.

Along with the music, Montiel – who plays María Luján, a gifted singer, specifically of the *cuplé* – holds most of the keys to the film's success, as we shall see. Apart from adolescent roles and a memorable part as an undercover, dispossessed Moorish princess, Aldara, in the historical drama *Locura de amor* (*The Mad Queen*, 1948) also directed by Orduña, Montiel's associations were Mexican, Cuban and North American (for example, *Veracruz* [Robert Aldrich, 1954]). As Terenci Moix reports, Montiel had two special sets of expectations to fill in Mexico in the early 1950s: to be Mexico's Marilyn Monroe, and to be a link for Spaniards in exile after the Civil War to home and Spanishness – the film was to prove hugely popular with this group. Playing Contreras, the impresario who discovers (and then rediscovers) María Luján was Armando Calvo who had played opposite Mexican star María Félix in *La mujer de todos* (*Everyone's Woman*, Julio Baracho, 1946) as part of an established Mexican career, but was also associated with imperialist-epic productions in Spain of the 1940s through his role as Lieutenant Martín Cerezo in the iconic war film *Los últimos de Filipinas* (*Last Stand in the Philippines*, Antonio Román, 1945). Some fascinatingly incompatible associations and a strong transnational flavour, then, were written into the film by its lead actors: a grave Iberocentric imperialist nostalgia and a sense of a new, sexy autonomous Mexicanness; liberal connections (Montiel's circle in Mexico) and reactionary agendas (Orduña's and Román's earlier films); sombre or heroic national histories of epic sweep and often flighty, entertaining stories fluffed up in the studio.

After a voice-over proclaiming the film as a homage to all those women 'who in days gone by knew how to move us with the magic in miniature of the *cuplé*', and the raising of a proscenium arch curtain, the outer frame of narration is established as being set in Barcelona in the 1950s (the exact year unspecified, as is the case with all the film's contextualising intertitles). At the beginning of the film, María Luján is a bloated, heavy-drinking and clumsy has-been, full of regrets for herself and for the genre that launched her career. The *cuplé* and its performers have been, she laments, successively downgraded to mere warm-up acts then pure and simple erotic titillation. A flashback takes us to the star's modest beginnings, living close to the poverty line with her ambitious, scheming and match-making aunt and working in the chorus at the Teatro de la Zarzuela in Madrid. In 1911, when she is happily courting her working-class boyfriend

Cándido, she is noticed and flirted with by Juan Contreras, who has been given encouragement by Maria's aunt. In a confrontation between Juan and Cándido the former establishes for the film a key narrative supposition by suggesting that María is in fact not destined for either of them, but rather for her art. He also suggests to her, countering her lack of confidence in the *cuplé*, her chosen form, that no art form is insignificant when the artist who performs it is great. Thus María Luján is inscribed in a familiar melodramatic show-business plot conflating and polarising art and life, performance and destiny. Seville, Valencia, Zaragoza and Barcelona lead to Paris in 1919 and an Armistice Day performance of 'Madelon' and, later that night, at the request of the Grand Duke Viscount Beaugency, 'La nieta de Carmen' ('Carmen's Grandchild'). A triumphant world tour follows. After her return from New York, at the start of the 1920s, she encourages the advances of handsome 19-year-old bullfighter Pepe (Enrique Vera) and has an affair with him which separates her from Juan, and brings intimations of tragedy: confronted by Pepe's good, simple girlfriend Trini and her affirmations of her love for Pepe, María's trump card is that she loves him more because 'ya sé que no volveré a querer más' ('I know I shall never love again'). In 1928 Pepe is killed in the ring, shortly after Trini, his fiancée, has persuaded her of Pepe's intention to go ahead and marry. An unspecified time later – possibly into the early 1930s – ill health manifests itself as María is singing on stage 'El relicario' ('The Reliquary'), whose plot involves the death of a young bullfighter. She is advised never to sing again. She recounts the passage of 'years and years' in voice-over punctuated by cameo scenes of gambling, drinking in a cheap café (in what looks like the mid-1940s), and then of her alone with the brandy bottle and a single bed in a cheap boarding house. We return to Barcelona in the 1950s and find the voice-over is her recounting her story to Juan in the dressing room. She is persuaded to sing on the big stage once again, in Madrid where she began her career; but the effort and the accumulated emotion precipitate her death, dressed in the black she had already chosen for her come-back, and prostrate on a *chaise longue* offstage.

As already suggested, the *cuplé* is thematically varied; similarly, as well as having an intimate capital city café feel, underpinned by risqué in-jokes designed for a specific demographic, it also ranges into rural folkloric or provincial neighbourhood territory (often getting conflated with the Andalusian *copla*, whose apogée came later in the 1940s and 1950s); joy, death, indignation and erotic power displays all find their place in the form; it can be – and is in this film – intense (as in 'Nena', María Luján's last song) and candy-floss and can-can trite (as in 'Ven y ven' ['Come here, come here']). The film's central, extended flashback goes to the 1910s and the mid-point of the *cuplé*'s period of popular cultural prominence. This part of the film recreates much of the *cuplé*'s usual simplicity – despite Montiel's elaborate style of perform-ance and manner of dress – and mixes pleasant, fantastical and quip-strewn recreations of back-stage life with sparingly placed, short-hand realist details of the period as experienced by the working and lower-middle classes in Madrid. However, when the film is charting María Luján's growing international success, and as the café gives way to the grand stage, other forms and styles impose themselves, notably the ever popular 'Valencia', a paso doble from the *zar-zuela* (light opera) *La bien amada* (*A Woman Loved*) by José Padilla (1924), which is given a hybrid Hollywood-cum-*zarzuela* treatment involving a gigantic set, two curving stairways for the entrance and exit of a large chorus, lavish orchestration, but folksy costumes and a topo-graphically coded set suggestive of the rice and reed beds, and the streams and channels of the Valencian foreshore. Another deviation from the Madrid- and Barcelona-based *cuplé* proper is the performance of Manuel Font de Anta's 'La nieta de Carmen', a *copla* with doubly Andalusian associations, through its Seville-born composer (and his collaborators) and, obviously, through its reference to the iconic Carmen. The geographical scope within the songs is matched, as the synopsis above points out, by María Luján's itineraries at the height of her career.

This blur and interchangeability of locations and emotional spaces contributes consider-ably to one of the film's aims, that is to offer an escapist, romantic 'cure' to a Spanish audience at the time all too aware of its own isolation and inability to travel as well as mindful of the recentness of hunger, strife, repression and war. In temporal terms the film is also radically unfocused: the following discussion will deal first with *The Last Torch Song*'s equivocal relation-ship to historical context and second with its star's own role as an agent of temporal impreci-sion, making the film and its motifs both entertainingly lacking in anchorage in any believable historical period and, at the same time, able obliquely to draw attention to some unexpectedly sharp, if very brief and sporadic, interventions of its plot and visual features in the contempo-rary story of Spain.

Marsha Kinder has pointed out that this is a film in which, in common with the 'escapist melodrama' of the period, and despite its strong emphasis on memory, 'all traces of contempo-rary Spanish political history are conveniently repressed'. Both the Spanish Civil War and World War II simply disappear into ellipses. Barcelona in the 1950s is determinedly and glamorously associated not with its recent history of marginalisation by a centrist and Castilianist state or with the emerging problems of super-fast economic development and difficult absorption of the immigrant labour force but with the freedom, bustle, glitter and elitism of the other cos-mopolitan locations selected for representation (though not costly on-site shooting, of course).

However, at a general level, María Luján's progress in the 1910s and 1920s into mobility and modernity, and the opening up of her career to the world abroad, might seem to chime with Spain's political progress in the 1950s; and there are references to historical events and trends. The film's second sustained Barcelona sequence, when we return to the narrative present, links Juan's dressing-room speech of encouragement to the theatre performance in Madrid by way of rapidly sequenced newspaper headlines on the economic crisis in France, audiences with Franco as Head of State, changes to the Spanish Congress, news of an upturn in industrial output, a general strike in Britain, and the Suez crisis. In terms of performance style the film charts (undoubtedly unintentionally) huge social changes: from the piquant coyness of María Luján's early, Madrid-based performances, indulging in an imitation of pre-Civil War artists; decorum in erotic matters seems to be in train, to the unrestrained sensuality of the performance of 'Fumando espero' ('Here I wait, Smoking') which makes the 1920s seduction of Pepe the bullfighter (and the outrageous open-mouthed kiss she initiates with him) look more suitable to the dawning of the 1960s. In the section of her autobiography which focuses on the film, Montiel makes strenuous efforts to put herself on some sort of historical stage. She presents a rehistoricised context for the film in terms of the text of her own career and her reception and positioning on the cultural scene. She stresses her own radical incompatibility at the time with Franco's Spain, and her left-wing or free-thinking connections and sympathies. The left-wing connections, though, are circumstantial rather than fed by a longer-term conviction, and her anti-Francoism seems due in part at least to her resentment at being used as a pawn in Franco's cultural politics of rapprochement with Europe and the East and to her stigmatisation (again, at the time of the return to Spain) as 'descarriada', 'mujer mala' ('off the rails'; 'a bad woman'), as the 'amante del americano' ('the American's lover'), her civil marriage to Anthony Mann being unrecognised in Spain.

The temporal profile of the Montiel image at this juncture was productively and entertainingly complex; and it continued to be so in the years after *The Last Torch Song*, with roles as a music-hall singer in Isabelline Spain in *La Bella Lola* (*Beautiful Lola*, 1962); in pre-and post-World War I vaudeville in *La reina del Chantecler* (*The Queen of the Chanticleer*, 1963), as a singer of *boleros* and *coplas* in early 1940s Casablanca in *Noches de Casablanca* (*Casablanca Nights*, 1963) and (with wonderful unbelievability) as a late nineteenth-century nun, disgraced by her rape while on a missionary posting and subsequently (again) living as a music-hall performer in *Esa Mujer* (*That Woman*, 1969). In all the roles subsequent to *The Last Torch Song* there is a flagrantly incoherent clash between historical authenticity (scarce) and the need (pervasive) of the star and her vehicle to showcase the best and most flattering in contemporary 1950s and 1960s coiffeur, couture and screen manners. Back-combed bouffant and Elizabeth Taylor-esque styled curls enter into dialogue with pseudo-period hats, drapes and dresses and contrast with the general dowdiness of frock coats and hats on her befuddled leading men. A similar frenzy of temporal simultaneity affects the sets. *The Last Torch Song*, while supposedly constructing its narrative charm around nostalgia in fact may be seen as itself a point of origin for the stylistic practices of much of the rest of Montiel's film career.

There are a number of particularly important constants in these productively unstable temporal horizons. Montiel is an unusually intense manifestation of the star as a mirage of transcendence, and while, as such, she can be consumed and appropriated by different kinds of audiences in different ways (straight men's object of desire, gay men's camp fantasy, a model for women looking for independence in a repressive culture), it resists very strongly indeed the inevitable truth that such a layered embedding in social and cultural meanings within the textual/filmic frame is perfectly stable: as she states, 'images change and develop over time'. Montiel, across the trajectory of her career, is glamorously all about not changing (though the stories she represents on screen frequently turn on tragic and traumatic alterations). The first extended biographical account of her uses the conventional sales tag of 'complete biography' but soon gives a more unusual sense of wholeness through its achronologically arranged photographic images which apply the same sumptuous fullness (of hair, lips, costume) to a diversity of represented historical moments. Her second (and rather more ironic) biographer, Javier Alfaya, fixes her with the sub-title 'the eternal return' (although he ends up signalling his own and the public's weariness with Montiel's reiterations, and acknowledges that he is writing at a time when film stars have given way to 'alternative deities'. The advertising tag on the boxed sets of Montiel films –'Siempre Sara' ('Forever Sara') – gives depth to the standardised and comforting compliments of many a magazine; especially in the 1980s, speaking of her unalterable physical charms, of how the passage of time seems not to affect 'esta maravillosa mujer' ('this marvellous woman'), of her ability to bridge past and future, fixing the myth in a space between Spain's pre-modernity and its post-modernity, and of 'la eterna Sara Montiel' who continues to be a myth, thirty years on from the premiere of *The Last Torch Song*. In New York to celebrate her 61st birthday she reportedly astonished American audiences, more prone to wearing tracksuits and trainers according to a playful piece by Maruja Torres, and who 'couldn't get over their astonishment at seeing an unadulterated, genuine diva of the sort that you don't see any more', appearing on the streets in white chiffon and at the party in the Waldorf Astoria with 'practically her entire jewellery collection on, and what she wasn't wearing was brought along by a friend, safely wrapped inside a nice little pouch in case of emergencies.'

A seven-episode spectacular at the end of the 1980s involving traditional and newly composed songs of regional topicality saw her dressed in an eclectic range of pseudo-traditional regional costumes (with the exception of that for the Seville-based episode, which was a hyper-Arabian number). Nominated in 1992 as 'Lady España' (an annual media and society prize since the 1960s), Montiel again dressed up as regional and provincial types both for the camera and in a series of appearances as part of her 'duties', each costume representing, for her, a set of (fuzzy) characteristics such as tradition and uniqueness for Madrid, gentleness and kindness for Extremadura, gaiety and femininity for Valencia and so on. As a media personality – dubbed 'our international Manchegan' or 'the universal Manchegan' – by the 1990s Montiel had appeared photographed in many hundreds of Spanish locations.

Finally, returning to Montiel as a disruptive physical presence, if Conchita Piquer had to rely to a certain extent on the lyrics of her songs and tone of voice, to offer the ancillary thrill to her audiences of the possibility of there being, as Silvia Bermúdez has said, 'a space for cultural difference in the Spain of the 1940s' which could 'reconfigure desire', Montiel's visible body does a similar trick, much more dazzlingly. *The Last Torch Song*'s emphasis on the eroticised body and voice and its tale of easy (if highly dramatised) transfers of amorous affection contributed to her becoming, in the words of Javier Alfaya, 'nuestro más acabado mito erótico' ('the most fully perfected erotic myth we have'). Spanish men no longer had to feel guilty about their attraction to foreign film stars as Montiel was able to provide what the Spanish scene had until then not been able or allowed to provide, 'un "sexy" cinematográfico claramente español' ('a truly Spanish sex appeal for the cinema'). The camera's attention to lips, teeth and tongue, and Montiel's aural glamorisation of the old-fashioned form of the *cuplé* was accompanied by glittering dresses, dense, shining hair, and gleaming, flatteringly-lit flesh at shoulders, bust and legs, all of which sexualise this film in no uncertain manner. The striking and unmistakable look of the body of Montiel – with her hips, bust, lips, nose and cheek bones always promising and withholding – her physical presence offers that 'iconic, transtextual sameness beneath variations' that has been singled out by Bruce Babington as characteristic of certain stars. The decoration of her body, and the way in which accessories, as well as camera work, draw attention to fragments of her anatomy, are excessive. On the one hand they remind the audience of what Terenci Moix sees in terms of earthy, primordial appeal – a reliable, robust, Spanish womanliness – and on the other hand they break scandalously through the diaphanous material of the 'very particular structure of the national sexual morality' of the time and push at the bounds of the officially acceptable. (These elements feature in Pedro Almodóvar's *La mala educación* [*Bad Education*, 2004].) The mixture of a cavalier approach to historical and geographical verisimilitude and stability, the rapid cutting to the tragic, sentimental chase, the visual flurries which lure the audience into attending to surface details which deliciously suck them in, above all the association of femininity with artifice (and masculinity with artlessness): this is part of the substance of camp. This is, perhaps, the final, strangely rehistoricising disruption at the heart of this film. There are signs there not simply that the past contains musical and visual treasures which might comfort and stimulate a 1950s audience in Spain, and delight and move audiences cut off from, or happy to idealise about, Spain, but signs too that a historically very specific way of being a (famous) woman is quickly revealed by fond parodic over-exposure to be fabrication, open to resistance; enjoyable, but politically avoidable. It is not for nothing that Sara Montiel has a substantial resonance in Spanish queer subcultures across a span of time and the polytonal theatricality of *The Last Torch Song* (complete with a director whose perhaps improbable gayness came eventually to be no secret) embeds it in that set of cultural contexts as well as emphatically in the Spanish cultural imaginary of the twentieth century.

Chris Perriam

REFERENCES

Alfaya, Javier (1971) *Sara Montiel*. Barcelona: Dopesa.

Ashley (1969) *Biografía completa de Sara Montiel*. Madrid: Ibérico de Ediciones.

Babington, Bruce (2001) 'Introduction: British Stars and Stardom', in Bruce Babington (ed.) *British Stars and Stardom: From Alma Taylor to Sean Connery*. Manchester: Manchester University Press, 1–27.

Bermúdez, Silvia (1997) '"Music to my Ears": Cuplés, Conchita Piquer and the (Un)Making of Cultural Nationalism', *Siglo XX/20th Century*, 15, 1–2, 33–54.

Kinder, M. (1993) *Blood Cinema: The Reconstruction of National Identity in Spain*. Berkeley: University of California Press.

Moix, Terenci (1993) *Suspiros de España: la copla y el cine de nuestro recuerdo*. Barcelona: Plaza & Janés.

Montiel, Sara (2001) *Memorias: Vivir es un placer*. Barcelona: Plaza y Janés.

Torres, Maruja (1989) 'Cumpleaños de Sara Montiel con sabor latino', *El País*, 13 March.

VIRIDIANA

10

LUIS BUÑUEL, SPAIN, 1961

Encouraged by various individuals working in Spanish cinema – including Carlos Saura – Luis Buñuel returned in 1960, for the first time since leaving the country after the Civil War, to make a film in Spain. His last films there had been those he produced (with the occasional directorial helping hand) at Filmófono studios (set up in 1931 by Ricardo Urgoiti, but in which Buñuel had also played an important administrative and, to a lesser extent, financial role): *Don Quintín el amargao* (*Embittered Don Quintín*, 1935), *La hija de Juan Simón* (*Juan Simón's Daughter*, 1935), *¿Quién me quiere a mí?* (*Who Will Love Me?*, 1936) and *Centinela alerta* (*Sentinel, Alert!*, 1936). His departure from Spain led first to an abortive spell in Hollywood where, unlike other European émigrés (Ernst Lubitsch, Fritz Lang, Billy Wilder, Douglas Sirk, and so on), he failed to re-launch his career, and then to Mexico where he resumed work as a director, with films like *Los olvidados* (*The Young and the Damned*, 1950), *Él* (*This Strange Passion*, 1952) and *Nazarín* (1958). His return home, drawing criticism from Spanish Republicans in Mexico, was perhaps a necessary journey to a country that remained dear to him in exile. Despite taking Mexican nationality in 1949, Buñuel remained, as he wrote in the *New York Times* in 1962, a Spaniard at heart: 'I went back to Spain because that is my country … We do not live in the best of all possible worlds.'

As expressed here, Buñuel's Voltairean outlook on politics disarmed any residual qualms about returning to a country still ruled by Franco, on whose regime, as a Republican, he had once turned his back. With characteristically wry humour, he points to the religious orthodoxy of the film, awarded a clean bill of health by the ecclesiastical adviser on the set, and decried only after its controversial screening at Cannes.

Nevertheless, despite Buñuel's disclaimers, the film clearly adheres to his customary practice and exemplifies another basic point in his *New York Times* comments – that his films aim to provoke and unsettle the viewer:

I would like to continue to make films which, apart from entertaining the audience, convey to people the absolute certainty of this idea … The true opium of the audience is conformity … Motion pictures act directly upon the spectator. To the spectator persons and things on the screen become concrete. In this darkness they isolate him from his usual psychic atmosphere. Because of this, cinema is capable of stirring the spectator as perhaps no other art. But as no other can, it is also capable of stupefying him.

Viridiana (1961) proved no exception to the rule, drawing praise and condemnation in equal measure. Critical acclaim from disinterested reviewers flooded in from all quarters. For instance, Alfred Fabré-Luce in *Arts* classified it as 'un grand film Catholique'; Pierre Marcabru in *France Soir* hailed it as 'Ce très beau film'. The Cannes Jury – which included the highly enthusiastic Catholic film editor of *Le Figaro*, Claude Mauriac – awarded it the Palme D'Or. On the negative side, Rose Pelswick in the *New York Journal American* denounced it under the heading: 'Spanish Film is Sick'. Much more damaging for the film industry in Spain, its screening at Cannes and general reaction abroad led to the collapse of *UNINCI* productions – which together with *Film 59* (Spain) and *Producciones Gustavo Alatriste* (Mexico) had financed the film – and to the replacement of José Muñoz Fontán as Director General of Cinematography by the Falangist Jesús Suevo. Furthermore, scandalised by the story of a violated nun's disillusioned surrender to the ways of the world, the Franco government prohibited any mention in the press of the film's success at Cannes. Mexico, like Spain a country governed at that time by an authoritarian regime, remained largely unmoved by the furore about *Viridiana*, and welcomed Buñuel back to an industry where he continued to make outstanding films like *El ángel exterminador* (*The Exterminating Angel,* 1962) and, in co-productions with mainly French companies, like *Belle de jour* (1966). He returned to Spain ten years later to direct *Tristana* (1970), a film that covers some of the ground of *Viridiana*, such as in its more direct inspiration by Benito Pérez Galdós, its interest in the relations between lovers of unequal ages, and its casting of Fernando Rey in the role of the older man obsessed with a younger woman.

Viridiana is really a film in two parts. The first concerns the life and times of Don Jaime (Rey), a widower with an illegitimate son Jorge (Paco Rabal), living in a ramshackle estate with his servants, who include Ramona (Margarita Lozano) his housekeeper, and her daughter Rita (Teresa Rabal, Paco's daughter). The second concentrates on Jorge's part inheritance of the estate and his attempts to modernise it. Viridiana (Silvia Pinal) features prominently in both: while in the first part her life is largely measured by the values of an antiquated Spain, personified by Don Jaime and the convent to which she is initially attached, in the second she opens up the part of the estate she has inherited to beggars who eventually abuse her kindness, run riot during her absence, and try to rape her on her return, a series of events that leads to the abandonment of her beliefs, and resignation to a *ménage-à-trois* life with Jorge and Ramona.

Don Jaime's story is a widower's attempt to reconcile himself to the death of his wife Elvira through the seduction of his novice-niece, uncannily resembling his wife, encouraged by her Mother Superior to visit her grieving uncle. When persuasion fails, Don Jaime drugs Viridiana, intent on violating her while unconscious but, after preliminary caresses, stops short of taking full advantage. Conscious again, and horrified by Don Jaime's confession, in which at first he falsely claims and then denies violation – both desperate measures to prevent her flight from his mansion – the distraught Viridiana rushes back to the convent. Later, after learning of Don Jaime's suicide by hanging, she returns to the estate she has now jointly inherited with Jorge.

Don Jaime's role has been read as Buñuel's view from exile of Spain's ruin by a patrician class: the sprawling estate, overcrowded with pine trees, surrounding a mansion in disrepair, its attic converted into a junkyard, is a metaphor for Spain itself – a country governed by ecclesiastics and authoritarian traditionalists, ripe for the kind of modernisation epitomised by Jorge, the representative of a new breed of businessman bringing material prosperity to Spain in the 1960s. The film's interest in class and politics is indisputable, but Buñuel's portrayal of the melancholic Don Jaime also raises questions of psychology that, in deference to his Surrealist affiliations, merit consideration through Freud's writing on dreams, the death instinct, and the links between mourning and melancholia.

Not made in the 1920s or 1930s, like *Un chien andalou* (1928) and *L'Age d'or* (1930), in the heat of Surrealism, *Viridiana* nevertheless pays tribute to Buñuel's endless fascination, originating in the Surrealists' interest in psychoanalysis, with the unconscious. Dreams, Freud's 'royal road to the unconscious', in *Viridiana*, as almost everywhere else in Buñuel, open up the psyches of their dreamers. Rita is troubled by her dream of the black bull entering her room; Viridiana is seen sleepwalking and performing acts of cryptic meaning while unconscious; and Don Jaime, not in the literal sense a dreamer, behaves in some ways like a somnambulist, living in the past, as if in a dream, viewing all around him from the distant horizons of memory. Buñuel read Freud's *The Interpretation of Dreams* (1900) and *The Psychopathology of Everyday Life* (1901) and, despite his later barbed comments about simplistic Freudian readings of his films, clearly recalled Freud's discussion of the mechanisms of the dream-work when staging some of his own complex dramas of the unconscious in, say, *Belle de jour* or *Le charme discret de la bourgeoisie* (*The Discreet Charm of the* Bourgeoisie, 1972). As with Buñuel's other dream-laden films, *Viridiana* challenges the viewer as much as its dreamers to interpret the latent meanings of its oneiric landscape.

To some extent, especially in the first, Don Jaime-related, part, this is a film about interpretation, about viewer response, voyeurism and complicity. In the early stages the little girl Rita is one of the film's most important watchers. Like the infant watching its parents make love in Freud's theorised drama of the primal scene, she is desperate to observe the private dramas of the adults, peering through windows, even climbing trees for a better view of furtive behaviour. Ramona, too, eavesdrops, looks through key-holes trying to decipher the sights and sounds of the mansion's secrets. Significantly these watchers are female. Excluded not just because of their status – Ramona, as a servant, Rita, as a child – but perhaps also because of their sex, they are eager to take control of the power of the look – defined by Laura Mulvey and others as the prerogative of the male – to satisfy their curiosity, libidinal or otherwise, through their concealed voyeurism. In watching Ramona and Rita we watch ourselves watching. Ramona's observation of Viridiana through the keyhole, motivated more by fascination with the latter's spirituality – though even here curiosity about the masochistic tendencies suggested by the crown of thorns and nails Viridiana carries around with her cannot be discounted – prefigures Rita's more determined attempts to witness Don Jaime's complementary perversions. The disclosure in these scenes of perversion committed by two pathological individuals reflects in the spectatorship of the characters on-screen the voyeurism of the audience, whose own complex drives and object relations are called into question through these vignettes of self-consciousness.

Rita watches Don Jaime place Viridiana, who had already agreed to dress up in his dead wife's bridal gown, on his bed. He sets a crown, not of thorns, but of flowers, on her head, converting Viridiana from Bride of Christ into a nuptial corpse, and sits in contemplation beside her. Placed at her feet, the camera zooms up her comatose body, as if in imitation of Don Jaime's savouring of Viridiana's inert beauty. Not satisfied with her vantage point, Rita climbs a tree for a better view. Now she watches Don Jaime raise Viridiana's limp torso to plant a kiss on her lips. He replaces her torso on the bed, unbuttons her top, buries his anguished face in her partially exposed bosom, and kisses her again. All of this is shot subjectively through Rita, the viewer's alter ego, here relishing as well as merely witnessing a scene of perverse desire.

Horrified by his own infamy, Don Jaime prevents himself from indulging it any further, and leaves the room, slamming the door after him. Rita climbs down from the tree and, when challenged by Ramona, replies, censoring the scene, that she has seen Don Jaime kissing Viridiana, immediately following the remark with another reference to her dream about the black bull who invades her room, in this way further deflecting attention from her shameful voyeurism. Rita here is both spectator and camera, one of various characters in the film who are viewers and creative observers, censoring, editing, reshaping as well as recording observed reality. Other characters who repeat the pattern include one of the beggars (El cojo) painting a picture of the Virgin Mary – modelled on Viridiana – attending to a poor, sick woman. Another beggar, Enedina (Lola Gaos), takes a mock photograph, not with a real camera but with one 'given to me by mum and dad': her sex. The perspective of one beggar-artist is limited by the struggle for survival; Enedina's, on the other hand, reflects an irreverent attitude to religion and its sado-masochistic tendencies – already signposted through Viridiana's Pandora's box of thorns, nails and crucifix – as she snaps the group of feasting beggars frozen sacrilegiously into a demotic Black Mass version of Leonardo's *Last Supper*. Enedina, the beggar artist, Rita and Ramona, are all Buñuel surrogates; elsewhere, Buñuel himself, without the intermediary of an artist figure, shoots a scene – when Viridiana compels the beggars in the field to down tools for the Angelus – in a way that, as Agustín Sánchez Vidal notes, unmistakably recalls not only a painting by Millet but also, as Vicente Sánchez-Biosca argues, Dalí's 'El mito trágico del Angelus de Millet' ('The Tragic Myth of Millet's *Angelus*'). Buñuel's viewpoint here mixes irony with empathy as he records the ultimately doomed attempts of a naïve young woman with little experience of the world to rescue the dispossessed in her care through the Gospels' message of charity. Through Rita, Ramona, the beggar-artist and Enedina, as well as through his own play-ful identification with Jean-François Millet, Buñuel fragments the processes of spectatorship, where viewers not only become witnesses to the action brought to their attention through these characters but also to their own complicity in the processes of observation. Like Viridiana, who reads her own sleepwalking collection of ashes as penitence and death, the audience is invited not only to look but also to interpret and, beyond that, to reflect on its own act of interpreta-tion.

We never discover the identity of the artists whose portraits of Doña Elvira and Don Jaime hang in the mansion, but their anonymous work contributes to the film's patterns of viewer response. The painter's eye here matches, in the portrait of Doña Elvira, Don Jaime's impressions of Viridiana; Don Jaime himself, though, is flattered by a pose of order and self-control out of keeping with the pathologically disturbed appearance of the man in the days leading up to his suicide. Don Jaime had earlier remarked, welcoming Viridiana to his home: 'Solitude has made me selfish.' He might have added that it had also led him to pathological depression, or melancholia.

The sight of Viridiana promptly unveils perverse feelings for his dead wife, leading to a comment on the uncanny resemblance between Viridiana and Elvira. From this first encounter between the pair, the film shifts to Don Jaime playing sacred music on the organ, a sequence intercut with shots of Viridiana in her bedroom, looking at herself in the mirror, removing her cap and stockings, freeing her snowy hair. The links between Don Jaime, Viridiana and their ironised contrasting activities – one surrendering through sacred music to unearthly yearnings, the other temporarily casting off the straitjacket of her other-worldly uniform – draw attention to extreme forms of behaviour that eventually lead in the case of Viridiana to life-affirming renunciation, and in Don Jaime's to death-dealing despair. Don Jaime's refusal to see Viridiana as anything other than the reincarnation of Elvira calls to mind Scottie's attempts to transform Judy into Madeleine in *Vertigo* (Alfred Hitchcock, 1958), made only a couple of years earlier by a director with whom Buñuel shared many passions and, from their mutual Jesuit education, forming influences. Don Jaime's obsession with Viridiana, climaxing in attempts to revive Doña Elvira through dressing his niece in his dead wife's garments, is a variant of Surrealist *amour fou*.

On a superficial, less controversial level, Don Jaime's mourning of his lost wife reflects the deeply-felt sorrow of a bereft widower, whose desire to end his life may be perhaps explained through Freud's theory, in the late essay 'Beyond the Pleasure Principle', of the death-wish, the desire for a 'return to the inanimate state', in which the instinct to be restored to an earlier mode of existence derives from Plato's account in the *Symposium* of the search by primeval humans for their unique doubles, in the process for a pre-cultural state of being, an earlier Utopia of death. In Don Jaime's *liebestod* wish to be reunited in death with Elvira, there are echoes not only of Buñuel's endless fascination with Wagner (for example, the *Tristan und Isolde* music in *Un chien andalou*, Silvia Pinal as a Walkyrie in *The Exterminating Angel*, the music of the *Ring* at the end of *Cet obscur objet du désir* [*That Obscure Object of Desire*, 1977]), but also of Fray Luis de León's great ode to his friend Felipe Ruiz. Like the painter Eben in another of Buñuel's favourite films, *The Portrait of Jennie* (William Dieterle, 1948), Don Jaime's perceptions of life are conditioned by dreams of death.

Quite apart from the sexual-political implications of a man's reconstruction of the identity of a woman through demands for her to put on clothes gratifying his sexual fantasies, the implicit necrophilia draws attention to the pathology, or melancholia, of the otherwise legitimate feelings of mourning by which Don Jaime is gripped. His attraction to the pallor and Gothic impassivity of Silvia Pinal's Viridiana-Doña Elvira points not only to a characteristically

Buñuelian predilection for submissive women but also to the deep depression that may ultimately explain his suicide.

With an already illustrious career in the Mexican cinema behind her, Silvia Pinal, the wife of the film's producer, Gustavo Alatriste, blanched her hair even more generously than in the comedies and melodramas in which she had made her name. Here she fits perfectly the image of necrophiliac fantasy where, as in *Belle de jour* and *Le fantôme de la liberté* (*The Phantom of Liberty*, 1974) the morbid desires of perverse men are incarnated in the allure of glacial women.

To some extent Buñuel's fascination is fuelled by his 'master', the Marquis de Sade, perhaps literature's greatest apologist for the entropic drives of love. In her study on necrophilia in literature Elisabeth Bronfen reads the connection between love and death as a tendency in the misogynistic traditions of Western culture. Admittedly, much Western art portrays the femme fatale as a dealer in death, visiting it through lubricity on her male victims, suffering it herself as the price of treachery. But, as David Punter and Lisa Downing point out, anti-life images in Western art, explained by de Sade as transgressions against nature as well as against social laws, cannot simply be read in reductive sexual-political terms. Nevertheless, in Buñuel's films the de Sade-inspired characters often give the impression that score-settling in the arena of sexual politics cannot be discounted where, beyond railing against providence, destruction as much as possession of the object is the spur to desire. In *Ensayo de un crímen* (*The Criminal Life of Archibaldo de la Cruz*, 1955), for instance, on glimpsing a woman to whom he feels drawn, Archibaldo comments with undisguised relish: 'La asesinaría con mucho gusto' ('I would gladly murder her').

In *Viridiana*, the action is focused on a desired but lost woman (Elvira), who returns in the imagination of her lover like a ghost – something emphasised in *Viridiana* by Silvia Pinal's wan expression, milky hair and bleached vestments – to haunt the body of another woman (Viridiana). When Don Jaime puts on his dead wife's high-heeled wedding shoe and corset – a transvestism repeated by the beggar accused of leprosy in the scene prior to Viridiana's violation – a number of possible readings of this eccentric behaviour suggest themselves: firstly, that traditional masculinity is finally cracking under the ultimately unbearable pressure of tradition; second, that, at any rate in the case of Don Jaime, and in a way ridiculed by the leper, this victim of *amour fou* can crave nothing less than some kind of symbiosis with his object of desire; but third, that Don Jaime's transvestism, in line with his melancholia, is a condition that targets both the self and the lost object with its growing anger and hostility.

As Robert Stoller argues in *Perversion: The Erotic Form of Hatred*, the pleasure of the necrophiliac is fetishistic in its focus on destruction, humiliation or deformation of the object of desire, reducing it to an inanimate state. But, as Stoller further argues, these negative drives also release more creative tendencies. Traumatised by the death of his wife, Don Jaime unleashes his fantasies through her re-apparition as Viridiana, reliving past happiness while simultaneously punishing her by treating her as a corpse.

Don Jaime's condition, ultimately readable through Freud's 'Mourning and Melancholia', is that of the melancholic, not someone who merely mourns the loss of the loved one, but whose mourning, while also reacting to that loss, highlights a disturbance in the mourner's unconscious: 'The melancholic displays something else besides which is lacking in mourning – an extraordinary diminution in his self-regard, an impoverishment of his ego on a grand scale. In mourning it is the world which has become poor and empty; in melancholia it is the ego itself.'

In reality these self-reproaches are assaults on the object of desire, displaced from that object on to the melancholic's own ego. Don Jaime's suicide may therefore be understood not simply as a wish to be reunited with Elvira, nor simply as self-reproach for the attempted seduction of Viridiana, but also as a way of treating 'itself as an object – if it is able to direct against itself the hostility which relates to an object and which represents the ego's original reaction to objects in the external world'. Through suicide, Don Jaime's ego becomes the object on which is displaced the hostility towards another, the object of desire, Elvira/Viridiana.

While Viridiana is oblivious of the obscure motivation behind her uncle's suicide, his death does lead to the first stage of her odyssey from innocence to experience. Charity, in the sense understood by her, an attitude compatible in origins with the sources of her uncle's paternalism – the Mother Superior significantly asks Viridiana early on whether she is aware of her uncle's 'caridad' – provides no cure to the material and social ills of 1960s Spain. Even though, as ever in his films (for example, *Los olvidados*), Buñuel refuses to confuse empathy with sentimentality, as the beggars turn their banquet into a saturnalian orgy, singing, dancing, fornicating, brawling and smashing up their mistress' dining room, the film's tone registers approval of radical social and political change. Viridiana's example of Christian innocence and self-sacrifice results only in making the desperate even more desperate. The destruction of the dining room, followed by the attempt to violate Viridiana, at least succeeds in making her rejoin the world, like Nazarin no longer able to remain immune to its vicissitudes. Jorge, whose task of regenerating the estate has already begun, may represent the country's more hopeful future. In his private life there is room neither for guilt – the starting point perhaps of Viridiana's charitable mission – nor for masochistic self-indulgence, nor for sexual narrow mindedness. When at the end of the film, disabused by now of her lofty ideals, Viridiana joins Jorge and Ramona in a card game of 'Tute', she does so on the understanding that exclusivity in love may be only one of the conventions henceforward under review.*

*I would like to express my gratitude to staff at the Filmoteca Nacional, Madrid, especially to Javier Herrera, Keeper of the Buñuel Collection, for making available to me research materials that helped make this chapter possible.

Peter William Evans

REFERENCES

Bronfen, Elisabeth (1992) *Over Her Dead Body: Death, Femininity and the Aesthetic*. Manchester: Manchester University Press.

Downing, Lisa (2003) *Desiring the Dead: Necrophilia and Nineteenth-Century French Literature*. Oxford: Legenda.

Fabré-Luce, Alfred (1962) '*Viridiana*, un grand film Catholique', *Arts*, 11 April.

Marcabru, Pierre (1962) '*Viridiana* de Luis Buñuel', *France Soir*, 7 April.

Mulvey, Laura (1975) 'Visual Pleasure and Narrative Cinema, *Screen*, 16, 3, 6–18.

Pelswick, Rose (1962) 'Spanish Film is Sick', *New York Journal American*, 20 March.

Punter, David (1998) *Gothic Pathologies: the Text, the Body and the Law*. London: Macmillan.

Sánchez-Biosca, Vicente (1999) *Luis Buñuel: Viridiana*. Barcelona: Paidós.

_____ (2004) 'Scenes of Liturgy and Perversion', in Peter William Evans and Isabel Santaolalla (eds) *Luis Buñuel: New Readings*. London: British Film Institute, 173–86.

Sánchez Vidal, Agustín (1984), *Luis Buñuel; obra cinematográfica* Madrid: Ediciones J.C.

_____ (1995) '*Viridiana*: un carrefour espagnol', *Textures, Cahiers c.e.m.i.a.*, no. 1, June, 167–81.

Stoller, Robert (1986 [1975]) *Perversion: the Erotic Form of Hatred*. London: Karnac.

EL VERDUGO THE EXECUTIONER

LUIS GARCÍA BERLANGA, SPAIN/ITALY, 1963

El verdugo (*The Executioner*, 1963) has always been regarded as part of the canon of Spanish cinema. Even with some fifteen minutes of cuts from the finished version (some of which have now been reinstated), there is a certain degree of consensus about Luis García Berlanga's masterpiece as a key anti-Franco film, that in spite of all difficulties managed to bypass the censor and express a critique of certain aspects of the regime. The cuts on the shooting script, as stated in the official report of the censors, have surprisingly little effect on the film's central idea. In particular, the censors showed prudish concern for the presence of women in the two execution scenes; the noise of the executioner's tool inside his briefcase was discouraged, as was the showing of the actual instrument; they also cut the erotic relationship between the protagonist and the executioner's daughter; and a rehearsal before the execution during which prison guards made jokes using the executioner's tools. All of these elements might have added some edge to Rafael Azcona and Berlanga's satire, but the story of a man trapped in the position of having to murder in order to keep a certain standard of living remains clear. Even if the traditional interpretation of the film as a statement against the death penalty (and against Franco, who was internationally known as 'the executioner' at the time) is the key to the film's reputation, it is the more general narrative of everyday compromises and comfort undersigned by death that brings forth its contemporary relevance.

The cuts show that the censors missed the most unsettling aspects of the script, but the reaction of politicians when faced with the finished film remains an illustration of the regime's paranoia. They did find the film provocative (after all, it was a film by Berlanga, a man who was regarded by Generalísimo Franco himself as 'worse than a communist: a bad Spaniard'), but their veredict on where provocation lay narratively was as wide off the mark as the censors'. Paradoxically, it was the ensuing scandal that focused attention on the film. One could suggest that if Berlanga, co-scriptwriter Azcona and 'assistant director' (who actually played a role as line producer and had a key role in its inception) Ricardo Muñoz Suay are responsible for the film itself, these functionaries and censors are responsible for the myth.

A few days before its presentation at the 1963 Venice Film Festival, Alfredo Sánchez Bella, the Spanish ambassador in Rome (who would become the government's highest authority for film in 1969), was shocked to realise that Berlanga's film was mostly a mockery of the Franco regime, that could be regarded as an attempt to erode the Spanish government's international reputation. It was a delicate period, in which Francoism was going through a process of diplomatic whitewashing, trying to counteract accusations of brutal repression and backwardness. The *Viridiana* affair in 1961, which had exposed high-ranking functionaries to ridicule and was the cause of resignations, was still recent, so Francoist officials were caught between the impact of another satire on the regime's ideals (and therefore letting the malcontents get away with it) or another international scandal showing them up as intolerant of dissidence.

The letter in which Sánchez Bella expressed his view of this situation has been quoted in full by Román Gubern in his thorough account of Spanish censorship, and constitutes a precious document on the attitude of Francoism towards unusual films that could be interpreted as giving a negative image of Francoism. Given international responses to films such as *Calle Mayor* (*Main Street*, 1956) and *Cómicos* (*Comedians*, 1954), both directed by Juan Antonio Bardem, or Carlos Saura's *La Caza* (*The Hunt*, 1960), there was a specific concern for any kind of ambiguity that *might* be a sign of such codes. This reflects one view held among authorities: whenever a film worked through indirection and ambiguity, it had necessarily something to hide and, furthermore, it was likely to articulate discontent with the regime; consequently ambiguity itself became suspicious in most cases, especially when featured in the films by such well-known malcontents as Bardem, Saura or Berlanga.

One section of Sánchez Bella's letter is particularly relevant in understanding the way in which the film was being read: 'This is a manoeuvre perfectly planned according to an actual revolutionary scheme. The film falls into what communists, in their dogmatic jargon call "socialist realism". The script includes all the clichés of communist propaganda regarding Spain, through a very Spanish version, that is to say, steeped in anarchism.' Communism, and its aesthetic expression in terms of Social Realism, becomes here a disqualifying term. (Finally, however, Sánchez Bella decided to make the best of the situation, and recommended that scandal be avoided at all costs.)

But a significant number of left-wing reviewers also found a lot to be desired in Berlanga's view. Berlanga himself, in a 1992 interview with Jean-Claude Seguin, recognised that even his more politically committed colleagues accused him of making 'evasion' films, of not militating in favour of any of the traditional parties. Such accusations subtly surface in the work of some Italian left-wing critics, who went as far as to suggest the film was really a pro-Franco film in nihilistically laughing off the serious issue of the death penalty in the country through circumstantial sketches which were too ambiguous.

It is worth noticing here that such commentators criticised the film precisely for *not* following the guidelines of social realism in incorporating a 'correct' conscience within the plot that stood for the opinion of the artist. Obviously, Berlanga's film was too slippery, too ambiguous in its message and in its satire. When his own opinions are considered, these critics seem to be eminently right. The central issue in this ethical debate is not whether one feels comfortable with the idea of the death penalty, but whether it is right to introduce laws about it: even today, reactionaries will claim that no matter how bitter the pill, in the end, the death penalty achieves definite results. The death penalty and the need of executioners is undesirable, and such criticism is not directed at Franco's regime alone. It is true that the pillars of Spanish government (the Church and the Army) do not come off very well, but, as Berlanga insists, his target was the way society crushes a man's dreams, something that Francoism obviously had in common with many other political systems.

As we can see, neither the regime nor the left as a whole felt comfortable about Berlanga's film. In spite of the scandal, *The Executioner*'s meaning is hard to pin down as belonging to any particular political position. This is brought out more clearly when considering Berlanga's credentials. He worked, not unproblematically, with Juan Antonio Bardem, a card-carrying Communist, in the early 1950s (in such films as *Esa pareja feliz* [*That Happy Couple*, 1951] and *¡Bienvenido Míster Marshall!* [*Welcome, Mr Marshall!*, 1952]), which marked him out as 'dissident'. His cinema had always had an affectionately satiric tone that seemed to mock authority, especially as represented by the Church. At the same time, *Welcome, Mr Marshall!* does not seem to undermine certain Francoist ideals; it grapples with the false hopes of a group of villagers who happen to be Spanish. If one had to place his early films in the political spectrum, we would have to consider them as 'liberal humanist', and he has defined himself as a 'libertarian that has in time become a libertine'.

The more bitter aspects of his view were stressed after his first collaboration with legendary scriptwriter Rafael Azcona on *Plácido* (1961). The film is set in a provincial town where a charity campaign is organised to have a destitute person sitting at the dinner table of all bourgeois families on Christmas Eve. Christian charity is shown to be a cover for meanness and hypocrisy: many of the wealthier families just want to be on good terms with the organisers, but nobody really cares about the poor. The counterpoint to hypocritical charity is the situation of the eponymous protagonist, trying to earn some money to keep up with the payments on the vehicle he needs for his work. At many points during the long evening, he despairs and is about to be rendered destitute himself precisely because of his efforts to assist in the campaign. In many ways, *Plácido* paves the way for *The Executioner* in presenting a character crushed by a grotesque social system. Both made use of a similarly bitter satire in representing social types and institutions, but with an emphasis on the individual.

An outline of the plot will help us focus a reading of the film beyond pre-established political positions. As the film starts, José Luis (Nino Manfredi), an undertaker, is on duty in a Madrid prison. He is there with his colleague Alvárez (Ángel Álvarez) to receive the corpse of a sentenced prisoner. As he leaves with the coffin, Amadeo (Pepe Isbert), the talkative executioner, asks them for a lift to the city. José Luis is reluctant, as he dislikes the idea of being too close to a man with such a gruesome job. As they drop off Amadeo, he leaves behind the briefcase in which he keeps the tools of his trade, so José Luis has to go after him to return them. The undertaker follows the executioner to his airless, cluttered flat, where he meets the executioner's voluptuous daughter Carmen (Emma Penella). A relationship develops between them, and soon they are attending picnics with Amadeo and Álvarez. José Luis tells her of his dreams: he is discontent with his job, and dreams of emigrating to Germany in order to become a car mechanic. One day, as the young couple are together in bed, they are caught by Amadeo. In order to placate the old man, he proposes to Carmen, although he has only the faintest intention of marrying her. But then Carmen tells him she is pregnant, which will eventually lead to José Luis reluctantly consenting to marriage, uncomfortable as he is of sharing his life with an executioner's daugher and being father to her son. Eventually, they all move into the council flat Amadeo has been offered after forty-two years of public service.

The first section of the film shows José Luis gradually becoming trapped in a spider's web: sex, marriage and a new flat are the bait. Amadeo appears to offer his daughter ('She is very clean') from the moment he introduces her to José Luis. He wants all of those things, although he is not comfortable giving up his dream in order to achieve them. The script is constructed so that there is a sense of fate in José Luis falling into the trap while protesting he wants to find work in Germany.

But the price to pay will be even higher. It turns out that, as Amadeo is soon retiring, he will be losing his entitlement to the flat. The solution, he says, lies in José Luis inheriting his job ('Traditionally, the profession of executioner was transmitted from father to son', scholar Corcuera will state, somewhat nonsensically, later in the film). Again, José Luis resists the idea, in spite of being reassured by Amadeo that he will never be called upon to fulfill his duty. At the same time, the need for accommodation and Carmen's insistence, as well as his duty as a father all conspire to make him take the job.

Months pass and things seem to be developing very smoothly. There is a sense of joy and achievement on the part of José Luis: the family has settled into their new flat and he is earning some extra money for his position, which he has not yet been called to exercise. There are a number of inconveniences (for instance, the flat is too small, and he is obsessed about street quarrels becoming serious in case he may be called up to carry out his duties), but they are all quite content. Then a letter comes summoning him to Mallorca's prison in order to carry out his duties as executioner. A long Calvary begins for him. Once more, Amadeo and Carmen talk him out of resignation, insisting that the trip could be regarded as a holiday ('We never had a real honeymoon', his wife insists blithely) and, after all, he can always refuse at the last minute. As they arrive in Mallorca (as a glamorous beauty contest takes place and surrounded by happy tourists, which help date the film's narrative at the time of the tourist boom of the early 1960s), the condemned man falls ill and José Luis is relieved to think that, should he die from illness, he may not even have to carry out his duty. José Luis and his family relax into their holiday and start visiting tourist spots and once again, he relaxes into marital bliss. One day, while they watch a show in an underground cavern, the police arrive with a summons to take José Luis to the prison. Once again, he attempts to resign, explaining his situation to the institution's director, but he is trapped in the machinery and cannot escape his duty. In a famous shot, he is accompanied to the room where the sentence is to be carried out. According to Berlanga, quoted in Carlos Cañeque and Maite Grani's biographical study, this image is the origin of the whole film: two groups of people, one supporting the victim, the other the executioner, crossing a great white hall towards a small black door; progressively, the group supporting the victim becomes smaller as the executioner is so nervous as to need more and more support: 'This image suggested to me that not only the condemned could "degenerate" ... but the executioner himself would crumble when he has to kill. Two groups dragging two persons who are to be executioner and victim, that is the film's key image.'

To what extent the film works as a specific critique of early 1960s Spanish society is open to discussion. Although the targets are recognisably Spanish, the film works best in the context of humanist narratives distorted through paranoia and absurdism. The rhetoric through which the film addresses real issues differs both from the manifesto aesthetics of left-wing intellectuals and from the Francoist idea of 'serious' film. The wedding sequence is an example of Berlanga and Azcona's perspective: as soon as Carmen and José Luis decide to marry, Berlanga cuts to a brightly ornamented church where a wedding is taking place. But this is not José Luis and Carmen's wedding. We soon realise that the protagonists are waiting in the background; as their turn comes, the couple walk down the aisle, and then the music stops as flowers and other adornments are removed and lights are dimmed; as the priest marries them even candles are blown out. This has been interpreted as a criticism of the Catholic Church's preference for wealthy customers, but in the film works as part of a broader conspiracy. Even if most of the signifiers are clearly rooted in specifically Spanish imagery, a reading of the film reveals it as closer to Kafka than to Valle-Inclán. Unable (or, rather, unwilling) to take a political stance, the film does take an ethical one.

The notion of frustration becomes the narrative's most consistent theme. The protagonist starts out as a man with dreams of a better life ('One day I'll achieve something great', he says to his brother and sister-in-law early on in the film), but his dreams are constantly let down by the chain of events. As in Kafka's *The Castle* or *The Trial*, a universal conspiracy seems organised to keep José Luis from ever achieving his goals. The character seems to be trapped in machinery that will push him ruthlessly into fulfilling a role which seems to have been always waiting for him: becoming someone who kills for money, a profession that disgusts him. In such a conspiracy there are elements that appear to be caused by chance, as when Amadeo forgets his bag in the undertaker's truck early in the film or the coincidence between José Luis being caught redhanded with Carmen and Amadeo being assigned the flat of his dreams. Only such happenings seem to follow a pre-determined (rather than merely accidental) development. Further, they suggest an articulation of narrative events in terms of paranoia: the thing most feared, which causes utmost revulsion, has a way of becoming reality. For instance, it is true that Amadeo may have simply forgotten his bag in the truck, but Álvarez also takes part in the conspiracy by insisting on José Luis running after him; similarly, in jumping the long list of applicants for the post of executioner, he is disinterestedly assisted by Corcuera, an 'academic' who will use his influence so that he can get the position more quickly, even if he states that José Luis is far from being the right person for the job (in the original shooting script, the intervention of the intellectual is even more absurd, as he clearly states he will not help Amadeo).

Paranoid narratives progress through the tension between the appearance of simple coincidence and the way they are subjectively reinterpreted by a character in terms of confabulation of reality. In *The Executioner*, there is a sense of 'normality' in the attitude of the characters towards their lives. Amadeo, Álvarez, even Carmen seem to go about their daily lives only taking the next step ahead. In this way, the transition between narrative sections is always smooth and communicates a sense of routine: whenever a difficulty appears, a solution is provided.

On the other hand, such smooth progress seems to have a fixed direction; he seems to become the protagonist of a prototypical success-story of early 1960s Spain, a keystone of Francoist ideological propaganda at the time. Even if the character's initial plans to become a mechanic in Germany never start coming true, it is clear that for more than two-thirds of the film, he is achieving some kind of dream-life in spite of the implication that such a life will mean that he has to end up as an executioner: despair continually alternates with euphoria. If we leave that detail aside, *The Executioner* obviously offers a narrative of happiness: José Luis finds a girl, leaves his brother's house, gets a nice flat, extra income and even holidays in Mallorca. In themselves, such events are vulgar and undramatic; what gives the narrative its relenting tension is that each of these is a step taking him closer to becoming something he regards as repulsive.

His attempts to escape his fate are unsucccessful because they are weak (after all he is only an individual up against the whole of society), but also because he cannot find any support within that context: there seems to be a reluctant but tacit agreement among all characters that his fate cannot be other than becoming an executioner. His ethics, in this way, are challenged by the allure of sex, extra salary, a flat, a tourist trip, and so on.

Killing people seems a terrible price to pay in order to achieve all of those things, but still he will pay it. In one remarkable scene, he retells his story to the prison's director, as part of his attempt to resign from his post. The prison director, looking as if he has heard all this before (as he pretends to listen he makes signs to the prison workers in order to proceed with the execution), and after stating that 'people understand each other talking', will calmly explain with perfect logic why, at this point, the best thing he can do is to perform his duty as an executioner: first, he would have to return months of salary and the trip's expenses, which José Luis is in no position to do. Yet he also proposes more humanitarian reasons: the longer the wait for the prisoner, the more possibilities there are of him falling prey to despair; and the punishment will take place in any case, whether he performs the deed or not, only the suffering will be worse.

A striking combination between stark realism (as in Amadeo's flat) and more dreamlike images (the ghostly entrance of the authorities, José's proposal at the undertaker's garage with a flower taken from a wreath, the wedding, the scene where José Luis is forced to do his job) is the sign of the tension between the real and the imagined. A certain kind of working-class realism constitutes the main principle of articulation in terms of images, but it is often invaded by intimations of menace. Berlanga's roots are in a short theatrical Spanish genre called *sainete*. As in *sainete*, humour results from broad characterisation, repetition and accumulation. *Sainetes* were short, character-driven plays enjoyed by the popular classes. Although a case has been made about their populism having a political impact, there is nothing within them that promises a change in social conditions.

It is death in the end that focuses the audience's attention. Death is constantly represented in the script and in the *mise-en-scène*: a coffin is prominent in the opening sequence, and the setting for José Luis' proposal to Carmen is an undertakers garage, surrounded by wreaths (minutes earlier we have seen the employees playing jazz among the funeral cars, accustomed as they are to such sordid backbround); death is, of course, central to the profession of both the main protagonist and his father-in-law, and news items concerning death fill the newspapers; Amadeo even has a picture of one of his victims adorning the living room, as if it was a member of the family; once he becomes an executioner, José Luis will be watchful that an argument between two customers at a bar does not end up in killing.

But at the same time, death's impact is somehow confused in the *mise-en-scène*, as if the narrative voice shared some of the disgust or discomfort of the characters in dealing with it. The first image of the film is a prison officer dipping a muffin in hot chocolate. Later we will realise that, just as he put the muffin to his mouth, an execution was taking place off-screen. Similarly, at the end, after José Luis is taken through the small door behind which he will have to carry out his duty as an executioner, Berlanga cuts to a close-up of a baby's bottle. Death is always hovering through the edges, but always ellided.

The presence of death, unusual in the *sainete* except as a joke, comes to disturb the placid surface of the film. And this is not a metaphysical death, but death carried out by humans. The aesthetics of *sainete* are reflected very clearly in *Plácido*'s long, busy shots, and they are also quite prominent in *The Executioner*. The long shot at the scene of the wedding reinforces the sense of temporal continuity between the luxurious ceremony afforded to the rich and the less than modest one for Carmen and José Luis. Comic distorsion of reality in this genre places the narrative beyond the social and the political. Finally, as Vicente Sánchez-Biosca has illustrated, ellipses also contribute to this paranoid vision by encouraging the audience to fill the missing pieces subjectively.

To conclude, *The Executioner* cannot be regarded simply as a veiled critique of Francoism. It is about a man becoming integrated into a social system. Amadeo's last sentence insists on this: nothing until that moment made us suspect that he also went through the trauma we witness in the case of José Luis. Suspicions raised throughout the film that the prison's director, the functionaries, Corcuera, Carmen and even Álvarez, were all part of the tacit conspiracy to force José Luis to carry out the dirty job, are almost confirmed. It is the nail in the coffin of the film's narrative. Up to that point, José Luis could be regarded as some kind of positive hero who might eventually manage to escape the pressures of society. But Amadeo's words make it clear that one does get used to the idea of killing. José Luis will never carry out his dreams of leaving the country, and, even worse, he will eventually get used to his job, as he gradually becomes as nonchalant about it as Amadeo was at the beginning of the film. After this the camera pans, following Amadeo's gaze, to a yacht on which a number of young people seem to be having a party. The yacht moves away fast, accompanied by loud pop music. Life will go on, but we have learned now the price of everyday comforts: happiness and a sense of belonging are only achieved at a high price.

Alberto Mira

REFERENCES

Cañeque, Carlos and Maite Grani (1993) *¡Bienvenido Míster Berlanga!*. Barcelona: Destino.

Gubern, Román (1981) *La censura. Función política y ordenamiento jurídico bajo el franquismo (1936–1975)*. Barcelona: Península.

Sánchez-Biosca, Vicente (1997) 'Un realismo a la española: *El verdugo* entre humor negro y modernidad', *Contextes*, 36, 79–90.

EL EXTRAÑO VIAJE STRANGE JOURNEY

FERNANDO FERNÁN GÓMEZ, SPAIN, 1964

It was Luis García Berlanga's idea to sketch out a story inspired by recent murder cases. Berlanga was fond of inventing imaginary solutions to unsolved crimes, and provided a fictional back-story turned into a script by Pedro Beltrán. The project had, then, quite a definite shape before it reached Fernando Fernán Gómez. The finished film *El extraño viaje* (*Strange Journey*, 1964) was ready, but the production company thought it had no commercial potential, and it subsequently remained in the vaults for five years before opening in 1970 as a part of a double-bill in a cinema in the outskirts of Madrid. It was then discovered by critics such as Manolo Marinero (*Film Ideal*), Miguel Marías (*Nuestro cine*) and Alfonso Sánchez (*Hoja del lunes*), who wrote favourably of it. It went on to become an inspirational film for such filmmakers as Pedro Almodóvar (who lists it as one of his favourite Spanish films), and in 1970 won an award from the Círculo de Escritores Cinematográficos, a film writers' association. It has steadily gained in reputation through the years. A 1976 survey among critics carried out by the *Reseña* magazine on the best Spanish films lists *Strange Journey* at number twenty. When the magazine *Nickelodeon* conducted a similar poll in 1995 Fernán Gómez's film came up at number five, with thirty-nine voters including it in their lists.

Marías' review is the most articulate at setting out the reasons for the film's interest and originality when it states the following:

> Keeping away from clichés – which are ferociously debunked – and the folkloric images of Spanishness (*españolada*), *Strange Journey* distinguishes itself for its real Spanishness, or even 'Castileness' … I would not hesitate to single out this film as an example of the kind of work that could not have been made elsewhere and is not even aiming to place itself on a European level. Each detail in the film comes straight from Spanish reality or from its plastic, literary or dramatic traditions.

He goes on to place the film in the tradition of black humour and *esperpento* (grotesque distortion of reality) that can be traced back the works of Quevedo, Goya or Valle-Inclán. Marías could only hint between the lines that not only was the film constructed according to Spanish traditions, its main theme, as developed in a tightly-structured script, through interweaved themes, motives and imagery, is Spain itself.

The scriptwriters and Fernán Gómez reworked the basic murder plot into baroque narrative structre and *mise-en-scène*, alternating conventions of the thriller, the horror film, the sex comedy and the comedy of manners. The very sense of disorientation it provokes in audiences may have actually helped the film to pass through censorship barriers.

The simplest way to describe the plot is in terms of the whoddunit: it centres on the murders of three members of the wealthy Vidal family (two sisters and a brother). Typically, we are first acquainted with the backstory to the crime, then the older sister is killed by the brother; the last part is concerned with the police investigation to find out who killed the brother and the other sister, whose corpses appear lying on a beach. After the bodies are discovered, we are led to suspect the older sister. For a significant amount of time, the film appears to have been transformed into a fantasy horror genre piece and audiences wonder whether the older sister (known by the neighbours as 'Mrs Dracula') has returned from the grave. The solution will be the last piece in a jigsaw that forms a perfect picture of a small Spanish village experiencing the shock of progress. By the end of the film, an almost terrifying image of the country's subconscious at the time has been perfectly articulated, the murders constituting only the excuse.

From the very beginning, attention is drawn to key motives that, even if only marginally relevant to the murder plot, are central to the film's meaning. The credits appear superimposed over a number of newspaper and magazine covers. A substantial number of them show starlets, celebrities and models (Jane Fonda, Jackie Kennedy and Sophia Loren), often teasingly showing their legs or wearing scanty swimsuits. This is the first manifestation of two themes that will be developed: the obsession with sex and the onslaught of modernity, linked to the tourist boom in the early 1960s, and the new habits foreigners were bringing into a country that had been officially dominated for several decades by the strict morality of the Catholic Church. One such cover, showing the wedding of king-to-be, Juan Carlos de Borbón, and Sofía, places the narrative in 1962, providing a political context to the plot.

Suddenly, within the same shot, a corset appears, held up by an outraged woman, Doña Teresa (Maria Luisa Ponte), crying that another such item of clothing has been stolen from her lingerie shop 'La Parisienne'. Censorship had made any allusions to underwear unheard of in Spanish films, to the point that its very representation could have a shocking effect. Indeed, there is no diegetic need to start with the item of underwear, and it is somewhat odd that Doña

Teresa has to drag one corset around as an example of the stolen merchandise. The gesture goes beyond narrative needs: it is straightforward provocation. Female underwear will appear in the same teasing fashion throughout the film (at one point we see Doña Teresa almost covered in a heap of brassieres), and a group of old women dressed in black will even come to chastise the shop owner for bringing such 'obscene' items into the village. Doña Teresa crosses the square in search of her shop attendant, Beatriz (Lina Canalejas), who is at the weekly dance organised by the town hall, with attention then shifting to the ball itself.

Loud jazzy music sends out signs that are in sharp contrast with the dancers, who are peasant couples in traditional clothes. Suddenly, the music becomes louder and faster and the camera focuses on a young attractive woman, Angelines (Sara Lezana), who twists in a wildly erotic way, attracting everybody's attention: a group of older men stop playing cards and most of the couples interrupt their dance, whereas the younger male villagers surround the young woman, excited by her dancing. To underline the shocking effect of the dance, the older women are shown in a tracking shot, leaning against the wall, like a frieze, both mesmerised and confused by such an outburst of modernity. The link between sex and modernity is thus reinforced.

The fascination of the villagers and their inability to join in speaks volumes about the situation of a village that cannot easily assimilate the kind of change promised by progress in the magazine covers that opened the film ('Progress' is the name of the dance hall itself). Together with Doña Teresa's outrage, they portray a society on the verge of change, and show how this society is bound to resist or to be baffled by innovation. The villagers leave the dance hall. A long tracking shot is used to describe the moment (this device proliferates in the film; space, in these early images is often represented as a frieze): placed outside, the camera moves to the right, following Angelita as she is harassed by a number of men, but then suddenly backtracks to follow a group of older villagers, who were distracted from their card game by the girl's dancing, and then cuts to show a couple (Beatriz and the orchestra's leading singer, Fernando, played by Carlos Larrañaga) saying goodbye on the threshold of the woman's house. He seems to want to come in, but she shuts the door abruptly.

At this point, there is a harsh change of pace and, after a flash of lightning strikes on the village, we are taken inside an old house that dominates the main square, very close to where the dance hall and the lingerie shop are. The darkness of the walls contrasts with the dance hall's white walls, and the old-fashioned furniture (clocks, chairs, cupboards) is the counterpoint to the sparse furnishings of the previous location. There is also a change of pace (the tracking shots become slower) that suggests a shift in genre conventions: up to that point, the film could be a satiric comedy of manners or even a realistic drama, but now we are clearly in the territory of the horror genre. The slow moves towards doors and the off-screen noises (suggesting creaking doors and floor boards), together with the menacing music and the sounds of thunder, invoke a gothic atmosphere. A stark contrast is established between the film's two main spaces: the village seems ordinary enough, similar to any small village on the Castillian plain, whereas everything in the house suggests menace. Finally, a grotesque woman cautiously opens a door, to be followed by her brother. The couple are terrified, but their comic demeanor seems to belie the sinister appearance of the place. Both Paquita (Rafaela Aparicio) and Venancio (Jesús Franco) are perfectly characterised in terms of appearance, gestures and language. It was important for Fernán Gómez that they looked similar. Aparicio (one of the best-known character actresses in Spanish cinema) is a dumpy lady with mannered gestures recalling the acting traditions of popular theatre. Franco (who had a prolific career as a film director) is also short and plump, and with a round baby face that recalls Peter Lorre. Both are presented as terrified grown children, who have been awakened by the sinister noises in the old house but are still curious enough to try and find out where they come from. They knock on the door of their older sister Ignacia (Tota Alba), a scary woman impatient with their fear. Again, Ignacia is portrayed as a caricature of the middle-aged repressed woman, but also in terms of a horror film stereotype: tall, thin, harsh and commanding, hair pulled back and intense, hard eyes. But Paquita has noticed someone else inside Ignacia's room, and on listening behind the door, she is terrified to learn that her sister is planning to get rid of her and Venancio during a trip they are all bound to be taking soon.

From that moment, the action shifts between the village and the house. The contrast of opposites becomes the basis of the film's narrative structure: the everyday events in the village contrast starkly with the dreamlike atmosphere within the house. If the village is one image of Spain coming to terms with change, the house represents another side of traditional Spain: the aristocratic families steeped in old traditions who are treated as the real ruling classes. In Ignacia we find echoes of two stereotypical women that have been used to examplify intolerance and hypocritical orthodoxy in Spain: Pérez Galdós' Doña Perfecta and García Lorca's Bernarda Alba. She appears as a stern, disciplined, repressed, authoritarian presence who makes decisions and imposes her point of view, who forbids her brother and sister to have any sweets, slaps Paquita, kicks about her beloved cats and keeps spirits locked in a cupboard. Everything in her recalls feudal oppressive order as if she was an emanation of the house about the furniture. We witness the growing fear of the younger brothers as Ignacia sells the family properties in preparation for a long journey. It will be precisely their fear that will lead them to kill her by accident: one night, as Paquita and Venancio pry in the wrong room, an outraged Ignacia surprises them and in the confusion is knocked unconcious by Venancio. Someone appears at that point and we cut to a shot of Ignacia's corpse being dragged down a staircase and dropped into wine containers. In ordinary narrative structures, such an event would constitute some kind of turning point in the plot. Here, it only adds to the mystery. We know who the murderers are, but a secret is introduced in the identity of the character who helped them to hide the corpse and why. On the other hand, the characters' lives seem to go on as if nothing happened. Even more strangely, Ignacia (or, at any rate, a tall thin woman dressed in black) is seen by the villagers as she sits on her balcony.

In the village, the motives set out in the early scenes are developed. We see Doña Teresa who is determined to discover who stole the corset from her shop and will try to impose her demands on the police and the clergy. The relationship between Beatriz and Fernando progresses: he is falling in love with her, and she has clear plans to get married in order to fulfill her dreams. At the same time, Angelines develops her plans to leave the village, eventually doing so with the musicians.

The whole village seems involved collectively in commenting on events, like a chorus. In particular, there is the group of older men, all characterised as Spanish rural stereotypes (the one who talks too much, the chemist who has pills for everything, the one who just never understands what the conversation is about). The second group, less individualised, is constituted by the women around Doña Teresa, always criticising the immorality of the times. In both choruses, modernity becomes an obsession: the men are fascinated by the new possibilities to ogle young women, the women are outraged by the loosening of habits.

The most obvious motive linking the characters in the house to those in the village is the need to travel, which appears in the film's title. Angelines finds the village boring and wants to run away from the men there. In the world of the house, Ignacia is also planning to go away, because, she claims, the village is too low for her and people there are not worthy of the Vidals' class. Travelling is presented with undeniable allure. She tells Paquita that abroad she will manage to get married, that things are always different when one leaves the country, reflecting one of the dreams of Spanish citizens under Francoism, having to put up with a gloomy reality, even as they were beginning to make out that things were different abroad.

A second motive is that of gossip as one of the recurrent motives in the life of the village: private life in the village becomes transparent, to the point that it soon becomes public and shared by everybody. Male villagers all gather nightly, even under pouring rain, expecting to see couples together, or to see Angelines trying her home-made bikini in front of her window. They also keep watch on the Vidal family: they know about their plans to leave the place and they know whether they go to church or not. The village is treated as a kind of whispering gallery where everybody seems to know about everybody else: references to people's private lives are tossed around quite casually in conversation. The prying motive has its parallel in the world inside the house: Paquita and Venancio are always curious to know what is going on behind closed doors, and it is because of their curiosity that they are caught in Ignacia's room, which will lead to her death. But whereas the village is almost transparent, the house is opaque and it will take until the very last moment to discover all of its secrets.

Sexual repression is also strongly represented and constitutes a third motive present in both spaces. This theme has already been stated in the opening scenes, and it is developed further in articulating relations among the characters both inside and outside the house. Characters are obsessed with sex and show all the signs of discourses on sexual repression that characterised the Spanish at the time. The group of older men represent the outcome of long years of repression. In women, repression has left a different mark. True, Angelita appears as the 'new' modern woman (in a malapropism, one of the villagers refers to her 'modernist' strut) who just wants to be free, but the rest of the women in the film are affected in different ways by sexual repression. Beatriz is reluctant to let Fernando kiss her until they get married: 'The first man who kisses me will be my husband' she states after Fernando's first attempt, only to change her mind when he invents the story about an invalid brother and a promise made to his mother to take care of him. Beatriz dreams about meeting her prince and getting married: she has spent all her life gathering her wedding dress and, in a scene that is both touching and ridiculous, we see her rehearsing her 'I do' in front of the mirror. Both women are grouped in two shots, as they say goodbye to the members of the orchestra with whom they have become involved, emphasising their common fate as attractive young women in a backward village. What further links both characters is that the solution to their problems lies with foreigners and their fantasies have to do with escaping the village's everyday reality. But most remarkable is Doña Teresa, who is obsessed by the vice she associates with modernity. When Angelines goes to her shop in order to buy a bikini, the lady is shocked about the request and sends her away.

Inside the house, an explanation for the sexlessness of Paquita and Venancio is suggested by one of the sayings that adorn the walls of every room in the house: 'Give up lust for a month and lust will give you up for three.' And of course, Ignacia represents another manifestation of sexual repression in the country: that of the woman who will not allow those around her sexual expression only to indulge in her own private vices. It is Ignacia, to a greater extent than everybody else, who shows the consequences of sexual repression. Obsessed by what the neighbours might say, she even has to listen to the radio through headphones in order to dance with her lover.

These motives are perfectly articulated through cross-cutting between town and house, as if to underline the continuity between both spaces: they are both complementary images of Spain. It is hard to miss the connection of all of this with the Spanish reality at the time. Tourism and the higher visibilty of sex are examples of this connection. Authority was identified with traditional ideas that somehow had to deal with this new situation. At the same time there was an infantilised nation that was both terrified of the authority figure and dreaming about the promise of a new brighter life, but without the emotional baggage to deal with it. If we develop the metaphor in terms of actual referents, Ignacia represents tradition and authority, a counterpart of General Franco, whereas her brother and sister suggest that the people he rules over are scared and childish, sexually castrated and always dreaming of something exciting that lies outside the house walls.

In one of the most moving sequences in the film, the brother and sister come into Ignacia's room after her death. They are curious to break into the forbidden place. What they will find there is their past that had been kept from them by their sister. First we discover she kept alcohol and sweets for herself. Then they find out she also indulged in other vices: the closet is full of stylish and 'modern' items of clothing (including sexy knickers and the missing corset) that are out of place in the stern woman's wardrobe. It is the first hint for the audience about Ignacia's secret life. With great caution they open drawers and closets to find the toys of their childhood which Ignacia had taken away from them: a hoop, a doll, some pictures. Memories are rekindled of a happy childhood that was taken away from them. At that point, there is a feeling of recovering the past they had lost. It is indeed moving to see two grown-ups feeling that they still have to catch up with their childhood, but at the same time we are reminded this has only been possible through murder.

Very shortly after this scene, the brother and sister will be found dead on a beach and the last section of the narrative is structured as a police investigation that will fill the gaps. But eschewing genre traditions, the truth will not be discovered through the efforts of a policeman and the appearance of witnesses. A taxi driver comes forward out of nowhere to explain that three people (the siblings and a tall veiled lady) left the house and had a good meal on the road the following day. A villager also saw three people getting into a car and claims 'Ignacia' waved at him as they took their planned trip. For the audience, it is plausible that the sister came back from the dead: authority figures, after all, have proved historically quite resilient (as Spanish audiences of the late 1960s knew very well). Then, the lady's corpse appears in one of the wine jars in the cellar, as they are being emptied.

This moment in the film is treated as black humour. There is a tradition in Castile to throw cured ham into the wine containers to give it a special flavour (and, in the words of a villager, to 'make it more nourishing'). As the old men drink the wine and comment on its wonderful qualities, we know that this comes from the same jars where Ignacia's corpse has been marinating since the murder. Then Fernando is offered a glass. He drinks up and then learns where it comes from: he immediately becomes sick, something that will give away his guilt when the corpse is finally found. In this way, the audience only begins to learn the truth at the same time as the villagers.

It is then that we learn the full truth through Fernando's confession, which contains a number of shocking revelations that dig deeper into the social situation of the village. He tells the chief of police (and the audience) about his secret affair with Ignacia, how he used to sneak into the house late at night (thus explaining the creaking doors and various other noises) and how he was seduced by the woman. He also tells the officer about her obsession with nice clothes and expensive lingerie that could not be expressed outside the walls because of rumours, and how he was forced to model so that she could indulge in it. The shots in which he walks in different female clothes while Ignacia looks on, placidly smoking a cigarette, are among the most remarkable in the film and the weirdest in Spanish cinema of the time. Then he confesses his need for money and their plans to run away. As he fell in love with Beatriz, he decided to tell Ignacia, but it was too late: the older woman was then killed by Venancio. In this way, pure, virginal Beatriz was about to achieve happiness by marrying a gigolo who had appropriated blood money and helped hide a corpse. Then we learn, in a series of flashbacks, that it was him helping the brothers to get rid of the body and taking the siblings on their trip abroad only to poison them accidentally when he intended to get them to sleep, in order to run away with his share of Ignacia's money.

This structure was criticised by the film's early supporters, and in a 1973 interview Fernán Gómez suggests that he was not sure it was the best way to organise the plot. But scriptwriter Beltrán's narration is a success in shocking audiences and sudenly revealing the secret workings of the social system. Had the events been narrated in chronological order the more grotesque elements would have been easier to follow. Here, audiences are amused by surfaces only to realise suddenly the hypocrisy that lay below them: the scary figure of authority was an underwear fetishist, the romantic *zarzuela* singer is a thief, a gigolo and a murderer. The supernatural element gives way to a story of corruption that shows a man who is seduced, who has to dress in drag, enter a house like a thief and is eventually adopted by the siblings (in the last flashback we can feel Paquita is beginning to fall in love with him). The key to this confession is that we do not feel Fernando is a 'bad' man. At every moment, we feel he is a victim of circumstances. And the circumstances, again, are remarkably reminiscent of the political atmosphere in Spain during the 1960s.

Alberto Mira

REFERENCE

Marías, Miguel (1970) 'El extraño caso de *El extraño viaje*', *Nuestro cine*, 94, 54–6.

LA NOCHE DE WALPURGIS SHADOW OF THE WEREWOLF

LEÓN KLIMOVSKY, SPAIN, 1970

Spanish horror cinema is enjoying something of a resurgence. It is being acclaimed in national and international circles and its reputation has grown among horror fans across the globe. The growing taste for Spanish horror is also contributing to the re-emergence/re-evaluation of a crucial part of the film culture in Spain during the late 1960s and early 1970s. One of the main participants in this horror 'boom', Paul Naschy, whose contribution to this popular genre in his different roles as actor, scriptwriter and director has been more recognised abroad than at home, is the focus of this chapter. While Naschy has enjoyed an established reputation in the international horror scene for decades, his work has only been officially acknowledged when he was awarded the 2001 Spanish Gold Medal in Fine Arts. This focus of the analysis here is on one of the most significant moments of Spanish horror, *La noche de Walpurgis* (*Shadow of the Werewolf*, directed by León Klimovsky and scripted by Jacinto Molina and Hans Munkel, 1970), both nationally, a box-office success according to contemporary publications, and internationally since it has been an object of cult following for more than three decades.

The cult of *Shadow of the Werewolf* and its lead actor Paul Naschy is just one example of the international and transcultural dimension of Spanish horror. Whether in specific spaces of exhibition (drive-in theatres, inner city cinemas, horror conventions) or via video, cable, satellite or Internet, Spanish horror films have been consumed, and are still consumed, throughout the world. Amando de Ossorio, Jesús Franco, Naschy and Klimovsky, as well as Narciso Ibáñez Serrador, Jorge Grau and Eugenio Martín, among others, have acquired *auteur* status as cult film directors for their horror productions, proving the strong relation between the genre and cult movie fandom. Their films are a common staple of mail-order video and DVD catalogues devoted to the genre. Yet these same figures have been relegated to the crypt of Spanish film history; many film historians suppress these films from their historical accounts. In other words, horror production is an unacceptable part of Spanish film history. Like other generic and subgeneric forms of Spanish filmic production which represent the trashier and exploitative end of the industry (the western, the sexy Iberian comedy, the popular musical, soft pornography), horror has been mostly ignored and, by extension, omitted from the Spanish cinematic canon.

However, the cultural history of the Spanish horror movie has been kept alive in marginal publications or resuscitated in popular publications and film festivals.

In tracing the history of Spanish horror between 1968 and 1974 one must begin by acknowledging that there was an already established market for the genre. The rise of the horror genre in terms of production and exhibition in the American and European markets demanded such products, which means that Spanish horror production needs to be considered within the wider historical context of international exploitation, and as part of a transnational approach to filmmaking. Spanish horror competed with other European popular cinemas who made horrors of their own (such as British Hammer, the Italian Gothic of Mario Bava, and so on). As is evident in the analysis of *Shadow of the Werewolf*, the appearance of horror in multiple cultural contexts raises interesting issues about the cultural specificities of Spanish horror. A closer look at the local cinematic regime, however, offers a second reason for the glory days of the genre in Spain. The economic crisis in the Spanish film industry during the late 1960s and early 1970s needs to be seen in the light of wider changes in the socio-cultural landscape, for example shifts in the media landscape (the impact of television in the country), as well as shifts in social mores (the new position of cinema within the leisure industry). But economic determinants lie at the core of Spanish exploitation cinema, in particular the economic failure of the New Spanish Cinema whose costly protection system left the administration with a huge debt. Furthermore, between 1968 and 1975 the Spanish film industry was witness to the closure of three quarters of its total screens, the loss of 75 per cent of its spectators, and a 50 per cent decrease in the sector's income.

Driven by pressing economic considerations and shaped by specific cinematic institutions and practices – censorship, co-production, double versions and exhibition – producers and directors exploited the rich seam of low-budget genre filmmaking. In the words of Carlos Aguilar, there was a 'systematic production of low-budget films, directed and interpreted by recurrent professionals that were destined for their indiscriminate consumption in double-bill cinemas and on rural circuits'. Spanish audiences saw a censored version whilst another more explicit (read: sexually explicit) was destined for international consumption. This practice was a common feature of international exploitation cinema, what is commonly known in the industry as hot and cold versions (they were distinguished as such by the amount of nudity or censorable material present); other production strategies to which Spanish exploitation horror movies in general and *Shadow of the Werewolf* in particular conformed were the rapid shooting schedules, the fact that shooting took place largely on location, and recycling techniques such as the re-using of old footage and characters from earlier films and formulaic story lines. Like other Spanish film directors working under the institutional restraints of Francoism, horror filmmakers had to abide by the censor's rules, resorting thereby to their own formal strategies, to their own 'aesthetics of censorship'. According to Carlos Aguilar:

> Spanish horror took care of obvious geographical and narrative questions (the action was set outside Spain, the story-lines dealt with universal archetypes, the shooting locations were unusual) and deployed more subtle resources, mainly concerning the cast: the actors were dubbed (so that the filmgoer could not identify the voices of the actors with those of other Spanish film genres) and they used to be either foreign (Americans like Jack Taylor and Patty Shepard, French like Silvia Solar and Howard Vernon, Central European like Dyanik Zurakowska, Barta Barcy and Helga Liné, Argentinean like Alberto Dalbes, Rossana Yanni and Perla Cristal) or Spanish who did not work – or hardly worked – outside the genre.

Jacinto Molina owes his artistic name to institutional and commercial imperatives. In the same way that the censors would not allow a horror film to be set on Spanish soil nor could they accept a Spanish monster; foreign producers on their part required a name with exotic central European resonance. To wit, *Shadow of the Werewolf*, an European co-production between West Germany (HIFI-Stereo 70, Munich) and Spain (Plata Films, Madrid), emerges in a historically-specific context of production and reception, which responds to industrial, commercial and institutional demands.

Often known as the Spanish Lon Chaney, Paul Naschy is considered a cult genre icon. A recent collection on the international horror scene, *Fear Without Frontiers: Horror Cinema Across the Globe*, devotes a chapter to Naschy describing him as 'a dedicated and passionate horror fan [who] deserves praise and recognition for pushing the envelope of sex and violence in horror, for defying the conventions of Spanish cinema and perhaps most importantly for caring enough to endow his characters with a level of emotional depth and intensity unseen in most of the world's horror films'. Mostly known in generic histories for his many horror roles, Naschy tried 'to play as many horror roles as Lon Chaney Jr had done: Dracula in *El gran amor del Conde Dracula* (*Dracula's Virgin Lovers*, 1972), a bandaged mummy in *La venganza de la momia* (*The Vengeance of the Mummy*, 1973), a hunchbacked body snatcher in *El jorobado de la morgue* (*The Hunchback of Rue Morgue*, 1972), Jack the Ripper in *Jack, el destripador de Londres* (*Jack the Ripper of London*, 1971) and Waldemar the werewolf in a series of films.' To this panoply of monsters, one needs to add many other villains like Gilles de Rais, Mr Hyde and even Satan. Although, as noted by Lake Regal, Naschy has played 'more monsters in films than any other actor', his generic popularity is mainly due to his role as Waldemar Daninsky, the werewolf. Naschy's own interpretation of the werewolf legend was inspired by the Universal horror classic *Frankenstein Meets the Wolf Man* (Roy William Neill, 1943) where Lon Chaney Jr plays Larry Talbot. From its first incarnation in *La marca del hombre lobo* (*Hell's Creatures*, Enrique López Eguiluz, 1968) to the latest in *The Unliving* (Fred Olen Ray, 2003) the Waldemar Daninsky saga comprises a total of twelve films. The Spanish *hombre lobo* was a persistent and disturbing presence in the 1970s (*Los monstruos del terror* [Julio Demichelli and Hugo Fregonese, 1969], *La furia del hombre lobo* [José María Zabalza, 1970], *Dr. Jekyll y el hombre lobo* [*Dr Jekyll and the Wolfman*, León Klimovsky, 1972], *El retorno de Walpurgis* [*Curse of the Devil*, Carlos Aured, 1972]), returned to haunt the screens in the 1980s under Naschy's direction (*El retorno del Hombre Lobo* [*Return of the Werewolf*, Jacinto Molina, 1980], *La bestia y la espada mágica* [*The Beast and the Magic Sword*, Jacinto Molina, 1983], *El aullido del diablo* [*Howl of the Devil*, Jacinto Molina, 1988]). The return of Jacinto Molina to the horror scene both in Spain and abroad is owed to films which partake of the contemporary revival of this cinematic tradition; films such as *School Killer* (Carlos Gil, 2001) and *Rojo Sangre* (*Blood Red*, Christian Molina, 2004) have repackaged Naschy for young audiences and revitalised his career.

As a natural self-publicist, the publication of his autobiography, *Paul Naschy. Memorias de un hombre lobo* is one of the latest additions to his own process of 'mythologisation'. As to *Shadow of the Werewolf*, he does not downplay the significance of the film: 'if *Shadow of the Werewolf* had not existed, none of this would have happened', indeed the film, he says, was 'a pivotal point for the existence of the Spanish horror film'. Fans are touched by his *sui generis* take on the wolf man for, as Fernando Savater observes, Naschy is 'not the authentic and artistic wolf man, but rather the *amateur* lycanthrope that the fans of the genre would have liked to interpret at least once'. His treatment of the werewolf has certainly left its mark on the sub-genre, what has come to be known as the *sello Naschy*, that is, the Naschy hallmark. Generic influences ranging from the classical Universal horror films of the 1930s to the Hammer gothic horrors of the 1960s, his particular conception of the werewolf myth based on continental legends and cinematic adaptations, the iconography invented by Naschy to accompany Waldemar Daninsky (the pentagonal mark on his chest, the Mayenza cross), his characterisation of the werewolf (make-up effects, emotional anguish, the sexual undercurrent) constitute his indelible mark. We shall see all these at work in *Shadow of the Werewolf*.

Shadow of the Werewolf was the third of Naschy's transformations into the wolf man. The beginnings of the cycle introduced us to the tragic character of Waldemar and announced the narrative template for his future wanderings. Cutting across time, the only connection between the films is the monstrous hero: the curse of lycanthropy gnaws at Waldemar, and death by a bullet or a cross forged of silver, his only cure, can be administered by a woman who comes into his life and falls fatally in love with him. At some point in the plot his beloved is threatened by a monstrous creature whom our *hombre lobo* is forced to destroy in order to save her and, in turn, secure his own death. Hero and victim, that is the sempiternally doomed nature of Paul Naschy's character.

Naschy's renditions of the werewolf myth respond to familiar narratives of metamorphosis in which generic appropriateness is fully observed in a ritualistic manner. 'Traditional metamorphants', writes Andrew Tudor, 'are caught up in a variously complex web of explicit ritual expectations. Werewolves traditionally metamorphose at the full moon, and most narratives make us aware of both that fact and the precise time of the lunar calendar.' The opening sequence of the film, to which we shall turn shortly, establishes as economically as possible the necessary narrative and generic elements for the return of the wolf man. Throughout the film Klimovsky rehearses unabashedly a number of firmly established generic conventions. Classic ingredients of traditional horror movies such as the remote locale, the main protagonists lost in the forest and stumbling across an isolated house or the 'scientific' and/or 'mythological' explanations given by some characters at different stages of the narrative provide the frame to the story, help to advance the narrative and reaffirm generic codes and conventions. Together with its formulaic and ritualistic nature, a detailed look at the story line shows how *Shadow of the Werewolf* conforms to and fulfils audience expectations. However, in order to understand the film within the parameters of exploitation production and reception, we need to move beyond its basic narrative qualities and turn our attention to the notion of spectacle, that is, those moments that 'fascinate the eye of the spectator'. In its privileging of spectacle over narrative, of visual excess over the logical development of the plot, exploitation cinema defies the conventions and reading protocols of mainstream cinema. Let us focus on the plot and alight on those moments of spectacle which attract the attention of the horror spectator.

Two forensic pathologists arrive at a morgue to carry out an autopsy on the corpse of a man suspected of being a werewolf. During the examination one of them notices a scar in the shape of a star on the chest of the corpse – a pentagram, the sign of the werewolf. Sceptical about this clear sign, an ironising Dr Hartwig shows his rationalist disbelief: 'It's supposed to be a werewolf, right? According to the legend, if the bullet that killed him is extracted from his heart, he should come back to life.' As soon as the silver bullets are extracted from his heart the corpse does revive and wildly mutates into a werewolf, killing the two pathologists. The wolf man Waldemar Daninsky is back and staring menacingly at us. An extreme close-up of the werewolf's face emphasises the distinctiveness of Paul Naschy's lupine alter ego; the make-up effects convey a creature far more bestial than the Universal werewolf: fangs in the upper part of the mouth, as well as the lower, and an excessive hairy guise. The metamorphoses of Waldemar are a major set piece of the werewolf subgenre since they announce the lurid moments of violence. The pre-title sequence ends with the monster on the loose encountering his next victim, this time a young female who is soon stripped of her clothes and murdered. Scenarios of blood and gore, as well as the first doses of sexploitation, whet our appetite. The representation of violence in Spanish horror is particularly graphic and finds its aesthetic precursor in *tremendismo*, a trend in 1940s Spanish novels which was characterised by detailed descriptions of violent acts and immoral behaviour.

Miles away in a sophisticated Parisian nightclub a female student, Elvira (Barbara Cappell) is telling her boyfriend Marcel (Andrés Resino), a police inspector working on international cases, about the research she and her friend Geneviève (Gaby Fuchs) are conducting: a study of the legend of a sixteenth-century sanguinary countess, who allegedly preserved her youth via the blood of thousands of young virgins. While Elvira narrates the sadistic methods of the bloody countess, a montage of images shows the satanic practices leading to the sanguinary attacks on young women's bodies. Elvira and Geneviève believe that they have found the tomb of the Countess Wandesa Darvula de Nadasdy in a rural area of the north of France. The film cuts to a scene of the two female friends on their way to the remote destination; they soon find themselves lost in an isolated spot in the countryside. Geneviève comments jokingly, 'perhaps Count Dracula will appear and he will invite us to spend the night in his castle'. None other than Waldemar appears to help them, inviting the women back to his conveniently isolated house, where he writes books on Gothic churches and lives the life of a 'lone-wolf' in the company of his mentally-disturbed sister. When Elvira and Geneviève mention the motive of their research trip to Waldemar, the camera zooms in to him showing a truly, yet excessively, horrified look on his face. A sudden flash of lightning and a storm raging outside are an omen for the terror to come. The spectral manifestation of the Countess Wandesa (Patty Shepard) fills the screen momentarily. Waldemar is also interested in finding her tomb since the silver cross with which she was killed is the cure for his curse. The following day the three characters stumble across the tomb close to an old abbey in ruins. In a scene reminiscent of Mario Bava's *La maschera del demonio* (*Revenge of the Vampire*, 1960) Geneviève cuts herself while extracting the Mayenza cross from the deteriorated corpse and blood drips over the Countess' rotting skull, awakening her spirit and unleashing her supernatural force. Geneviève, we are led to assume, has provided the virgin's blood that brings Wandesa back to life. The supernatural manifests itself in the shape of a skeletal, menacing monk who erupts from nowhere and attacks Elvira only for her to be saved by Waldemar, thanks to the newly-found Mayenza cross. That same night Wandesa vampirises and possesses Geneviève mentally and sexually. This and other supernatural manifestations of the female vampire are filmed in slow motion, conferring to the scenes an unrealistic and eerie atmosphere. Such moments of aestheticised horror fulfil a double function, since they provide both visceral and carnal gratification. In these scenes sex and eroticism come to the fore: Wandesa's nocturnal activities are highly sexualised and lesbian, with sexual consummation reached through biting and sucking. The inclusion of such 'forbidden' moments of spectacle in *Shadow of the Werewolf* are a response to international trends within the genre; by the early 1970s American and European audiences expected representations of sexuality to feature large in horror, while Spanish horror audiences in a climate of hardened censorship were content with suggestiveness.

Waldemar's and Elvira's doomed love (and sexual) affair is set in motion; a medium close-up of Waldemar, staring into space, frames the confession of his tragic fate to Elvira. Both are in mortal danger for Wandesa's blood lust has no limits; the night of Walpurgis, after which vampires will reign supreme, is approaching. Meanwhile Marcel has received a letter from Elvira (when and why she sends it remains unaccounted for) and finds his way to Waldemar's house. In an act of tragic love Waldemar asks Elvira to leave with Marcel to protect her from the ensuing horror. In their escape they fall prisoners to the Countess who is ready to sacrifice them to the Devil. The climactic and long-expected moment of confrontation between the werewolf and the vampire sees the destruction of both monsters: the vampire queen at the clutches of Waldemar (defying the internal logic of the film since it was stated that she can only be destroyed by a silver cross), the werewolf destroyed by the woman who loves him, Elvira. The film's grand finale, albeit brief, offers the horror fan another 'spectacular' moment, this time special effects: the death of Wandesa is shown by means of white wax melting off the bones of her face, whereas the werewolf's murder returns Waldemar to his normal state in a series of effective dissolves. Such cinematic trickery would evolve through the saga with the improvement of make-up and special effects technology in the industry so in a film like *Licántropo* (*Lycantropos*, 1996), for instance, the transformations of Waldemar Daninsky are achieved by means of computer morphing.

As Tatjana Pavlović argues of the cinema of Jesús Franco, 'international circulations of Franco's low-budget, cult, trash, B-production and sexploitation films have transnational implications posing questions about co-productions, market and movements across national borders'. The consideration here of *Shadow of the Werewolf* can only scratch at the surface of one of the most understudied subgeneric trends of Spanish cinema. A revision of a popular subgeneric form that occupied such an important aspect of the Spanish film culture of the late 1960s and early 1970s demands an inclusive approach to the history of Spanish cinema, as well as a critical engagement with the complex conjunction of industrial, commercial and cultural factors which made these films possible. As part of the sleazy European horror of the 1960s and 1970s, this was arguably Spain's most international cinema for its commercial fitness in foreign markets and for its awareness of changing trends within the genre.

Antonio Lázaro-Reboll

REFERENCES

Aguilar, Carlos (ed.) (1999) *Cine fantástico y de terror español*. San Sebastián: Donostia Kultura.

Naschy, Paul (1997) *Paul Naschy. Memorias de un hombre lobo*. Madrid: Alberto Santos.

Pavlović, Tatjana (2003) *Despotic Bodies and Transgressive Bodies: Spanish Culture from Francisco Franco to Jesús Franco*. New York: SUNY Press.

Regal, Lake (1984) 'Spain's 'Mr Monster', *Classic Images*, 114, 10–11.

Savater, Fernando (1998) 'Hermano lobo', *Nosferatu*, 27.

Schneider, Steven Jay (ed.) (2003) *Fear Without Frontiers: Horror Cinema Across the Globe*. Godalming: FAB Press.

Tudor, Andrew (1989) *Monsters and Mad Scientists: A Cultural History of the Horror Movie*. Oxford: Basil Blackwell.

EL ESPÍRITU DE LA COLMENA SPIRIT OF THE BEEHIVE

VÍCTOR ERICE, SPAIN, 1973

Víctor Erice's first feature film *El espíritu de la colmena* (*Spirit of the Beehive*, 1973), as most of his scant later productions, belongs to the reflective tradition described by Susan Sontag in her 1984 essay on Robert Bresson's cinema as one in which 'the form of the work of art is present in an emphatic way.' According to Sontag, 'awareness of form does two things simultaneously: it gives a sensuous pleasure independent of the "content" and it invites the use of intelligence' – a sidestep from the stern critical discipline of the Brechtian 'alienation effect' which is one of the theoretical signposts for this type of work. Following Sontag's argument we can add that sometimes the 'content' owes more to the eye of the beholder than to the material displayed in the film – at least that is the case in *Spirit of the Beehive* – and it may require the use not only of intelligence but also of imagination.

Set in a small Castilian village in 1940, the film tells the story of a little girl, Ana, literally mesmerised by the image of Frankenstein's monster after seeing James Whale's 1931 classic for Universal Studios starring Boris Karloff. In one of the first dialogues of the film, Ana's concern about the fate of the monster is met by her sister Isabel's pragmatic response: in cinema everything is a lie and therefore the monster's death in the film is only a trick. But then, taking heart from the impact of her words, Isabel goes on to assert her ascendancy over her younger sister telling her that in reality Frankenstein is a spirit in disguise which Ana can befriend and summon at any time if she closes her eyes and repeats her name. Stunned by this double revelation in which the constructed nature of what had appeared as reality on the cinema screen is compounded with the creative power of imagination, Ana begins her personal quest to conjure up the spirit of Frankenstein.

It is also this assertion of the creative vision alongside of an awarenes of the conventions of filmmaking that characterise the equally elusive spirit which informs *Spirit of the Beehive*. Paul O'Flinn's commentary on screen reworkings of the Frankenstein story notes that it is in times of crisis that Frankenstein's monster re-appears before an audience. In the case of Whale's film, released in the depths of the Depression with 14 million unemployed, O'Flinn suggests that it articulated the fear of working-class insurrection. Comparing the film to its nineteenth-century source in Mary Shelley's eponymous novel, he notes: 'Where (mass) activity might be assertive and democratic (the Walton story) it is removed and concealed; where it is violent and insurrectionary (the monster's story) it is systematically denigrated; and where it is traditional and reactionary (the mill-burning) it is ambiguously endorsed.'

Interestingly, in its use of Whale's film, *Spirit of the Beehive* employs those instances which mark Universal Studios' departures from the literary original. First, the introduction of a criminal brain in the monster's assemblage; a revelation disclosed in the off-screen dialogue between Dr Waldemar and Dr Frankenstein which Ana's father, Fernando, overhears from his balcony. Then, the episode which records the encounter between the monster and the little girl by the lake which Universal's edited version left incomplete, thereby casting a dark shadow on the monster's behaviour. We see the whole sequence on the village cinema screen, alternating with images of the audience's intent faces. The excerpt follows the narrative line starting with the farewell scene between a peasant and his daughter outside their lakeside cottage, followed by the appearance of the monster who then plays a game with the little girl which consists of taking turns to throw flowers into the water. At this point there is a brief cross-cut to an exterior with Ana's mother, Teresa, cycling back home, and then we are back at the village hall at the moment when the cinema screen shows the peasant holding in his arms the corpse of his little daughter. The scene of the monster and the little girl by the waterside is given prominence in *Spirit of the Beehive*, and will be re-enacted later in a climactic scene with Ana as the protagonist. Finally, the images of the villagers searching for Ana with torches and dogs on the night of her disappearance is almost identical in design to that of the lynch mob hunting down the monster, another addition of the 1931 film version.

In O'Flinn's analysis these revisions to Mary Shelley's novel convey a view of the monster's behaviour as rooted in nature rather than social circumstances, a view which legitimises its demonisation and which, at a symbolic level, justifies counter-revolutionary violence. Examining the history of Frankenstein's myth, Fred Botting argues that, 'the adaptability of the monster, its plural and constantly changing significance, stems from its construction as other.' In *Spirit of the Beehive*, the excluded and suppressed otherness represented in the monster is eventually internalised by the protagonist.

The fact that the film is set in a specific historical background in the aftermath of the Civil War at the beginning of the most sombre decade of Francoism, and that it is cast in a gloomy, secretive and stagnant atmosphere, makes the critique of the regime self-evident, at least for Spaniards used to reading between the lines after more than thirty years of censorship. Even though the film resists a naturalist approach to history, some of the characters have a political identity whose connotations exceed their roles. The references and allusions that ground the narrative in the oppressive reality of post-war Spain are clear: the yoke and the arrows, the symbol of the Falange at the entrance of the village, men in Nationalist uniforms on the train, a letter written to a Red Cross refugee camp in France, a fleeing Republican soldier executed by the Guardia Civil. The fugitive is taken by Ana as an embodiment of the monster in an attempt to endow its spirit with the fullness of a body. He represents a literal return of the repressed in the historical context in which the story is set. Ana's friendly behaviour towards the Republican is followed by her distress at his violent disappearance. Following the critical line which interprets the family dynamics in the film in terms of political allegory, Ana's affiliation with the monster symbolises a rebellion against Francoist repression and society's conformism.

However, it has been noted that the reality of the events in the film is constantly undermined. Erice's elliptic description of the killing of the fugitive, his ambiguity in the characterisation of the Guardia Civil and of the republican intellectual in the figure of the father, distinguishes his treatment of history from many of his contemporaries. Whereas *Spirit of the Beehive* offers an indictment of the Francoist rule by showing its devastating effects, the film does not enter into a Manichean argument about the past. Rather, by relating the film to a historical circumstance, Erice is urging his counterparts to go beyond that past. In this respect the central motif of the beehive is significant.

Fernando first appears tending beehives in the guise of an apiculturist, and at several points in the film we see him writing about the behaviour of bees in his diary. The passage he writes, or perhaps merely translates, comes from a treatise in entomology written by the Belgian Symbolist poet Maurice Maeterlinck called *La Vie des abeilles* (*The Life of Bees*, 1903). The traditional comparison between the beehive and human society has had a long history from classical antiquity to modern fable and educational texts. In most cases the bees are taken as models of virtue, industriousness and selflessness, but these social insects, which instinctively embody the often cruel, unthinking laws of nature, can also evoke images of an impersonal and mechanical existence. The expression 'L'esprit de la ruche/the spirit of the beehive' is used by Maeterlinck to refer to the invisible, enigmatic and paradoxical force that seems to shape the beehive's life 'a spirit to which everybody submits and which itself submits to a heroic duty always turned towards the future'. In the passage Fernando's diary records, the machine-like organisation of insect society fills the casual observer with a feeling of 'grievous dread'. In fact, the life of his household is akin to that of the beehive, hierarchical and compartimentalised. When the father is absent there is a palpable relaxation in the atmosphere of the house. The maid's light-hearted remark 'The republic is here and ready!' at the children's riotous laughter and noisy playfulness is eloquent in itself. Also, the film's characteristic lack of establishing shots re-inforces the feeling of alienation. An illustrative example is the montage sequence of the family breakfast in which we never see all members of the family together. Instead, except for the initial shot of the two girls sitting side by side, the parents and the children appear one at a time, in close or medium shots, which frame each of them individually as if they were in self-contained cells.

Moreover, the film's *mise-en-scène* confers a beehive-like quality to the site of those earlier institutions of socialisation: family and school. The montage sequence of the children entering the school is made with shots of the same action taken from a single high angle and then superimposed on each other to produce a flickering effect which recalls the flight path of bees returning to their hive, and the same effect is achieved in the sequence of the two girls running downhill towards the abandoned barn which stands in the empty plain. At the level of the cinematography, the honeycomb-like leading of the house's stained-glass windows filters the light indoors in the golds and warm browns of the hive. The final image of the film in which Ana opens the window panes with their hexagonal pattern, for her invocation of the spirit, represents an epiphanic breaking up and breaking out of the self-enclosed world represented by the beehive.

If the presence of Frankenstein's monster is an indicator of cultural anxieties, an examination of the historical context from which *Spirit of the Beehive* emerges should provide an explanation of the threat it signifies and the warning in which it is couched. In the years which preceded Franco's death a feeling of malaise was experienced by Spanish society. The financial destabilisation of the late 1960s which resulted in recession, together with the uncertainty about the political future of the country, stirred social unrest and raised the alarm of a violent break with the past: after Franco's death, two alternatives for the future appeared – one was a simple reform of political structures, the other a more extensive break with the established order. Since public debate was unfeasible at the time, some artists and intellectuals felt compelled to express in their works their own position regarding Spain's future; a task which required a skilled obliquity in order to avoid censorship. Gradually, political commentaries became an imperative for dissident filmmakers. Aggravated by an acute crisis in the film industry, this pressure added to the sense of cultural disorientation that Spanish cinema experienced during the last years of Franco's regime and the beginning of the country's transition to democracy. The obliteration of an original tradition, the ideological constraints imposed by censorship, and the colonisation of the national market by the American film industry had deprived modern Spanish cinema of a sense of cultural orientation.

In this context it comes as no surprise that the film's socio-political implications are linked to a self-referential reflection on the practice and experience of film. After all, the image of Frankenstein's monster, made up of parts of dead bodies galvanised into life, is in itself a metaphor for the medium of film. Moreover, the creature does not appear as a floating signifier but comes attached to a cinematic text. Whereas there is an implicit homage to Hollywood's classical period in the fascination the monster evokes, its presence is also a figure of the dangers implicit in the very nature of film, in its potential to become a rampaging monster endowed with immortality, and particularly in Boris Karloff's iconogenic performance it becomes a reminder of the commodification of the image. But, the cinematic references of Erice's film also extend to other traditions.

Looking at the filmic associations of *Spirit of the Beehive*, Peter Evans has seen in its *mise-en-scène* and low-key lighting reminiscences of early German Expressionist cinema, noting the use of some of the motifs and conventions of the horror films produced by Val Lewton at RKO in the 1940s, particularly the ones directed by Jacques Tourneur. These films, which followed the German visual conventions and therefore conform to a fear-by-suggestion tradition introduced a connection between the supernatural and repressed desires, which Evans underlines in his interpretation. More recently, discussing the mysoginistic ideology of the 'monstruous feminine' in the traditional horror/woman's film, Susan Martín Márquez examines the development of the two sisters as contrasting responses to female socialisation in a patriarchal society, with Ana's rebellion set against Isabel's behaviour as a budding *femme fatale*. She argues that in showing the constructed nature of cinematic representation, *Spirit of the Beehive* both exposes and subverts the genre's conventions.

Indeed, whereas the compelling and mystifying power of film is displayed in Ana's response to *Frankenstein* through the film-within-a-film technique, Erice's film also makes a point of dispelling the illusory transparency of cinematic discourse. The reference to the conventions of fiction in the sentence 'Once upon a time' superimposed at the end of the front credits on a child's drawing depicting the screening of Whale's film is duplicated later with the inclusion of *Frankenstein*'s preliminary scene where a compère introduces the story as a cautionary tale and stresses the materiality of the medium in his address to the audience, which starts with the sentence: 'Good evening. The producer and the makers of this movie didn't want to show it without first giving some warning.' Erice is both self-conscious and explicit about the fictiveness and textuality of the reality he portrays. However, the contrast between Ana's creative imagination and Isabel's more knowing make-believe, also suggests that behind the film's strategies of detachment there is an impulse which goes beyond the promotion of critical distance in the spectator, into a more self-referential reflection.

Even though *Spirit of the Beehive* follows a linear narrative, the method of constructing the story is fragmented and contains many instances of overt directorial intervention. Some scenes are cut short and then set end to end without an obvious temporal progression. Time is stylised and compressed in the American montage sequences mentioned above such as that of the school's entrance, or the one with Ana and Isabel making their way to the barn in the field. Time can also be suspended – as in the freeze shot of Isabel over the bonfire – or even expanded, dwelling on apparently sterile images that seem to add nothing to the narrative, as in the scene where Fernando, on his way home, stops and ponderously lights a cigarette. Overall, the pace – at least for the spectator used to the current action movie – is almost unbearably slow. Whereas these strategies interrogate the nature of time, and represent a visual approximation to its subjective experience, the power of the visual is explored in the treatment of the image.

The equivocal nature of perception is made evident by the way the camera lingers on certain images, such as those of Isabel pretending to be dead, so that what we see becomes uncertain and we begin to doubt the reality of her pretence. At the same time sound is used to extend perception beyond the field of vision into a wider off-screen space, for instance when we are made aware of the absent presence of the monster as Ana closes her eyes for its invocation while we hear the distant whistle of the train. The relationship between sound and image is no longer one of subordination but instead it has become more autonomous and dynamic, as when the characters read written material and their voices flow off their corresponding shots into the surrounding sequences without any apparent causal link.

The disjunction of sound and image contributes to the eerie sense of silence which pervades the film. Together with the presence of the silent cinematic monster, so unlike its literary original, the conventions that *Spirit of the Beehive* re-appropriates from silent cinema make of silence a central theme which should be read in terms of the historical context of Franco's dictatorship. Not only are the dialogues sparse and laconic, even at times, as in the whispers between the children, almost unintelligible, but there are whole sequences in which speech is totally absent – the family breakfast and the scene between Ana and the fugitive are two examples among many. The atmosphere of unnatural silence invests the image with a sense of readability associated with silent cinema, intensifying the visual impression. At the same time the auditory, detached from the image, also acquires a new resonance, as when the two girls overhear Fernando's steps on the floorboards above their bedroom.

The effect of these narrative and compositional dislocations is to dissolve the temporal and spatial limitations which define the horizon of the perceptual in order to create an area of experience beyond the space of the visual frame. The camera is no longer the eye which objectifies the fantasies of the spectator but a centre of consciousness where the present coexists with the past, the represented with the unrepresented, just like the real and the imaginary coexist in Ana's consciousness.

The aspiration to capture that which is absent from phenomenal perception has been identified with the films of the *nouvelle vague* of the late 1960s. The renovation of the cinematographic language undertaken by the filmmakers associated with this movement represents, in the view of recent film theory, a turning point in the history of the audiovisual image. Their reformulation of the modernist advocacy for an art that renews and alters perception marks the definitive departure from the classical narratives of sound cinema (John Orr refers to this movement as neo-modern due to its manifestation of 'a return to the earlier moment of high modernism between 1914 and 1925 when cinema was still in its technical infancy'). Although the use of narrative dislocation is not pushed to the extremes which characterised some of the most radical productions of his French counterparts, Erice's film shares with them a lyrical reflexive quality and a similar concern for the processes of generating meaning, as well as a sense of film heritage and film culture, with a reappraisal of Hollywood cinema.

If the film shows Erice's affiliation to the dominant trend of European cinema, his dissociation from a national tradition whose present has become stagnant is articulated in Ana's quest for a compensatory order, and her escape which breaks the ties with her family. Her alienation from the stagnation that afflicts her parents illustrates the turn from filiation to cultural affiliation which Edward Said has described in his study of the literature of high modernism.

Ana's break from the world that encloses her parents also invites us to consider the film's position within Spanish cinema through the iconic associations on which the actors and their performances draw. Ana's family structure is used as a metaphor by which Erice's filmic parentage can be examined. The parents are played by well-known actors whose presence brings a set of extra-textual connotations to the film. On the one hand, Fernando Fernán Gómez is a many-faceted, popular actor with a long career behind and in front of the camera. His style goes back to the neorealism of Luis García Berlanga and Marco Ferreri and like them he is at his best in bitter-sweet comedies which focus on his characters' inability to transcend their own circumstances. His presence conjures up the whole spectrum of a tradition which has been either directly imposed or shaped by political circumstances. Moreover, the combination of the actor and his screen persona in the film points to a specific type within that spectrum: a cinema made by dissidents who nevertheless had to compromise in order to secure the viability of their productions: a tradition of realism which developed into the so-called New Spanish Cinema. On the other hand, Ana's mother is played by Teresa Gimpera, a Catalan actress and model closely associated with a short-lived movement of the late 1960s known as the Barcelona School. The type of film it promoted was experimental, strongly influenced by Godard's semiotics and had adopted some of the formal advances of the *nouvelle vague*. It is clear that *Spirit of the Beehive* does not entirely conform either to the circumspect style conjured up by the presence of Fernán Gómez and re-created in the realistic premises and sombre atmosphere of the film, nor to the experimentalism of the Barcelona School with which Teresa Gimpera is identified, although it displays some of the conventions of the fantasy and horror genres favoured by this tradition. The necessarily composite nature of the cinematic art and the inflections Erice gives it through the film's affiliative strategies make of the Frankenstein myth a particularly apt vehicle.

From its release in Madrid in October 1973, *Spirit of the Beehive* enjoyed a box-office success unprecedented for a Spanish film of its kind. That same year the film was awarded the Golden Shell at the San Sebastian Film Festival – the first time that a Spanish film had won the first prize. Other distinctions followed such as the Silver Hugo award at the Chicago Film Festival, and the film was selected for many other international film festivals in Europe and America. The audiences' acclaim was almost unanimous. The critical reception of the film marked the emergence of Víctor Erice's persona as a fully-fledged *auteur*. Only recently has some critical attention been directed to the collaborative and 'bee-like' industrial elements within his cinema. In the case of *Spirit of the Beehive*, the contribution of the cinematographer Luis Cuadrado, the co-scripter Angel Fernández Santos, the producer Elías Querejeta and the actors (particularly Ana Torrent) has been substantially overlooked in favour of a view of the film as the product of an *auteur*'s vision. Formalist commentaries concerned with the film's quality of introspective reflexivity and technical accomplishments, have contributed to the mystique of auteurism which surrounds Erice's persona, investing his work with an aura of abstraction and remoteness. The filmmaker's own declarations to the press have certainly colluded with this perception, reinforced by his subsequent maverick reputation built on a series of industrial disputes. Erice is a well-informed film critic, co-founder of the leftist magazine *Nuestro Cine* modelled on the French *Positif* and a collaborator in *Cuadernos de Arte y Pensamiento,* where he shows himself to be conversant with the current debates in film theory, and partial to Pasolini's *cinema di poesía* and the filmmakers of the *nouvelle vague,* in particular Godard. He has also co-written a book on Nicholas Ray.

With the release of *Spirit of the Beehive* Erice was hailed as the new hope of the Spanish cinema. Whether the film's impact continues to influence the new generations of Spanish filmmakers is less easy to say, but the film has certainly acquired the status of a modern classic. Twenty-three years later, the image of Ana Torrent's transfixed gaze watching a snuff film in Alejandro Amenábar's *Tesis* (*Thesis*, 1996), is an acknowlegement of its permanence.*

*I am grateful for this reference to Glenn-Østen Anderson, who establishes this intertextual connection in his unpublished M.St Dissertation, 'Looking Through the Thriller: Sight and Suspense in the Early Films of Alejandro Amenábar' (University of Oxford, 2003).

Xon de Ros

REFERENCES

Botting, Fred (1991) *Making Monstrous: Frankenstein, criticism, theory.* Manchester: Manchester University Press.

Evans, Peter William (1982) '*El espíritu de la colmena*: The Monster, the Place of the Father, and Growing Up in the Dictatorship', *Vida Hispánica*, 31, 3.

Martín Márquez, Susan (1999) *Feminist Discourse and Spanish Cinema: Sight Unseen.* Oxford and New York: Oxford University Press.

O'Flinn, Paul (1983) 'Production and Reproduction: The Case of Frankenstein', *Literature and History*, 9.

Orr, John (1993) *Cinema and Modernity.* Cambridge: Polity Press.

Sontag, Susan (1964) 'Spiritual Style in the Films of Robert Bresson', in *Against Interpretation* London: Vintage, 1984.

CRÍA CUERVOS RAISE RAVENS

CARLOS SAURA, SPAIN, 1975

Carlos Saura's work as a filmmaker has been extremely diverse and has seen him direct both political allegories, like *La caza* (*The Hunt*, 1965), in which hunting articulates a critique of strongman politics by dramatising the sport so cherished by Franco, and fantasies such as *El amor brujo* (*Love the Magician*, 1986), one of several films Saura made in the 1980s and 1990s centred around ballet and other traditional dance styles. Shot in 1975, during the death throes of Francoism, and released in 1976, just as Spain was entering the uncertain antechamber to democracy, it is perhaps fitting that *Cría cuervos* (*Raise Ravens*) should fall between these two polar opposites in Saura's œuvre. With strong musical elements – the film's success was aided by the catchiness of British chanteuse Jeanette's rendition of 'Por que te vas' and the inclusion of 'Maricruz', an Imperio Argentina favourite – *Raise Ravens* also has elements of political allegory, though these are not as starkly drawn as in *The Hunt*. Like the earlier film, however, *Raise Ravens* shades a portrait of a morally bankrupt political system with hues drawn from a contrast of gendered behaviour patterns. The interiors in which much of the film takes place are so lugubrious that it can be easy to forget that, unlike *The Hunt*, the later movie was shot in colour. For viewers who know David Lean's film version of *Great Expectations* (1946), there is a similarity between the gloomy household where much of *Raise Ravens* unfolds and the tomb-like stasis of Miss Havisham's mansion.

The comparison with *Great Expectations* may also owe something to the fact that both stories develop from a child's point of view. In *Raise Ravens* the child at the centre of the story is Ana, one of three daughters (Maite is younger, Irene is the eldest) who are orphaned when their parents fall as casualties to the lingering malaise that has endured three decades on from the Civil War. Ana's father, Anselmo, is a high-ranking and decorated officer in the armed forces and has the mistresses, the rambling Madrid home, and the neglected and abused wife to go with his station. 'He was a terrible skirt chaser,' the maid Rosa recalls. As a little girl Ana witnesses her father dying from a heart attack whilst in the middle of a sex act with his mistress. Ana mistakenly believes that she has poisoned her father with bicarbonate of soda – which she thinks is a deadly poison – that she had added to his night-cap. As well as an officer in the army, this man is also shown to have been a tyrant in his home, so much so that his own daughter wished him dead. While the tyrant dies an easy death, his wife writhes in agony from a cancer that takes its time to kill her.

If these deaths are figurative of the death of the larger regime outside, Saura seems to be saying that while Franco may slip away peacefully, his legacy will take longer to fade and will visit itself on his victims and on those not necessarily responsible for his tyrannical acts. When their mother dies, the three children are looked after by their Aunt Paulina, an unmarried woman whose hysteria comes to take the place of the deceased father's brutality. She feels robbed by the children of the chance to attend to her own romantic desires and sexual needs. Her life seems to be repeating the pattern established by the children's mother who had given up a promising future as a pianist to pursue domesticity instead. Ana reflects that her mother may have chosen the life of a homemaker over that of a pianist because the domestic option offered the chance of shared responsibilities. As the film progresses, we see that Ana's mother was doubly disappointed in having a husband who was uninterested in his household. Presiding over the house left behind by the domestic tyrant seems to produce similar behaviour in anyone tasked with the job, as if the edifice itself were given to despotism: Aunt Paulina becomes disciplinarian in her dealings with her nieces. Silently overseeing this regime change is the children's grandmother, a mute woman confined to a wheelchair (and reminiscent of Joan Crawford in Robert Aldrich's *Whatever Happened to Baby Jane?* [1962]). Ana puts on the grandmother's favourite Imperio Argentina records and talks her through a pinboard of her photographs and mementoes, the child reiterating and voicing over the older generation's history. The grandmother is drawn to a picture of another woman and is upset by Ana's repetition of the story of her marriage and honeymoon, a reaction suggestive of an unspoken, unspeakable and unlived experience outside her accepted biographical history represented by the pinboard. The grandmother assents to Ana's offer to help her to hasten her death but rejects the offer of a lethal dose of bicarbonate of soda.

The narrow dimensions of this seemingly uncomplicated scenario are widened through an unusual use of narrative voice and through multiple perspectives. Critics have pointed to the film's mercurial narrative as being inseparable from what makes it stand out from other projects of the same period. Marvin D'Lugo writes: 'Its development of a unique visual structure which interrogates the significance of the historical moment [is] what makes the film so notable. Saura structures the film around a special project within which the viewer is made to discern his own psychic and perceptual features in the figure of the nine-year-old spectator-in-the-text. Through the course of the narration, the film posits a number of repositionings of cinematic perspective, which eventually bring the spectator to move beyond the constraints of contemporary visual and social illusion.'

Geraldine Chaplin – who was Carlos Saura's partner when *Raise Ravens* was being made – plays María, the terminally-ill mother. In terms of screen time Chaplin would have had a rather more minor role in the film had she played only this part, but in fact she plays two, coming back as an older Ana reflecting from 1995 on the double bereavement she lived through as a child in the mid-1970s. Chaplin's English accent is easily discerned in her role as the mother: as an adult Ana her scenes are voiced-over by a native speaker which helps to distinguish the two parts. In her 1995 scenes Ana is shot in a kind of photo booth enclosure that gives nothing away about how the director imagined 1995 might look. All we see is Ana against a plain white background. Perhaps 1975 was too soon to imagine what a post-Franco future might look like. Saura has Ana as an adult comment in a vague and meandering way about her childhood with no explicit reference to the politics of the time in her analysis of the stultifying atmosphere in which she grew up. Her confusion may owe more to the continued threat of the censor (government censorship of film was not abolished until 1977) than to a character deliberately portrayed as unable to reach any conclusions about the relationship between her past and present. 'The only thing I recall precisely', says the adult Ana, 'is that at the time my father seemed responsible for all the sadness my mother suffered in her last years.' Her observations also reflect the director's distrust of the romanticising of childhood when she says 'I don't understand why some people say that childhood was the happiest time of their lives.' In real life, by 1995, Ana of 1975, or the actor who played her, Ana Torrent, would be about to achieve great success in Alejandro Amenábar's *Tesis* (*Thesis*, 1996) and in Helena Taberna's *Yoyes* (2000), the latter a film whose approach to the subject of Basque terrorism would have been unthinkable in 1975. Saura's explanation for the narrative structure of the film is more straightforward than some of the critics': 'The fact that the story is told by Ana as an adult woman ... was not a gratuitous choice, but the only way I found to approach the present with the eyes of the past.'

In *Raise Ravens*, Ana Torrent plays the kind of child orphaned by the enduring effects of conflict familiar from René Clément's *Jeux interdits* (*The Secret Game*, 1952). Like her counterparts in the earlier film, she tries to come to terms with death by acting out funeral and internment scenes with a dead pet, her loneliness used by the director to comment on the lasting divisions and wounds left behind by a war. Like Clément's earlier film, *Raise Ravens* attempts to picture grief from a child's angle and to demonstrate the absurdity of weapons and the military through a contrast of an adult blind acceptance of conflict and children's incomprehension of its causes. Also in common with *The Secret Game*, *Raise Ravens* has scenes of children play-acting adult scenarios in order to demystify them. Irene, Ana and Maite act out a scene of domestic jealousies and in doing so the full-size version of the situation is reduced to a series of formulae and clichés revealed as laughable. John Hopewell notes the way in which Saura uses unexpected editing to reinforce the impression of Ana's isolation: 'A shot of Ana's face is likely to introduce some reverie which isolates her in the solitude of her own imagination. Ana's stare is … opaque, completely neutral, fixed in a wax-like pallor, a blank look designed more as a passive defence against inquisition than a means of making contact.'

The opening scenes of *Raise Ravens* reveal a tableau of photographs, which, as the film progresses, we realise must belong to Ana as an adult, though we are never shown a scene of her looking at it (some critics refer to this tableau as a family photo album as if it belonged to the 1975 strand of the narrative). Her voice is conveyed through hand-written captions to photographs depicting scenes from the three girls' shared childhoods: 'Maite, mouth wide open as usual', 'Me and my mother'. Other pictures show Ana as a newborn baby. Under one of these she has written 'Hard to believe that *that* was me'. Captions like this one suggest a difficulty in reconciliation with the past as well as a sense of alienation between Ana's child and adult selves. 'I remember my childhood,' she says 'as a long, interminable, and sad episode in which fear touched everything, fear of the unknown.' In the course of the film, cutting back to the adult Ana's tableau of photographs serves as a means of modulating between 1995 and 1975. The adult Ana comments on a recollection prompted by one of her photos and this takes her twenty years back in time, a switch rendered visually by a horizontal wipe between the tableau and the 1975 interiors. If the grandmother's silence later in the film points to the historical self-censorship that would be called for by the *pacto de olvido* (pact of silence), so too do the adult Ana's incompletely elaborated captions to her own past. The 'pact of silence' had still to be agreed upon when Saura was making *Raise Ravens* and yet the film seems to predict the generation gap, internalised in Ana's own divorce from her childhood self, that would grow out of a historical and political blackout. Like her grandmother before her, Ana will, as an adult, be searching for some kind of chronology or closure from a series of moments captured by photographs. In the 1975 sequences, Irene and Maite are shown cutting out pictures of sexy ladies from magazines for their scrapbooks. Irene's bedroom space is given over to portraits of matinee idols and the 'Por que te vas' song the children repeatedly play predicts for them a future identity as women who hanker after and lose the love of wanton men. The lyrics describe the fate of their mother, someone who gave up her own life for a neglectful husband: 'All the promises of my love will be with you [but] you will forget me.' Ana, the rebellious daughter, mimes along to the song with a sceptical look on her face. She prefers to spend time with the mute granny rather than in dressing up with her sisters although she is no more impressed by the grandmother's 1930s favourite, 'Maricruz', which similarly describes a woman whose great achievement was to be attractive to men. The only place of refuge from her sisters' play-acting of adult mores is the kitchen where the maid Rosa listens to romantic radio serials and Aunt Paulina operates a sewing machine with eager determination. The house seems to offer no escape from the mechanisms which condition little girls to make them become in their turn women like Amelia, Paulina, María and Rosa.

The initial anonymity of the photographic tableau means that its moment in time, 1995, does not automatically become the film's present tense. Several distinct episodes from 1975 are recalled in the course of the film, not remembered one within the other as some critics have suggested, but alternated through reference back to the future of 1995. Because of the visual emptiness and claustrophobia of the 1995 scenes, their logical status as chronological degree zero is blurred. A child can hardly be imagining the kind of monologue associated with the adult Ana's scenes of self-reflection and yet, as some critics have noted, the Ana of 1975 seems more level-headed and philosophical than the arrested adolescents who surround her. The ambiguity over the film's internal narrative chronology adds to its sense of mystery and to its evocation of time as a series of thresholds which can only be determined with hindsight. Ana the child sees her mother pass the threshold to her bedroom several times in succession, a device that would have been a gag in Buñuel and which here becomes a surrealism of history where a child's daydreams merge with a studied chronological laxity. The film's internal ambiguities are reflected in the variety of artwork used in various parts of the world to publicise the film. In America, for example, the publicity used was a twin headshot of Geraldine Chaplin and Ana Torrent, thus emphasising the mother/daughter or older-self/younger-self relationship. In Poland the poster for the film depicts a forlorn and jaundiced Ana with her deceased pets, emphasising the film's focus on childhood and orphanhood. The poster created for the film in Cuba brings to the fore the film's references to the nationalist version of Catholicism (*nacionalcatolicismo*) with a series of cross-shaped tombs looming in the distance over abstracted ravenous ravens. The capacity to produce a variety of fluid interpretations (or the incapacity to indicate any firm meaning) is an aspect of the film which has been used to underscore its art-house credentials. As John Hopewell notes: 'Rather than diffusing the protest implicit in *Raise Ravens*, its ambiguities distance the film's political passions, so rendering them both more subtle and more convincing.'

It is a commonplace of criticism of Spanish cinema to equate the prevalence of children in film of the 1970s and 1980s with the youthfulness of a country newly emerging from forty years of isolationism and *nacionalcatolicismo*. *Raise Ravens* seems to fit this formula, along with Víctor Erice's *El espíritu de la colmena* (*Spirit of the Beehive*, 1973). In both films, a focus on Ana Torrent's dinner-plate eyes is connected with youthful vision. In *Raise Ravens*, however, Ana is more than a child. She is an orphaned child. This status lends her position another layer of political allegory since the Falangists had made so much political capital from harping on the plight of young evacuees and children orphaned by the Civil War. Children left without parents or removed from their homes were crimes ascribed to the 'infamy committed by the reds' and Nationalist publications of 1939 and 1940 trumpeted the saintly work done by the Falangist women of the Auxilio Social in bringing children home or finding them foster parents. Here, by contrast, Saura depicts a home shaped by the outcome of the Civil War where children have been left without parents not by the infamy of the reds but by the selfishness of the fascists. By destroying his wife's morale, an army officer's egotism leaves his children with neither parent. Anselmo 'is distinguished not for his fascism but for his adultery, the prerogative of the Francoist *pater familias*', says John Hopewell. If the focus on childhood is connected with the rebirth of the nation, then, it is also about setting straight a one-sided record of parental neglect and lack of concern for children unfairly levelled by the regime exclusively at its opponents. Official women's magazines of the regime had proclaimed that 'Spain's primary concern is the care and well-being of its children.' With its provocative title from the proverb 'Raise ravens and they will peck out your eyes' ('Cría cuervos y te sacarán los ojos') Saura's film contests the sincerity of such pious statements and goes on to challenge the fascists' record in claiming exclusive rights to good parenting.

The young Ana's homicidal fantasies can also be read as a domestication of a political legend involving childhood and exploited by the victors in the Civil War. To this day, a shrine in Toledo's Alcázar commemorates the site where Colonel Moscardo, a Nationalist officer besieged in the fortress, received a telephone call from his son who had reputedly been kidnapped and was being held hostage by Republicans outside. The ransom for his release was the surrender of his own parent and of all the other Nationalists holed up in the Alcázar. In a sequence of events disputed by historians, the officer instructed the child to give up his life for the greater cause: 'Commend your soul to God, shout Long Live Spain! and Long Live Christ the King! and die like a hero.' Here again Saura turns this kind of myth-making on its head by depicting a child who is not ready to die for any cause of her parents but is instead ready to kill a military father to avenge her mother. The plucky boy of the Alcázar legend has become an inscrutable little girl, a further illustration of how Saura uses translations of gender to construct a narrative in opposition to the official record. Ana emerges from a cleaning session in her late father's study with one of his loaded firearms, which she aims with an impressive sangfroid at Aunt Paulina. Trying to wrest the weapon from Ana's grasp, Paulina's uniformed boyfriend tells the girl, 'What do you want with a pistol? That's a boy's toy, isn't it?' Far from associating death with a cause, the young Ana imagines her end as a way out and contemplates suicide by throwing herself from the roof of a building (pre-empting a similar scene in *Abre los ojos* [*Open Your Eyes*, 1997] many years later).

The same Falangist magazines which had claimed children as the progeny and property of the *patria* also told women that as mothers they should be models of self-sacrifice: 'With your work and self-sacrifice as Spanish mothers we will lose few of our Spanish children' (*Anuario* of the Sección Femenina, 1941). In *Raise Ravens* neither the terminally-ill real mother nor Paulina, the adoptive mother, seems to correspond to this self-denying model of motherhood. The children's real mother's wants are concentrated on gaining some attention from her absentee husband and their adoptive mother is unwilling to give up any hopes of finding happiness for herself with a man outside the parental role thrust upon her by a sister's untimely death. Another commonplace of criticism of Spanish cinema is to see these 'bad' mothers as characters created by the displacement onto women and onto motherhood of the evils committed by men and by patriarchy. Another way of reading the 'bad mother' scenario is to suggest that in creating women characters like those in *Raise Ravens* Saura was adding another dimension to his domestic allegory of national politics. When Ana's mother tells her father 'I can't stand this anymore' it is not only a message of despair and defiance about her situation at home but about the plight of all the put-upon women taken advantage of by the regime. Being a rebellious mother, having cancer, disregarding the children, being middle-aged and looking for a boyfriend are as much the actions of female characters charged with reacting against years of enforced saintliness as they are the pranks of arrested adolescents. The film does not specify what kind of cancer Ana's mother is suffering from and yet the pain she endures and the way she writhes in her bed clutching the space between her legs suggest that it might be cancer of the womb, as if her body itself were closing down on the reproductive role assigned to it by the years of dictatorship.

Compared with other Spanish films from 1975 and 1976, *Raise Ravens* has had a durable appeal for audiences within Spain and overseas. Part of this may be down to luck: Saura happened to be making a film about dictatorial death just when the tyrant passed away, as he was bound to do, sooner or later. More than this, however, the film's outreach towards a moment in the future lends it a kind of timelessness. The Ana of 1995 is in an outer space which can never become dated. Added to this is the film's enduringly challenging reference to learned behaviours in children. Saura's own analysis, in an interview with Linda Willem, of his film's response to the relationship between adults and children is as arresting in the twenty-first century as it was in the twentieth:

> I think the idea which motivated me to make this film is simply that of the identification between a little girl and her mother, and the extent to which this child … is immersed in what we call a child's world, a world which is, in fact, much more the doing of adults, a repressive world in which children are no more than the reflection or the projection of adults. I don't know how we can feel proud of the fact that children imitate us; in this respect, they are merely perpetuating our errors. I think children would have to kill the adults in order to be able to be themselves. Ana … subconsciously understands this. But, of course, she doesn't buy the stories of a childhood paradise, nor of childhood innocence, nor all the stupidities that we adults happily recite.

Ryan Prout

REFERENCES

D'Lugo, Marvin (1983) 'Carlos Saura: Constructive Imagination in Post-Franco Cinema', *Quarterly Review of Film Studies*, 8, 2, 35–47.

Hopewell, John (1986) *Out of the Past: Spanish Cinema After Franco*. London: British Film Institute.

Willem, Linda (2003) *Carlos Saura Interviews*. Jackson: University Press of Mississippi.

EL DIPUTADO CONFESSIONS OF A CONGRESSMAN

ELOY DE LA IGLESIA, SPAIN, 1979

Eloy de la Iglesia's *El pico* (*The Fix*, 1983) and *El pico 2* (*The Fix II,* 1984) depict the misfortunes of people whose lives fall apart when they become caught up in the world of illegal drugs. The director's life seemed to imitate his art when he became inactive in filmmaking for more than a decade due to a drug-dependency problem. He is quoted as saying, however, that his addiction to film was always stronger than his addiction to narcotics and in 2003 he made a comeback as a director with *Los novios búlgaros* (*Bulgarian Boyfriends*). Set in contemporary Europe, this film explicitly conjoins the politics of homosexuality and of 'Fortress Europe' as its Spanish character, a 40-year-old middle-class man from a respectable family, falls in love with a 23-year-old Bulgarian and finds his social status and security challenged as a result. Made and set in 1979, *El Diputado* (*Confessions of a Congressman*) is seemingly worlds apart from *Bulgarian Boyfriends*, being firmly anchored in the politics of the transitional era of Spanish politics. Nevertheless, the explicit attempt to integrate sexual politics with party politics demonstrates the common parentage of the two films.

Confessions of a Congressman concerns the personal and political odyssey of Roberto Orbea, a prominent socialist politician who is about to be nominated as the general secretary of his Marxist political party when the film opens. Through a protracted flashback, the film explains, from Orbea's own viewpoint, why this promotion is not going to be the happy occasion it might have been. While in prison for his political outspokenness, Orbea had met Nes, a gay-for-pay hustler who introduces the older man to the world of the street and the gay brothel after his prison term, thereby reawakening homosexual appetites the politician thought he had left behind him when he married. Nes introduces Orbea to Juanito, another gay-for-pay adolescent with whom the socialist begins an intense affair, largely conducted in the secrecy of the offices the party had used for its underground meetings before the process of transition to democracy began. Orbea's wife accepts her husband's young lover and they establish a *ménage à trois*. Whilst Orbea is successfully refining Juanito's tastes and raising his political consciousness, right-wing extremists are simultaneously encouraging the teenager to take part in a plot to expose his mentor and lover as a clandestine homosexual. The fascists do not tell Juanito that

THE CINEMA OF SPAIN AND PORTUGAL   159

they plan to murder him later and to force Orbea to be discovered with the dead boy's body. The scandal coincides with Orbea's promotion and the flashback finally catches up with him as he contemplates the best way to handle this violent turnaround in his circumstances.

De la Iglesia uses Orbea – a party-political Orpheus – to force the well-meaning Marxist's class-consciousness into the world where his political theory resides in the abstract but rarely travels for real. Orbea's homosexual reawakening obliges him to confront an underworld of real poverty, of expectation as well as of material goods. His world and Juanito's mingle in the soundtrack's inclusion of strident rock music and Vivaldi's *Four Seasons*. This aural simile for the forced encounter between the working class and the bourgeoisie demonstrates the aestheticising modus operandum of the film's would-be synthesis of political cultures. De la Iglesia was very clear in the 1970s, in an interview with Isolina Ballesteros, about his intended wish of playing off political cultures against each other to demonstrate their interdependence: films like *Confessions of a Congressman* were made, he says, in the belief that 'sex cannot be detached from politics and neither can politics be detached from sex'. Orbea's dialogue is frequently used to reinforce the point. He reflects, for example, 'My political activities went forward in parallel with the development of my relationship with Juanito.' José Luis Téllez says the film sets out to ask 'how far a sexual option can interfere in the accomplishment of a political function'. But does the film actually succeed in politicising the marginal sexualities explored by Orbea's descent into the underworld? By the same token, does it successfully shift party politics into the register of sexual identity? Its use of a juxtaposition engineered around taste and aesthetics arguably undermines its chances of success in either of these tasks. In the opening titles, for example, the internal political debate is meant to be suggested by the interpolation of icons of homosexual desire, such as a classical David sculpture, within a series of representations of Marxist political gatherings in the Soviet Union. De la Iglesia's composition in this sequence aligns him with generations of artists who, in the words of Germaine Greer, 'constantly revisited the art of Rome and found in the classical nude the correlative of their notion of the rational body politic, regardless of whether it was imperial, revolutionary, republican or fascist'. This initial identification of the homosexual with the aesthetic also undercuts one of Orbea's perorations later in the film where he insists on a distinction between his gay lover and the homosexual love objects of famous aesthetes. He tells his wife:

I suppose you had imagined that [Juanito] would be a fragile adolescent, a Visconti character who might pop up on a beach in the Venice Lido with Mahler playing in the background. No, Carmen. He's not a little Lord for Oscar Wilde to fall in love with and he's not a Greek ephebe nor a Petit Prince. See for yourself: he's a prole, a street urchin from the suburbs. No Mahler. No operatic arias. No Venetian beaches. Nothing like that. Tacky music. Loud discos. Stolen mopeds. Poverty. That's his world.

No Mahler, perhaps, but there is Vivaldi's music emoting in the background, as Orbea and Juanito get to know each other. Orbea's distinction between *his* young lover and others' is undermined not only by the introduction of homosexuality into the initial terms of reference through Greek statuary but also by Orbea's own definition of who Juanito is through aesthetic criteria. And if Juanito *was* an urchin from a poor housing development when Orbea met him and no Lord, the politician seems resolved to change that as soon as possible. While the inseparability of sex and politics may not be persuasively demonstrated by the film, the mutual dependence of high art and the bourgeoisie is never in any doubt. For Juanito to become part of Orbea's family he must be groomed in museum-going, gastronomy and chamber music. When the *ménage-à-trois* assembles at Orbea's home to play music, Juanito is posed like one of Caravaggio's decorative lute players and the role he plays as trophy boy for Mr and Mrs Orbea recalls, furthermore, the role of status symbol occupied by boys in the society depicted by the court painter. If the film's Vivaldi soundtrack pushes its aesthetic reference back to the seventeenth century, the depiction of the politician's male love objects as ravishing street urchins ennobled by boyish beauty shifts the film's aesthetic register back as far as the Baroque easel painting of the sixteenth century and to an era when, as Germaine Greer observes, 'Western painters and poets, themselves no longer boys, vie with each other in depicting the untimely deaths of boys.' Insofar as the film inherits a tradition of depicting young male nudes as martyrs, like Saint Sebastian, Juanito's fate is sealed by an aesthetic logic even before party politics and transitional intrigue have intervened. Juanito's status as a trophy can also be understood within the film's visual reference to a centuries-old pictorial aesthetic tradition which dictates that licentiousness in the artistic representation of young males is acceptable so long as they are street urchins. The arrangement and photography of Juanito's bloodied body at the end of *Confessions of a Congressman* recalls images of dead fighting boys from art belonging to previous centuries as catalogued by Greer who argues that there has been a 'perennial holocaust of boys' brought about by older men's willingness to see them go into battle in their place and die before they become a threat in the sexual marketplace. *Confessions of a Congressman*'s reflection of this further aesthetic tradition makes sense given Juanito's role of intermediary between political factions bequeathed by the Civil War. Juanito is the male sacrificed to the battle over the future direction of Spain, not Orbea, and his untimely death has the added benefit for Orbea, the fascist bogeymen, and all their generation, of eliminating a younger male who was becoming increasingly attractive to the likes of Orbea's wife.

The creation of the aestheticised working-class homosexual presents both Orbea and the film's political agenda with a problem: what about all the other Juanitos? Are they all to be rehomed by charitable Marxists with understanding wives and reprogrammed by weekend picnics and museum visits? The answer to this conundrum arrived at by Orbea is hardly a persuasive one. Newly alerted to the cultural disenfranchisement of Juanito's world and attempting to make the personal – and the sexual – political, Orbea tells his fellow party members: 'We must begin by taking the town halls ... and cultural centres so that civic life is where it ought to be.' Are we really supposed to believe that opening a few cultural centres will change the lot of the working class and the internal marginalisation therein of dispossessed homosexuals? Or does de la Iglesia give us in Roberto Orbea not the good homosexual, but a picture of the inevitable price to be paid by others for his misguided Trotskyite entryism? Orbea's reflections towards the end of the film could be read as suggesting that his goodness resides in being an example of how not to carry out social engineering: 'I saw myself as being among those who were going to make history and nevertheless it's turned out to be me who's going to suffer it instead.' Juanito was not going to be able to trade on his youthful good looks forever. What would have become of *Confessions of a Congressman*'s gay Pygmalion? The fascists' murder of the boy absolves Orbea of any responsibility for the future of his protégé and from having to answer these more difficult questions. The project to galvanise identity and party politics by fusing them together comes apart at the seams where the revolutionary rhetoric is haphazardly sewn into a classical iconography of homosexual and class martyrdom. Duleep C. Deosthale attributes Juanito's demise and Orbea's scandalous predicament not to the fascist bogeymen in the film's plot but to a global scenario of homophobia where 'many believe that the only way to move the public and make them recognise this [homophobic] injustice is by presenting a reality that culminates repeatedly in tragedy'.

Although *Confessions of a Congressman* ends with a level of ambiguity about the details of how Orbea will organise his outing as the older gay lover of a dead 'golfillo de barrio', it remains relatively clear that the event will become news and will enter the public domain.

Despite the film's opening caveat that all its characters are entirely fictional, the camera nevertheless picks out details and names recognisable from the real political scene of the time. Among others, Felipe González is recognisable on a television screen seen in shot. Within this context of a blend of fact and fiction, we might suppose that the Orbea-Juanito scandal should be understood as having some documentary value. De la Iglesia hinted that the film was in part a response to a real-life scandal surrounding a left-wing politician. He recalled in 1985 that in the late 1970s 'there were rumours in the corridors of political power that there was a case like the one I deal with in *Confessions of a Congressman* and I took this as inspiration'. From the perspective of the early twenty-first century we can see that the rumours which became a full-blown scandal in the film amounted to nothing in the real world of Spanish politics. While there are notable exceptions in the realm of regional parliaments, in the 25 years after the film was released there has never been a case of a Spanish politician belonging to the central government coming out of the closet, either voluntarily or as a result of some hideous kind of extortion such as that presented in de la Iglesia's imagined transitional political landscape. The openness of the Spanish political establishment to the possibility of a central government deputy espousing his or her *individual* homosexual identity as part of a political platform (and thereby accomplishing the fusion which was *Confessions of a Congressman*'s theoretical motive) is no more developed than it was when de la Iglesia and his co-writer scripted their gay political thriller.

Although legislation to recognise gay partnerships was unexpectedly accelerated following the elections of 2004, when José Luis Rodríguez Zapatero announced plans to put gay union and marriage on an equal footing, in the run-up to those elections, rumour and innuendo continued to act as an interface between the central establishment and homosexuality. The political leanings of those caught up in these rumours had changed since the 1970s. In the early 2000s they were the heirs apparent to prominent right-wing figures of the political landscape about whom gay innuendos circulated. In August 2003, Alfonso Guerra, a former vice-president of the Spanish Labour Party (PSOE), described Mariano Rajoy, the then Prime Minister Aznar's deputy, as a political 'gadfly'. The word he used in Spanish, *mariposón*, can also be used to describe a man as effeminate or homosexual. José Luis Rodríguez Zapatero, defender of gay marriage, was photographed bent double in laughter at his comrade's use of the pun which also saw the audience, comprised of members of a mineworkers' union, in fits of laughter. Later, during the 2004 elections, posters depicting Rajoy would be defaced with lipstick. While on the one hand the left courted the gay vote, on the other its same liberal constituency and politicians were happy to taint the right wing with homophobic insinuations of effeminacy. The real Juanitos of the 2000s are scarcely more represented in the legislature than was the fictional one in 1979. No minister of the central government has ever been identified as gay, so we do not know whether a real life Roberto or Roberta Orbea would be hunted down in the same way as the fictional one. However, the first openly gay priest in Spain was forced out of the Church in 2002, something which did not augur well for homosexual public figures.

Is the Spanish political scene so enlightened that it has moved fast forward to a post-gay rhetoric and is able to bypass the outings and scandals witnessed by other democracies, or have the forces of conservatism exercised such a powerful latent control in Spanish politics that the clumsy terror tactics of the fascist bogeymen in *Confessions of a Congressman* are simply unnecessary? Gay politicians being outed by homicidal neo-Nazis is hardly a sign of democratic evolution and yet the continuing mystery over the real-life events which inspired *Confessions of a Congressman* and the persistence in the 2000s of the same kind of rumours which were common in the 1970s suggest that *Confessions of a Congressman*'s fiction still looks to the future. Although dismissed by some as a simplistic political pamphlet on release in 1979, the ambiguity of the film's political message was enough to see it win opprobrium from columnists for *ABC* as well as *El País*. For the right, Pedro Crespo dismissed the film as 'laughable', summing it up as 'an opportunist film, gratuitously crude in its depiction of sex acts and tendentious in its politics which are marked by a puerility rendering them rather comic'. For the left, Fernando Trueba also finds the film opportunistic and declares that the director 'uses dates, moments and characters from our recent history to lend verisimilitude to a story which is false from beginning to end'. Of the two reviews, it is Trueba's which is the most scathing. He finds nothing to recommend the film whatsoever, while Crespo concedes that some of the actors perform well and that José Sacristan convinces viewers of Orbea's 'humanity'. A film which sees a critic of the right take sides with a gay Marxist-Leninist character may be many things but not a pamphlet with a monotonous single message.

Perhaps what neither critic can forgive *Confessions of a Congressman* is its pessimism. The film was made just at the time when 'homosexual acts' were being erased from the Ley de Peligrosidad y Rehabilitación Social (Law on Dangerousness and Social Rehabilitation), a piece of legislation in force between 1970 and 1978 and which allowed the prosecution of men found to be habitual homosexuals. Coupled with the general ambience of progress and advance heralded by the transitional politics of the time, this legislative development might have seen the director make films with a brighter outlook. Not *Confessions of a Congressman*. Firstly, de la Iglesia casts as his closeted politician José Sacristan, an actor whose face was already familiar to Spanish audiences from *Un hombre llamado Flor de otoño* (*A Man Called Autumn Flower*, 1978) where he played a doomed 1920s homosexual transvestite. Secondly, the narrative structure of the film allows little room for any sense of progress, on any front. As Isolina Ballesteros observes 'the film ends where it began'. This teleological static bleeds into *Confessions of a Congressman*'s treatment of history and politics which are similarly running to stand still. This is not to say that the film is unable to tell us anything about why de La Iglesia is pessimistic about the future. On the contrary, the way Orbea's personal history is mediated points to a critique of a cross-party system of surveillance and nosiness. It has also been suggested that Orbea's first-person narration, which frames and sits over the unravelling of his story, ties him into an old-fashioned confessional discourse. Ballesteros, for example, says that the film is structured 'like a confession'. However, Orbea's story is not in fact mediated by the metaphor of confession. What he uses to tell his story are the archives and files which have been built up on him in the past and those which will be written about him in the future. The pessimistic continuity of the film, then, resides in its projection of a state apparatus which will continue to keep records about individuals and to track them regardless of constitutional changes or the success of political parties espousing liberal progressive rhetorics. The politically-neutral filing cabinet is more of a threat in *Confessions of a Congressman* than the fascist party-political father confessor.

The inclusion in the film of elements of a dystopian view of the future seen as an information tyranny is clarified by looking at the film alongside de la Iglesia's earlier *Una gota de sangre para morir amando* (*Murder in a Blue World*, 1973). Described as the Spanish *A Clockwork Orange* (the US title is *Clockwork Terror*), de la Iglesia's earlier film seemingly could not be further removed from *Confessions of a Congressman*. However, both films deal with anonymous killers of adolescent boys and with gangs of fascistic thugs. A young homosexual slated for murder in *Murder in a Blue World* recalls being given a punch card stamped with the letter 'H' when he finished his education, while some of the film's horror scenes are centred on the all-knowing computer room. Like all dystopias *Murder in a Blue World* is grounded in the present, and therefore refers as much to its own then-present moment of late Francoism as to any future world. However, the film's marginals, who protest a desire to be socially useless, have as much in common with those disenfranchised by the politics of the 2000s as they do with those considered beyond redemption by Franco. The futuristic, science fiction element of de la Iglesias' politics, more self-evident in the earlier film, perhaps makes some sense, if carried over into *Confessions of a Congressman*, of that film's maladjustment to the evolving political consensus of its own era. The film's pessimism anticipates a future homogenisation of party politics readily accessible to later audiences if not to those of its own time.

Another of de la Iglesia's earlier films, *La criatura* (*The Creature*, 1977), casts light on certain elements of *Confessions of a Congressman*'s visual and aural style. *The Creature* depicts an inter-species relationship between the disenchanted wife of a conservative politician and a German Shepherd. It brings to the fore visual elements of *tremendismo* (exaggerated realism that focuses on the grimmer aspects of life) characteristic across de la Iglesia's work. They find an echo, if not a reflection, however, in *Confessions of a Congressman* where the fascists' interrogation scenes with Juanito are overlain with an intense insect buzzing. The use of a tradition of Spanish black humour known as *esperpento*, another feature of de la Iglesia's style, is also brought to the foreground in *The Creature*. In what could almost be a definition of de la Iglesia's cinematic autograph, the disenchanted wife explains her intense relationship with her German Shepherd boyfriend by saying: 'Being a monster, surrounded by monsters, in a world made by monsters, the only way out is to aim for a monstrosity even more extreme than the average.' Seen in the context of *The Creature*, where the *esperpéntico* and the *tremendismo* of de la Iglesia are more clearly in evidence, perhaps it would be a mistake to try to read an elaborate and refined politics in *Confessions of a Congressman*, even if its ostensible narrative context is the world of party congresses and meetings. Could it be that while the Eloy de la Iglesia of interviews was elaborating a political rhetoric for his film, the visual style he had worked up in his previous dozen or so features was more interested in depicting the monstrosity of politicians of every persuasion?

Ryan Prout

REFERENCES

Ballesteros, Isolina (2001) 'El despertar homosexual del cine español: identidad y política en transición (Eloy de la Iglesia, Pedro Olea, Imanol Uribe y Pedro Almodóvar)', in *Cine (ins)urgente: textos fílmicos y contextos culturales de la españa postfranquista*. Madrid. Editorial Fundamentos, 91–127.

Crespo, Pedro (1979) '*El Diputado*, de Eloy de la Iglesia', *ABC*, 9 February, 66.

Desothale, Duleep C. (1992) 'Sex, Society and Oppression in post-Franco Cinema: The

Homosexual Statement in Iglesia's *El Diputado*' in George Cabello-Castellet, Jaume Marti-Olivella and Guy Wood (ed.) *Cine-Lit*: *Essays on Peninsular Film and Fiction*. Corvallis, OR. Portland State University; Oregon State University; Reed College, 10–18.

Greer, Germaine (2003) *The Boy*. London: Thames and Hudson.

Téllez, José Luis (1979) '*El diputado*', *Contracampo*, 1, April, 51–2.

Trueba, Fernando (1979) 'Sexo y política, un cóctel que vende', *El País*, 27 January, 21.

ARREBATO RAPTURE

IVÁN ZULUETA, SPAIN, 1980

The premiere of *Arrebato* (*Rapture*), on 9 June 1980 at the Azul cinema in Madrid, went almost unnoticed. However when, a few months later, the Alphaville cinema in Madrid scheduled this unusual Spanish film, with its crude, no-punches-pulled depiction of drug use, in its weekend late-night programme, it remained there for an entire year, ultimately gaining the popular cult status which it retains to this day. Not only is the success of this strange, experimental film with audiences who would normally have paid it little or no attention, surprising, but also the fact that neither its author, Iván Zulueta, nor its style have spawned either a sequel or an imitation in more than two decades. Its very originality would seem to have ensured *Rapture*'s immunity to imitators and the film has risen to become an object of veneration over the years. The journey which Zulueta's film took from the smaller circle of the faithful to that of the much wider mainstream arena could be justified through its unashamed cinematic flourishes, its reflections on the essence of cinema itself, its treatment of drugs and drug use and the way it spoke for a generation.

Interweaved in a relatively conventional, although at times enigmatic, linear plot are some of the key elements of experimental film: home-movie style is used to adopt an analytic perspective on the dispositive of capturing images and the practices of recycling and re-shooting. What is unique is how all these phenomena appear together, woven into a highly original tale, a tragic adventure in which heroin becomes the metaphorical driving force and which heads to a passionate climax which the author not unintentionally baptised with a name of mystical resonance: the Spanish word *arrebato* actually means 'rapture' but also 'ecstasy'.

Let us begin with the attractions which this film offers to its public. An unashamed celebration of the cinema, *Rapture* is very much of its time, as references to and quotes from other films are embedded throughout, which one would most certainly not consider to be of the intellectual elite but of the mainstream. First and foremost, film features centrally within the film via its protagonist José Sirgado (Eusebio Poncela), a mediocre filmmaker specialising in Z-series horror movies; it also features as background in the numerous cinema posters which cover the walls of José's apartment and the editing studio in which he works (Zulueta himself is renowned as a poster artist). It makes an additional ambiental contribution at the beginning of the film with billboards for *Quo Vadis*, *The Humanoid*, *The Deer Hunter*, *Phantasm* and *Bambi* oozing film fetishism and accompanying Poncela on his night-time drive down Madrid's Gran Vía.

Even more relevant is how cinema is present in *Rapture* as a re-elaboration, reference or whimsical allusion. Thus, throughout the film, we see frames and fragments of lesser or greater relevance to the story, to remind us of, for example, the enigmatic 'Rosebud' of Charles Foster Kane immediately prior to his death in *Citizen Kane*, the mysterious monolith of *2001: A Space Odyssey*, the fall of the brutally-butchered Janet Leigh in the infamous *Pyscho* shower scene, the cross of Saint Andrew which forebodes the violent murders of Howard Hawks' *Scarface*. For a generation brought up in the cinema and in a period where pastiche equalled style, *Rapture* contains much for those looking for familiar territory.

Such elements, although not totally unique within the Spanish cinematic panorama, are no doubt relatively infrequent. Nevertheless there is nothing closer to a postmodern rhetoric than these frequent nods to popular culture, a tapestry of varied references often discordant amongst themselves, where irony, parody and pastiche capriciously combine. A brief examination of a contemporary instance of similar elements will help us discover the originality of Zulueta's view. In *Pepi, Luci, Bom y otras chicas del montón* (*Pepi, Luci, Bom*, 1981) Pedro Almodóvar hangs his story on a very similar collection of meetings to that which serves as the starting point for Zulueta. The origins of the film only confirm this: *Star* magazine asked the filmmaker for a short story parodying the punk movement, from this sprang the idea for a script which started life being filmed in 16mm before growing to 35mm and then jumping to unexpected success on the commercial circuit. The result is an eccentric film which tells us of the deeds and misdeeds of three girls, interspersed with grotesque-penis competitions, publicity spots and musical numbers. Eccentric but weak on structure *Pepi, Luci, Bom*, like *Rapture* makes innumerable cultural references to comic book culture, uses cheeky musical and cinematic quotations, and turns day-to-day events bizarrely on their heads.

In spite of all such connections, *Rapture* and *Pepi, Luci, Bom* are still separated, in terms of materials, by an enormous gulf as Zulueta seeks to create not a pastiche burlesque but a real drama, at the centre of which is cinema, and a story which gains more and more force and ultimately winds up sweeping away the life and soul of the protagonists. What is more, as we shall see, Zulueta ponders a series of questions and problems more specific to the cinematic avant garde.

Cinema is the real crux of *Rapture* in the most intense and radical manner imaginable; it is seen as cruel, vampire-like and capable of nothing short of draining the very life-blood from the characters. Within the first few moments of the film a vampire woman looks into the camera from her sepia-toned celluloid and we soon learn that this is the film which José is busy editing. With this simple look which is echoed in the final moments the film will come full circle; as well as inspiring the closing image of the film it also closes the protagonist's mind to all that exists outside the camera. In fact the camera is transformed into something of a free spirit and given a life of its own, deciding what it chooses to film and when, selecting objects and people at will, and moving with an unnerving liberty which results in the successive disappearance of the two main characters in some kind of technical vampirism.

Rapture opens with a prologue where a husky voice, bordering on inaudibility, is heard recording words of invitation onto a cassette for an absent listener. These words of instruction, which are seen to have come from some type of pallid, living corpse, are packed on their audio cassette into an envelope along with a spool of Super 8 and a key. We also hear the recorded plea that the addressee should study the enclosed reel of images and then set off to look for a final film which one presumes has yet to be made. As the envelope is sealed with a red stamp the titles are suddenly superseded by fragments of a vampire woman in black-and-white celluloid, the very fragments which José, the recipient of the parcel, is editing together.

These recorded words contain the central theme of Pedro's (Will More) cinematic suffering, namely images and their capturing in the eye of the camera. The first fortuitous meeting between Pedro and José in a country house in Segovia for the filming of a subsequently uncompleted film, is followed in the recording by the different stages of his cinematic experimentation and his obsession for interval shooting. Back home, José listens to the cassette and, after shooting up, the story continues, mixing his memories with an overdose of hallucinatory imagery. Amongst this mosaic of memory we see the meetings and separations of José and his partner Ana (Cecilia Roth), their fall into the world of drugs, and their sexual and spiritual decadence. These and other changes offer some backbone to an otherwise broken up and deliberately ambiguous tale. But what exactly *is* the journey on which Pedro invites José?

At 29 Pedro remains an infantile being, obsessed by the simple act of filming the people and objects which surround him: his aunt, his cousin, the different rooms of the country house where he lives, the trees, and of course himself. One might say that his films are a species of home movies but lacking in the individual passion which drove filmmakers like Jonas Mekas (the writing of memory), Stan Brakhage (the inner eye and the transfiguration of reality),

Carolee Schneemann (the representation of intimacy) and so many others. Still, behind the apparent banality there lurks a deeper question about the mechanism which connects with the other great movement of the avant-garde: the conceptual. Pedro in fact proclaims himself to be spurred on by an anxiety to investigate the interval (the suspension of time between frames). On more than one occasion he claims to have spent hours (he could spend days, weeks he adds) observing a single frame of *King Solomon's Mines* (1950) and other such works. He also feels unspeakable pain when viewing what he himself has filmed. It would seem that, unnoticed, the meeting with José must have sparked off, deep inside, the investigation which he is close to finishing.

The majority of what José sees on that reel is indeed made up of home movies (a sightseeing trip through the highlights of Thailand, the Ganges and Los Angeles amongst others and which may itself have been pirated from someone else; a high-speed trip from Segovia to Madrid; emblematic images of the Spanish capital). Here again Pedro's work draws deeply on experimental cinema: on one hand it connects with the travelogue style of amateur filmmaking while on the other, much more importantly, it practises re-shooting (the recycling of images for other ends; so-called found footage), an idea which Zulueta had already practised in his short films and which has come to be one of the most successful crops in the cinematic avant-garde of recent years.

Pedro's obsession with filmmaking brings up another source for reflection which also belongs by rights to experimental cinema, namely the analysis of the base mechanisms, the minimalist elements of cinematographic expression. The use of interval shooting, of perception, the capturing of images, and the transformation of said images are questions which have, since the 1970s, interested Michael Snow, Ernie Gehr and Hollis Frampton in North America and also Kurt Kren and Peter Kubelka in Europe. Even so, Pedro seems little moved by theoretical and abstract discussions and is more concerned with an enigmatic emotion about the capturing of real images, as if his experiment were to be attributed not to a cold study of the camera as machine but to the possibility it offers of revealing reality and causing tears and shock.

To recapitulate then, in one way *Rapture* touches on the themes of domesticity and family, following in the footsteps of the American avant-garde led by Marie Menken and Jonas Mekas, while at the same it aims at a seemingly opposite current which analyses film as a dispositive. *Rapture* certainly feeds on such distinct sources and equally certainly it blends them together in a path of initiation, a tragic path along which the subject discovers something which leads him to delirium, something which cannot become either a memory or a treatise for reflection, something truly devastating. It is right here where the innovative power of heroin intervenes becoming a source of rhetoric, governing delirious connections and boundless experiences.

Rapture is the story of a journey and a learning process, a highly original *bildungsroman* which demands that the viewer look deeply but disconnect from logic and reason. From this comes the first and most evident paradox: the complete story of the adventure which Pedro lives seems to respond, in its own language, to a hidden agenda minutely plotted by something unknown (the camera) and to an initiation process whose keys are slowly to be revealed after a series of challenges. The key script device consists in presenting this journey as something shared between the two protagonists or, more accurately, initially shared and later experienced successively. Their two stories are superimposed, metamorphosing and mingling into each other and the joins barely show; two delirious minds collide in a pained voice, pained for reasons we do not know and a tortured look at the very edge of the abyss. Thus we start from this blind spot, this intimate, irrational communion born from Pedro's voice and the abyss which opens up before José's eyes as he starts to absorb the mysteries hidden within the seemingly harmless reel of Super 8.

The voice invites him to dive head-first into his own adventure. José ponders the grainy image from a car advert, a series of compulsively repeated shots as a car crashes against a rock placed in the centre of the road, and this image blends into a more familiar road and a more familiar vehicle. José and his friend Marta (Marta Fernández Muro) are traveling together as the voice from the tape recorder summons up the images, going back to the first meeting of the two protagonists. In so doing, José infiltrates Pedro's story but goes beyond what he could possibly have seen and known and imposes his own memories within Pedro's words. Pedro's adventure thus becomes José's and the coherence of a single viewpoint is discarded as unnecessary and the ties with daily life are cut as this is a journey which can only be made alone.

Everyday life, the central theme of all home movies, is treated in *Rapture* simply as irritating background noise. The spectator will never feel more asphyxiated than in those moments where cotidianeity bursts into the film (the banal conversation of Marta's aunt about movie stars of yesteryear, Ana's reflections on couplehood). Amongst complicities and fake ecstasies managed only with help from the drug, the projection of the enigmatic spools filmed by Pedro sentence the element of cotidianeity, and the unstoppable interior adventure to oblivion becomes clear: 'You have to remember,' the voice says, 'that I still believed in the cameras that filmed, the things that they filmed and the projectors that projected them. You must understand that I could never have guessed how far I was from my real course in life.' To the sound of Pedro's words, once the projection is over, there is a hallucination uncertain in origin, as images from all over the world appear with that grainy, aged quality which makes them seem somehow more distant, unusually pure, uncontaminated and for this reason strangely incomplete. Some blank frames precede the arrival at Hollywood Boulevard in Los Angeles before both sound and picture are inexplicably interrupted. The interruption is external to the sound and to the images themselves and is in reality ludicrously prosaic, we see how Ana ham-fistedly puts on a record and this simple action returns us to a totally empty 'here and now'. She breaks this feast of images with her puerile chatter about giving up heroin and implausible proposals for fraternisation of the couple. Rarely has domesticity and everyday life been so ruthlessly and publicly X-rayed.

From the brink of the abyss, once again it is the cracked voice which heralds the next development: the contents of the reel of film accompanying the cassette tape. At the same time José, and the audience, are brought back to earth with a bump as Ana, masquerading as Betty Boop, performs an entertaining little number in front of the screen, lit by the projector's glare. In this vignette she plays out a scene from her relationship with the dual José/Pedro character in which she gives free reign to her ecstasy. José gives a satisfied smile, willingly enjoying her uninhibited performance but nevertheless proceeds to violently reject her attempts at lovemaking, embarking instead upon an infinitely more interesting and risky venture which will erase the girl from the picture forever.

In the projection which follows there is a moment in which José's gaze is finally possessed by whatever lies deeply hidden inside Pedro. The appearance of a red frame in Pedro's home movies marks this point of no return. In fact it is another cinematic reference, this time to *Schwechater* by Peter Kubelka, a publicity film commissioned by the Austrian brewery Schwechater Bier. The piece is composed of 1,440 different black-and-white fragments, some of which appeared in red. Kubelka filmed with an old hand-crank camera from the 1920s without a viewfinder and, during the editing process, printed a sequence of 30 frames based on the red element which recur throughout the film at ever decreasing intervals in line with his 'Metric Cinema'.

There is, however, no other similarity between the two filmmakers' use of the red frames. In *Rapture* the development of Pedro's untiring filming of himself sleeping and waking, locked away in his apartment, carries with it an enigmatic extension related to the red frames which, in contrast to Kubelka's usage, represents not a cold, analytical principle but a fatal chance intervention. Pedro's disembodied voice draws attention to this fact when, before the red frame appears, there is something which the camera appears to refuse to film. Later the camera recovers its regularity and continues filming according to the conventions of submission to reality.

At one point Pedro asks his cousin Marta to stay awake and observe the behaviour of the camera while he falls asleep within its gaze. As he drifts off we see the camera turn on its tripod, focusing its attention menacingly on the girl. This is the very sequence mailed by Pedro at the beginning of the film and it has had the desired effect, as by this point José finds himself inextricably caught up in the delirious whirlpool into which his friend and colleague has thrown him.

Zulueta closes the circle by repeating the pre-credits sequence to avoid confusion: the husky voice of the decrepit Pedro returns, the cassette with its explanation of the itinerary, the key to the apartment, and of course the Super 8. José, intrigued by the mysterious and incomplete summons arrives at the apartment. From the shadows we hear the click of the shutter as the camera, still running on its self timer, continues to take shots of the bed where Pedro is no longer to be seen. José removes the film from the machine and takes it to be developed. After three days of walled-up waiting, three days reminiscent of the entombment of Christ, three days of which the viewer sees and learns nothing, José, wrapped in Pedro's overcoat, begins to pore over the developed images. This physical transformation is an eloquent metaphor for the inner metamorphosis which has been taking place within him.

The projection of the final reel confirms our suspicions – the red frames come thick and fast and the camera has captured nothing of reality except for a single frame of Pedro in close-up, the final trace of the meeting of camera and the outside world. But when José freezes this frame it suddenly and unexpectedly comes to life on the screen, denying its own inanimate condition as the face of Pedro trapped in the celluloid hints that his friend should take his place on the bed. José feels like the prey of some optical hallucination and consequently waves his hand in the shaft of light coming from the projector only to discover that it is in no way affected by this intrusion. The intrigue becomes still greater for José, who, we must not forget, has spent days shut away in this room wearing Pedro's coat and reliving his disturbing disappearance. Suddenly the image of Pedro becomes his own face projected on the wall above the bed and immediately the two images begin to alternate. Behind José the camera begins to move towards him and José finally makes the decision to move to the bed and takes up Pedro's last known position. The camera tacitly follows José and resumes its regular shots. José surrenders completely to the situation and the moment, searching among the sheets for the blindfold which Pedro used to protect himself from the sun's glare. When he does not find it, he tears off a strip from the sheet and binds his eyes. The shutter clicks speed up to a ferocious crescendo like a frenzied machine gun which leaves José's convulsing body weakened and broken on the bed. And there *Rapture* ends, cutting to some fragments of an old movie, a black-and-white sequence of José which echoes that of the vampire woman of the opening sequence and finally includes José in the film-*within*-the-film.

One reading of the film, not only transparent but almost banal, is that the camera progressively consumes the protagonist since the first revelation symbolised by the red frames. This is probably the interpretation which Pedro himself gives Marta when he asks her to start her bedside vigil but, as if aware of its own banality, the idea is not expressed by any of Zulueta's characters caught up in the drama. Such an allegory, although not completely false, would dilute the tragic nature of the process though which the characters pass when, in fact, both Pedro and José revel in the experience, surrendering to it completely as if to an investigation in which they knowingly offer their lives. In one of his moments of weakness on hearing the shutter click on automatic Pedro says, 'And then … I knew who my allies were and I only had to place myself in their hands. They possessed me, they devoured me and I was happy in that surrender. I had needed to stand on the edge of the abyss to understand what was happening. It was the point not to do but be done to.'

The film stands at the edge of a precipice. Subject becomes object within the film and only in seeing this process can we understand why Pedro and José walk so close to the edge of that abyss. And there at the cliff's edge, mixing delirium and ecstasy, heroin plays its key role. It is not an inducement to action nor is it sign of the times, it is an instrument for discussion. *Rapture* is not a film made about drugs but a film made *on* drugs, with all the hypersensitivity, fascination and leaps of imagination which they induce. Augusto Martínez Torres noted in the preface to the published version of the script that the shooting of *Rapture* was plagued by drug-related problems, both in front of and behind the camera, including those of Zulueta himself.

To conclude then, the film's originality lies in its desire to go beyond the conventional bounds. When considered as a home movie we see how, rather than providing a crutch to get through life, it winds up tearing apart the subject who films his daily life. When viewed as a studied analysis of the technical aspects of capturing images and cinematic reproduction, *Rapture* is passionate, even ecstatic, overheating the already hot world of conceptual experimentation and investigation. If looked at from the point of view of recycling and re-shooting we see how it annihilates not only the idea of re-shooting, but the very idea of film itself. Compared with the other films on drug-related themes which began to circulate in the 1970s, *Rapture* makes no statement on heroin but merely explores the world as seen through the drug. Perhaps for this very reason Zulueta chose such a resonant title, a title which signals both toward the lower limit of cinema (pause, interval, absence of movement) and that mystic ecstasy where one becomes the channel for forces beyond ourselves. Translating *Rapture*'s ineffability into words or beyond to the realms of allegory would be to strip the film of its essence. Maybe that is what makes *Rapture* so unique and unrepeatable.

Vicente Sánchez Biosca

REFERENCE

Martínez Torres, Augusto (2002) 'Prólogo', in *Arrebato. Guión cinematográfico de Iván Zulueta.* Madrid, Ocho y medio, 7–21.

LOS SANTOS INOCENTES THE HOLY INNOCENTS

MARIO CAMUS, SPAIN, 1984

Mario Camus' *Los santos inocentes* (*The Holy Innocents*, 1984) has been singled out by historians of Spanish cinema as a showcase for the aspirations of the early Socialist government (PSOE), implicit in the Miró Law of 1983, to support 'quality cinema'. It was the greatest box-office success in Spanish film history up to 1986, and also received wide critical acclaim in Spain and abroad: its director was awarded the Prize of the Ecumenical Jury and nominated for the Palme d'Or at Cannes, while its leading actors, Alfredo Landa (Paco, the short one) and Francisco Rabal (Azarías) shared the Cannes Best Actor award. Its leading actress, Terele Pávez (Régula), won the Bronze award from Madrid's leisure listings magazine *Guía del Ocio*. The following year, Camus obtained Spain's National Prize for Film Production.

Camus is best known abroad for his screen adaptations of literary works centred on Francoist Spain. *The Holy Innocents* represents the harsh living conditions of a family of landless laborers (Paco, his wife Régula, his retarded 61-year-old brother-in-law Azarías, his son Quirce, and daughters Nieves and the mute, crippled, mentally handicapped 'Niña Chica') living on a Marchioness' remote estate in Extremadura (near the Portugal border) in the mid-1960s, the last decade of Franco's regime. The aristocrat's estate is used primarily for family celebrations and for bird-hunting parties in which her thirty-something son Iván (Juan Diego) entertains influential acquaintances (such as ministers and ambassadors), boasting both of his shooting prowess and the dog-like retrieving skills of his loyal hunting aide, Paco, who crawls following the smell of the dying birds and fights over them with other aides to ensure his master obtains his entire catch. The estate's 'quasi-feudal' hierarchical social structure includes an intermediate position, that of the manager, Pedro (Agustín González), who has to put up with Iván's flirtations with his idle wife Pura (Ágata Lys) but lets off steam by bossing the laborers around. The only turning point in this otherwise static plot (and social formation) is when Paco falls off a tree and breaks his leg. He is pushed to continue helping in the hunt but, after the unhealed leg breaks a second time, he is replaced by his sulkily rebellious son and by his brother-in-law.

In terms of fulfilling the requirements of the Miró Law, the quality of *The Holy Innocents* project was doubly guaranteed: the script was based on the homonymous novel by the established award-winning anti-authoritarian author Miguel Delibes (who won the prestigious Nadal Prize in 1947) and its director, Camus, had won the Golden Bear award at the Berlin Film Festival in 1983 for his literary adaptation of Camilo J. Cela's *The Beehive*. Thematically, the film appears to have perfectly fitted the aims of the PSOE government in reconstructing the Spanish cultural heritage, and counteracting the Francoist propagandistic use of the media and cinema to show social harmony, progress and political achievement: Barry Jordan and Rikki Morgan-Tamosunas emphasize the PSOE's efforts to re-appropriate the past which had been 'hijacked and aggressively refashioned' during 40 years of Francoism, and see Camus as 'perhaps the Spanish director most consistently associated with film adaptations of literature focused on the dictatorship'. On the one hand, this film's depiction of the Civil War's losers as the endearing victims of a violent *señorito* was coherent with the emphasis placed in the early 1980s on the 'intellectual representation' of the subordinated classes, marginalised by Franco's regime. On the other, its portrayal of disability (the howling, crippled Niña Chica, devoid of any cognitive powers, and the retarded Azarías) could potentially link this film to the tradition of Buñuel and help to establish its 'art-cinema' status abroad.

The Holy Innocents also benefited from further state subsidies thanks to the agreement signed by Spanish state television, TVE, and independent film producers' associations in September 1983. This collaboration excluded projects based on controversial topics, which raises questions about the extent to which Camus' screen adaptation of Delibes' novel complied with the ideology of consensus promoted by the PSOE in the early 1980s. Focusing on the three different types of power relations established between the landowner Iván and the main male characters, here we will look at the film's ideology on three different levels: the social roles within the film, its production and the level of filmic narration.

On a social level, the film's characters are social types, rather than individuals. Iván is the stereotype of the ill-mannered, tyrannical *señorito* who swears continually and establishes his masculinity and his superiority through hunting and seducing his employee's wife. Paco, with his eyes filled with admiration for and, later, fear of his master, acts as an unconditional servant. Régula's act is limited to that of the submissive wife: washing, cooking and sewing, showing maternal caring for her retarded daughter and brother, and bowing to her superiors. Quirce, with his evasive looks, represents the taciturn rebel. Azarías behaves as the village idiot, smiling gratuitously or crying disconsolately (joy and sorrow being the only two states of mind he expresses). They are defined by the ways they interact with each other within a rigid quasi-feudal social configuration, as well as by their own (ideological) perception of their own position within that hierarchy.

The film shows power being exercised primarily through a system of differentiations of an economic and cultural nature, in which the dispossessed who live on the estate are kept virtually illiterate, with whole families working for the landowners in exchange for basic housing and a few sporadic handouts, presented as spontaneous generous gestures, rather than as fair payment. The precariousness of this arrangement is made manifest by Azarías' dismissal from the neighboring estate of La Jara, where he has lived his whole life, sixty years.

In terms of production, John Hopewell has suggested that the casting of Alfredo Landa, 'the hangdog lecher of the Spanish sex comedy' of the 1970s, as the strikingly humble peasant Paco only serves to divert attention from the world represented in the film to 'extra-fictional speculations'. Such speculations would, of course, only have worked for cinema audiences in mid-1980s Spain. For critics abroad, the casting can be justified solely in terms of the requirements of the script: in the words of Patricia Santoro, Landa 'typifies the sturdy peasant with his strong, compact body and quick movements. Moreover, he has the face of a loyal hunting dog.' But this choice, together with the casting of actress Ágata Lys, known for her significant contribution to the low-quality *cine del destape* (nudity boom) of the late 1970s, can also be seen as part of the joint attempt of Spanish filmmakers and politicians of the early 1980s to dignify the national cinema. Both Lys and Landa play characters with fixed identities, but any extradiegetic connotations associated with their personae are re-contextualised here by the seriousness of the topic and its literary background. What better means of reconstructing, relocating and re-presenting the recent Spanish cinema tradition? Besides, the film's casting helped to ensure its appeal to a broad mixed audience, as would be expected of a project supported by state television.

Hopewell sees the film as 'an acid portrayal of the Spanish authoritarian mind in the figure of the *señorito*'. But he then goes on to criticise the film's use of polished camerawork and its aim of being 'visually pleasing at any cost' as being incoherent with the squalor it portrays, as well as with the filming tradition inherited from Buñuel. He concludes that by creating 'an effect of picturesque poverty', in his film Camus appears to suggest 'a glossier fictional reality' which deludes viewers. This interpretation, however, denies the ideological value of aesthetic representation.

It is possible to see this film, and the novel on which it is inspired, as explicitly fulfilling the ideological role which Catherine Belsey attributes to literature: 'it may have an important influence on the ways in which people grasp themselves and their relation to the real conditions in which they live'. Rather than offering a radically new vision of the peasant class, *The Holy Innocents* appears to engage with the tradition of representing the 'popular classes' as subservient, docile and contented, to which the National-Catholic ideology of the early Francoist years had strongly subscribed. Nonetheless, this film also stresses the unbridgeable gap between the attitude of the older generation of laborers and that of their children, whose sharper perception of their living conditions leads them to discontent and change.

On the level of the narration, the characters are constructed through verbal interactions and symbolic processes and practices which are visually codified in ways recognisable to the spectator through a number of aesthetic choices, such as setting, *mise-en-scène,* casting and characterisation. While the original narrative takes place in an unnamed hinterland location, the setting chosen by Camus, Extremadura, is a region historically known for its *latifundia*, landless laborers and absentee landowners (as well as a land of conquistadors and emigrants). At the start of the first framing sequence we see Quirce getting off a train, in military uniform and entering a bar where he painstakingly writes a note to his sister Nieves. The railway station metonymically represents the whole of the Francoist period: a few soldiers, indicating Franco's omnipresent military dictatorship, a young priest, symbolising the ubiquitous presence of the Catholic Church, and two women in black pointing at the importance of religious traditions such as mourning. The only unambiguous time references in the film are the second Vatican Council, the clothes worn by the young aristocrats, their cars and the tractor. Whereas in the novel there is no explicit reference to Franco, the film shows his photograph prominently displayed in the aristocrats' sitting room, overtly stating the family's alliance with the winners of the Civil War. Iván's complaint about Quirce, 'today's youth did not fight a war', and his later remark 'we are no longer in 1936', also denote his belief that the war and the dictatorship had brought progress. By contrast, the poorer characters appear to belong to a 'timeless' setting, marked by the station bar's aged cheesecloth table covers, the gatehouse's single light bulb and the clothes they wear, which suggest that progress was circumventing them.

The film begins with a tracking shot of the most innocent of the characters, Azarías, racing through wooded land at dusk, running after a tawny owl, with which he is exchanging communicative noises. These primeval sound exchanges soon give way to traditional percussion music (tambourine, drums and cowbells), which links Azarías' fast movements to the next shot, a still black-and-white shot of the whole of his family outside the whitewashed wall of the small house they share. The stillness of this long shot and the strangeness of the extradiegetic percussion music, both of which seem to be taken from an ethnographer's archive, accentuate the remoteness of the story narrated by the film. The family photograph provides the backdrop for the opening credits, while the extradiegetic music changes from the rhythmic percussion to the equally obsessive sounds of a jarring, discordant *organillo*-like violin, which will recur in each of the four parts into which the film is divided. Named after four of the characters – Quirce, Nieves, Paco, Azarías – these four segments are interspersed with five framing sequences added by Camus, with the percussion sound introducing every flashback to the main narrative. Quirce acts as the unifying thread in all the flashbacks, though they are presented as the subjective points of view of each of the four characters: the first is introduced by a succession of three stills (long, medium and close-up) which zoom in on Quirce; the second by the same succession of shots focusing on Nieves; the third by a medium shot of Paco cleaning his shotgun, the fourth by a close-up of a rosary's cross held by Azarías against the light. The transition back to the present tense of the framing sequences is consistently marked by a fade to white and, in all except one, by the use of percussion. Besides giving the narrative a structure and a point of view, these five framing sequences help to develop the rather static original plot and also add an ideological layer to it.

The characterisation of Paco and the laborers of his generation can be read, in general terms, as a practical illustration of Althusser's notion of the role of ideology in transforming individuals into subjects by giving them a sense of identity in which they can (more or less consciously) recognise themselves. They simply take up the pre-determined subject positions of the loyal servants, marked by the refrain used by Régula in all her exchanges with the landowners: 'Just give us orders, that is what we are here for.' Their identity is shaped through processes of social division and exclusion, which the film depicts in a blatant way, as when Azarías is shown addressing his landlord from outside a barred window (asking for permission to call a healer for his sick pet owl) and being sent away with critical, confident laughter, or when Paco travels on the outside of his master's Land Rover, holding on to the door, while happily talking to him. The system of privilege and exclusion which define different social groups in this hierarchical structure needs to be supported by an ideological framework which will keep people subject to their 'fixed' social positions.

The old laborers' subservient attitude is underscored through a number of unambiguous visual arrangements and camera movements; for instance in the long shot in which they are lined up, looking up and cheering with a 'Long live the Marchioness, and may she live for many years!', while a low-angle shot of the Marchioness at the balcony accentuates her authority and importance. This is only one of the institutional rituals and practices employed by ideology to fulfill the role of reproducing social relations and maintaining the privileges and status quo of the dominant classes. When such objectives cannot be attained through consensus, coercion is used.

In the film there is a contrast between the Marchioness' 'consensual' relation to her subjects and the increasingly coercive means which Iván needs to use to maintain his position of superiority. In one of the first hunting scenes, for example, Iván is shooting behind the bush and Paco, shown slightly lower than him, is asking his permission to move. His words, '*suélteme…*' ('let me go', or 'untie me'), may suggest that he imagines he is on a leash, like a dog, but can also be read as his unconscious need to be freed from the utter control and fascination his master exercises over him. When, later, Paco is on all fours, tracing the missing partridge, the high camera angle shows him from Iván's position, alternating with point-of-view shots from his. At one level, he may be seen as a dog loyally running around his master. At another level, though, he appears to be acting out of his sense of duty towards Iván, he is also enjoying the attention he is receiving from the other hunters.

The visual hierarchy established in these early scenes is challenged when Iván needs to enlist the help of Quirce and Azarías for his hunting activities. But, all along, Iván is seen increasing his coerciveness: bullying Paco through his repeated insults, intimidations and challenges, and, later, trying in vain to buy Quirce's loyalty with his generous tips.

There are other visually-marked displacements of the established hierarchy, as in the fluid montage which combines three different space and time frames with Iván's words: 'You might say that nowadays young people are annoyed at having to accept a hierarchy. I may be mistaken minister, but, some more, others less, we all have to accept a hierarchy: some below, others above. It's the law of life, isn't it?' This monologue begins at Paco's bedside, continues as voice-over while the camera cuts from his face to his earlier exchange with Quirce, and then cuts to Iván relating it to his guests in his sitting room. This editing somewhat creates the effect that Iván is thrown off-balance by Quirce's attitude, and is trying to re-establish his dominant position by talking at others. But it also invites the spectator to question the established hierarchy.

In contrast to Quirce, the retarded Azarías does not resist power; he simply appears to be unaware of it. He is not directly bound by power relations. Having been asked to leave the estate on which he had lived since his birth, doing menial jobs such as plucking the hunted birds, he enters a new relation of dependence with his sister's family, based on her righteousness and her identification with the pre-determined role of the mother ('a son of my mother's will not die in an institution as long as I am alive'). But, unlike his sister, he cannot be seen as a subject recognising himself within a pre-determined role.

Azarías spends most of his time communicating to his pet birds and to his mute crippled niece, either imitating the birds' sounds ('eh, eh'; 'quiá, quiá') or repeatedly referring to both girl and bird with the affectionate phrase '*milana, bonita*' ('my beautiful kite'). That he does not seem to have a clear idea of his position *vis à vis* the social hierarchy around him is made clear when he grabs the hand of the Marchioness' daughter and makes her run, eager to show her his caged bird and his crippled niece. Being outside the symbolic order, he is not bound by the same laws as the others, or by any ideology; only by his emotional attachments. When Iván, in his frustration after a bad hunting session, kills his '*milana*', he can only show as much respect for the master's life as the master has shown for his pet; dropping a noose around his neck, he hangs him from a tree.

In the last framing sequence, Azarías is seen sobbing, uttering the words '*milana, bonita*' and looking out of his barred window, while watched by his silent nephew. Up to this point the camera had shown him looking from outside bars: watching his pet bird in its cage, talking to his landlord from outside the window, or staying outside the gate which separates the manor from the rest of the estate. Now he is being contained within the symbolic order, finally becoming subjected to the law.

Conversely, the characterisation of Quirce and Nieves suggests that a subject's (ideological) relation to his or her conditions of existence may change more rapidly than the conditions themselves. Quirce watches his father being bullied, and remains silent, following the kind of behavior his sister is taught to follow when in the presence of their superiors: 'Watch, listen and shut up.' Though he also works for Iván, he is not bound to him by the same sense of loyalty. When coerced into helping, his form of rebellion is to refuse to accept tips. This, together with his sulkiness, makes Iván uncomfortable, undermining his confidence as a hunter and making him worry about his own image in the boy's eyes. The fact that Quirce's silence can be such an effective form of resistance suggests that Iván is also a subject, rather than an individual: besides being bound by his addiction to hunting, he is subjected to his own image as master, and feels obliged to keep proving his superiority through his hunting prowess.

Judging from Iván's comments, Quirce and his sister may be seen as the product of the ideological renovation brought about by events such as the Second Vatican Council. But their change in attitude also appears to be related to a change in the characters' relation to language:

while Paco and Régula are shown struggling to sign their name, in the framing sequences we see Quirce writing a note to his sister and her smiling while reading it.

The framing sequences thus not only add a narrative viewpoint, but also an optimistic note to an otherwise sordid plot. They show Quirce on a train and a coach, symbols of progress, which offer new connections to the outside world for the estate workers, who in the main parts of the story are seen traveling by foot (Azarías), by cart (Régula), on horseback or on a tractor's trailer (Quirce), while the landowners come and go freely in their expensive automobiles. The train and the coach also serve to mark the transition between the old rural setting and the urban spaces which the younger characters inhabit in the screen additions.

In the first framing sequence Nieves is shown working in a factory, wearing white overalls and a cap which contrast with her dark skin. The cleanliness of her outfit, the orderliness of the tins on the production line placed between her and the camera, and the sound of the busy machines shown in the next traveling shot, also contrast with the stillness of the ensuing scene: a pack of famished street dogs and two young children and their mothers in a squalid semi-urban setting, presented through four *cinéma verité*-style shots from the viewpoint of Quirce, who is watching in silence, while waiting for his sister. Nieves, like her brother, has succeeded in leaving behind her old static rural life and her old rural clothing.

In the final scene, Quirce, on his way out of the asylum in which Azarías is kept, looks up to the sky and sees a migratory flock of birds flying over the city, undisturbed by hunters. While the birds underscore in symbolic terms the young protagonists' fleeing from the stifling social configuration of the estate (with its bird cage, its barred windows and barred gate), the characters on the screen echo the massive rural exodus in the extradiegetic Spain of the 1960s, summed up in Pedro's earlier remark: 'Now everyone wants to be a *señorito*, Paco, you know, it is not what it was. Nowadays, people don't want to dirty their hands, some go to the capital, others, abroad.'

The optimistic slant which the screen version adds to the original narrative, juxtaposing the young laborers' new beginning to the tragic end of the upper-class villain, can be justified as part of the film's strategy to comply to its agreement with television by targeting a broad audience. Nonetheless, Camus has been accused of endorsing the Spanish Socialist Party's pragmatic ideology of consensus by giving the impression that the problems depicted in the film had been left behind with the rural exodus of the younger characters, and by being, as John Hopewell points out, 'vague about the relevance of that criticism to the present'. In contrast with such claims, it may be argued that the film does act as a reminder of the not-so-distant past from which some of the conflicts, aspirations and disillusions of the Spain of the mid-1980s had emerged. After all, Nieves has simply replaced one set of relations of power with another: she has left behind the quasi-feudal conditions in which she had been forced to work as an unpaid maid in the manor ('cleaning other people's dirt') and replaced them with the stultifying working conditions of a production line. But she has somewhat succeeded in freeing herself from the ideology of serfdom which had bound her parents to the estate. Around the noisy machinery, she is no longer forced to see, hear and shut up.

Overall, the film supports the PSOE's goals of promoting social awareness and renovation through the media. By drawing on literary and cinematic conventions, it shows how social relations are not purely economic, but depend to a great extent on ideological mechanisms which shape a subject's self-perception. Here, far from embracing the PSOE's dominant ideology of consensus, the film depicts a variety of processes of self-construction through differentiation: imposed social division (Paco and Ivan), separation (Azarías), self-detachment (Quirce). Through the representation of Spain's recent history, *The Holy Innocents* stresses how the positions available to Spanish subjects have been determined by their inherited socio-historical configurations, and how these, despite the goodwill of politicians, filmmakers or critics, are slow to change.

Elena Carrera

REFERENCES

Belsey, Catherine (1980) *Critical Practice*. London: Methuen.

Hopewell, John (1986) *Out of the Past: Spanish Cinema after Franco*. London: British Film Institute.

Jordan, Barry and Rikki Morgan-Tamosunas (1998) *Contemporary Spanish Cinema*. Manchester: Manchester University Press.

Santoro, Patricia (1996) *Novel into Film: The Case of La Familia de Pascual Duarte and Los Santos Inocentes*. Newark: University of Delaware Press.

JOÃO DE DEUS TRILOGY TRILOGY OF JOHN OF GOD

JOÃO CÉSAR MONTEIRO, PORTUGAL, 1989/1995/1998

In his review of the *politique des auteurs,* launched in the 1950s by the young critics of the *Cahiers du cinéma,* Jean-Claude Bernardet compares the cinematic auteur to God, 'the prime cause'. Radicalising the auteurist principle, the Portuguese filmmaker João César Monteiro invented a protagonist for his mature work called João de Deus (John of God), combining his own name with that of the supreme creator, to feature in a famous trilogy, *Recordações da casa amarela* (*Recollections of the Yellow House,* 1989), *A comédia de Deus* (*God's Comedy,* 1995) and *As bodas de Deus* (*The Spousals of God,* 1998). The character is played by Monteiro himself, who is also the director, the author of the screenplay and virtually the exclusive source of the trilogy's style.

If Monteiro's divinised character and overwhelming personality are reminiscent of the mythic *auteur* worshiped by the *jeunes Turcs* in the 1950s, it is not mere coincidence. Only seven years younger than François Truffaut (1932–84), Monteiro shaped his cinematic taste in the wake of the *nouvelle vague*'s cinephilia. His kinship with the French is noticeable from his first films. *Quem espera por sapatos de defunto morre descalço* (*He Goes Long Barefoot that Waits for Dead Men's Shoes,* 1970), early evidence of Monteiro's creative force, basks in a typical *nouvelle vague* atmosphere, featuring, like the early works of Truffaut, Jean-Luc Godard and Claude Chabrol, non-conformist youths living out of illicit expedients. One of the characters even writes in his notebook that 'Cinema is a fraud (Godard), but that fraud may be overcome'. *He Goes Long Barefoot...* launched its charismatic, self-reflexive Belmondo in the figure of the actor Luís Miguel Cintra, who would soon become an icon of Portuguese cinema, especially for his performances in Manoel de Oliveira's films. Here he plays Lívio, a mysterious character who will reappear in Monteiro's trilogy as an envoy of God.

Monteiro's assertion of the almighty *auteur,* after the poststructuralist and postmodern interventions which had shattered the author and his work in theory and practice, reinstates an authority aimed at organising the chaos caused by the lack of narrative. In a way, therefore, Monteiro's output is conservative, displaying a peculiar atemporal style, which seems entirely immune to fashion. On the other hand, however, few contemporary films could be more radi-

cal than his. Authorship, in his case, means the absence of limits and total freedom of expressing his obsessive world.

Monteiro's great achievement is to carry out such a project without ever resorting to
any messianic romanticism. Indeed, it is an essential part of his style to show, at each step,
the ridiculousness of his divine pretension. His cinematic representation of God necessarily
includes irony, humour and self-deprecation. Accordingly, the construction of the character of
João de Deus is based on two opposing principles: on the one hand, the use of strictly realistic,
almost documentary shooting techniques; on the other, the use of the fable through a citation
system derived from cinephilia. It is a dialectical, critical and self-reflexive approach, which
single-handedly affirms and negates its subject, thus solving and overcoming the question of
cinematic authorship.

In *Recollections of the Yellow House*, Monteiro appears for the first time before the camera
as the leading actor, in the role of João de Deus, whom he once called his 'heteronym', in the
fashion of the heteronyms used by the Portuguese poet Fernando Pessoa (1888–1935). But,
unlike the poet, Monteiro's heteronym is not meant to disguise his true personality, but to reveal
it. *Recollections of the Yellow House* is a turning point in the director's production, in that the
Portuguese medieval fables of his previous feature films give way to his own contemporary urban
environment of old Lisbon, where he can comfortably deploy his autobiographical features.

Here begin the adventures of João de Deus, the middle-aged paedophile, who collects
the pubic hair of teenage girls (which he calls 'Ariadne's threads'), lives out of small, often illicit
jobs and is impermeable to social impositions of any kind. Like an English lord, his cultivated
speech is always uttered in a moderate, cordial tone, even when it is sheer vulgar language. His
slim, elegant figure never loses its poise, even in the face of disasters. As to his 'divine' quality, it
is nothing but the result of the camera work, which concentrates obsessively on him, regardless
of the insignificance of his acts, thus making him the centre of the universe.

The erotic bias given to this peculiar character finds its roots both in the director's biography and the history of Portugal. Monteiro used to describe himself as raised in a family
'dominated by the spirit of the First Republic', that is to say the anticlerical system reigning in
Portugal from 1910 onwards. According to him, in this milieu, 'anticlerical jokes were abundant', even though his father wanted him to pursue a religious career. In the trilogy, religion is
deconstructed via the depiction of God as a consummate pornographer, echoing a Portuguese
tradition of anticlerical art with prominent representatives, such as the obscene poet Manoel
Maria du Bocage (1765–1805). João de Deus, instead of the pious activities his name suggests,

devotes himself to the realisation of his sexual fantasies, dissipating all the money that falls into his hands in this unproductive job.

Indeed, his aristocratic manners never allow him to work for money, to which he has access through unconventional means, such as gifts from mysterious friends, withdrawals from his ageing mother's meagre savings and minor frauds. One of his favourite forms of entertainment is to throw it away or waste it on women and gambling. As a consequence, he lives in permanent instability, constantly changing from a beggar into a multimillionaire and vice-versa. Thus obscenity in the trilogy acquires an anticapitalist aspect that recalls the notion of 'waste' (*dépense*) formulated by Georges Bataille, according to which unproductive activities such as gambling and perverse sex derive from aristocratic traditions of purposeless expenses.

In his first appearance, in *Recollections of the Yellow House*, João de Deus is an old bachelor living in a boarding house in Lisbon where he struggles against bedbugs and venereal diseases. He slyly manages to pocket the savings of a prostitute living next door, who dies after having a back-street abortion, and plans to elope with the young daughter of the owner of the boarding house. Rejected by her, he tries to rape her, but is caught in the act by her mother. He then throws all the money over the girl's body and goes out into the streets to live as a beggar. Finally taken into a mental hospital, he meets the mysterious Lívio, who gives him his own savings and sets him free.

In *God's Comedy* João has got back on his feet and works as the manager of an ice-cream parlour, thanks to the charity of its owner, Judite. But his skills as an ice-cream maker are soon unmasked by his boss as the activity of a 'sexual pervert', who assaults and disgraces the innocent teenage employees of the business. Thrown back into the streets, João recovers once again in *The Spousals of God*, in which an envoy from God (again Luís Miguel Cintra) offers him a suitcase full of dollars. He thus becomes the proprietor of a huge *quinta* (estate) but ends up losing everything when his beautiful fiancée runs away with his fortune.

With his phlegmatic character, his inscrutable countenance and his disdain for the bourgeois accumulative spirit, João de Deus again resembles the film director, known for his low-budget films. In his early works, he even used to include the negligible figures of his budgets in the credits. The result, rather than precarious, is a peculiar aesthetics based precisely on the visibility of its gaps. In his early career, Monteiro made some films of great visual sophistication, exploring maritime views (*Sophia de Mello Breyner Andresen,* 1969), country landscapes (*Veredas,* 1977) or using techniques of frontal projection (*Silvestre,* 1981), which enabled him to add natural landscapes to the background of studio scenes.

However, the trilogy excels in austerity, as its real aim is to 'document' the director's erotic imaginary as realistically as possible, thus turning money into something superfluous, even counterproductive. Originally, *God's Comedy* was a much more expensive project, in scope and format, with parts shot in France, a large crew and foreign actors. But a month into the shoot, Monteiro suddenly brought it to a halt, discarded the shot footage and restarted it from scratch in his own way, that is, with the same frugal means used in *Recollections of the Yellow House*.

With regard to the genre, Monteiro opts categorically for comedy. *Recollections of the Yellow House* is described in the credits as a *comédia lusitana* (a Luso comedy). The designation is repeated in the title of *God's Comedy*, which parodies the title of Dante's masterpiece, *The Divine Comedy*, bringing it down to the prosaic level of Portuguese daily life. The choice of the comedy genre is consistent with Monteiro's documentary tendencies, for the wit derives from the clash between João de Deus' supreme pretensions and the minute scale of their actual realisation. To attain such an effect, realistic techniques are applied as dogmas to the shaping of the character and his environment.

Crew and cast are witness to the forceful quality of the director's style. For example, Mário Barroso, director of photography in *God's Comedy* and *The Spousals of God*, when asked in an interview (featured in the DVD version of the film) how much freedom he had to do his job, answered categorically: 'None.' Indeed, from *Recollections of the Yellow House* onwards, Monteiro radicalised his view that the camera should not participate in the drama, but only record it. Thus the camera is kept at a considerable distance from its object, often immobile and unable to follow the characters' movements or looks. The result is a predominance of sequence-shots and long shots, and virtually no reaction shots. Close-ups and detail shots are reserved for the few moments when, for example, there is a need to stress the simple, plain beauty of an adolescent face. Artificial lighting is only used when absolutely necessary, whereas natural light is explored as much as possible, sometimes requiring complicated manoeuvres of the camera. Although all sorts of sounds are added in the editing, voices and music tend to be diegetic, recorded on location, and the music is often played during the shoot itself. If you add to such techniques the extensive use of non-professional actors, the real outdoor and indoor locations and the contemporary settings, the result is the perfect realist film, as André Bazin used to describe it.

The inevitable consequence of such a pronounced auteurist style is the narcissistic effect derived from the imposition of the director's sovereign will and the 'divine' quality of the character he portrays. But this is counterbalanced by the hilarious clumsiness with which Monteiro plays his character, reducing him to the trivial status he deserves. The name João de Deus itself reunites the opposite trends of the character's will to power and his actual insignificance. On the one hand, the name is reminiscent of the Portuguese saint São João de Deus (Saint John of God, 1495–1550), the founder of the order bearing his name; on the other, the surname 'de Deus', given to those of unknown family origin and preceded by a common forename such as 'João', suggests a 'João Ninguém', or a nobody. This duplicity is constantly reflected in his behaviour, made up of delusions worthy of Don Quixote and resulting in comic effect.

Let us look at some examples from *God's Comedy*. At the very beginning, Dante's cosmology is parodied with an animated sequence representing the Andromeda galaxy, while a child's voice announces: 'Joaquim Pinto presents *God's Comedy*, João César Monteiro', and laughs when pronouncing the director's name. The galaxy, in this opening (replayed in *The Spousals of God*), looks like a child's toy, and the self-reflexive laugh derides the fact that God is directed and played by João César Monteiro.

The scene preceding the protagonist's first appearance can be read as a discussion about his divine status as the manager of the ice-cream parlour Paraíso do Gelado, or Ice-Cream Paradise. Two of the parlour's young assistants are standing at the door, waiting for Mr João to open it. They see him approaching with 'British punctuality' at a slow pace. The camera, without offering a reverse shot of João, carries on focusing on the girls, while one of them observes: 'The slow movement is essentially majestic,' and the other replies: 'For me it is a waste of time.' In this dialogue, João's (lack of) timing makes him oscillate between the almighty and the useless. Indeed, not only João de Deus, but the films starring him are slow, conferring on both an authoritative as well as an idle quality.

João maintains his solemn pace while supervising the hygiene of his subordinates and checking his business accounts. Upon declaring that 'infallibility is his motto', he sends one of the girls to wash her overall that is stained with menstrual blood, and the other to clean the toilet messed up by the girls themselves, while they make fun of such orders. However, his lessons in tidiness and work-related skills are invariably betrayed by his own clumsiness in funny passages, such as when a tangerine segment he throws into his mouth misses its target, or when he squashes the cone upon which he tries to fit a ball of ice-cream.

The fact that such moments can sometimes reach the sublime seems to suggest, through Monteiro's dialectics, that the character's divine quality resides precisely in his typically human fallibility. A good illustration is the scene in which, in *God's Comedy*, João acts as a swimming instructor to Rosarinho, the new innocent teenager hired by the ice-cream parlour. To the sound of the final aria of Wagner's *Tristan and Isolde*, 'Mild und leise wie er lächelt', Rosarinho, lying on her stomach on a suspended board, moves her arms and legs as if swimming under the direction of João, who waves his arms like an agitated conductor. The inexplicable power of this scene turned it into one of Monteiro's most brilliant moments.

At several moments, João's clumsiness turns into slapstick, starting with his odd and disgusting fetish involving female pubic hair. João keeps a collection of it, carefully wrapped in small envelopes stuck to the pages of an album called 'Book of Thoughts', complete with names, dates and comments. João apparently corresponds with other experts in the field, for, among his letters, there is one containing some of Queen Victoria's private strands. João expands his collection by inviting teenagers for dinner in his home, where he entices them into carefully prepared milk baths. The butcher's youngest daughter, Joaninha, not yet 15 years of age, is one of his guests. While massaging the girl's body with a sponge and looking for her private parts, João ends up falling into the bath head first. After the ritual, he fills up containers with the bathtub milk with his usual clumsiness, spilling milk all over the place. The aim of this activity is twofold: to filter the girl's pubic hair and to reuse the milk in his ice-cream.

Monteiro's trilogy presents several of the characteristics ascribed by Roger Odin to the family or home movie: the temporal indeterminacy; the absence of flashbacks or flash-forwards; the absence of simultaneous actions and parallel montage; the absence of connection shots between the scenes, composed exclusively of relevant shots; the absence of reaction shots; the predominance of long shots; the abundance of sequence-shots; the abrupt cuts; the lack of artificial lighting and other tricks; real indoor and outdoor locations, and so on. Indeed, as observed by the actress Maria de Medeiros, Monteiro used to form something like 'an artistic family' or a friendly relationship among crew and cast which often replaced formal rehearsals (as they comment in the interviews included with the DVD version of *Silvestre*, *God's Comedy* and *Vai e vem* [*Come and Go*, 2003]). Not only the supporting actors, mostly recruited from real life, but also the main cast frequently included lay actors, especially the attractive nymphets, usually first time actresses whose mothers Monteiro had to approach for permission for them to act.

The protagonist João de Deus is mostly shown in intimate, indoor, homely situations. In *God's Comedy*, the ice-cream parlour's young and sexy assistants relate to the manager as their equal. The seductive games as well as the arguments among them resemble those taking place among family members on the brink of incest. The film has therefore the flavour of a home movie, in which João de Deus performs his daily activities, including shopping at the street market, gossiping with neighbours, cooking, maintaining his personal hygiene, bodily needs and onanistic eccentricities, which of course include lots of voyeurism, leading to multiple takes through mirrors, doors and windows. The public exhibition of his intimacy soon becomes exhibitionism, also in the sexual sense. João de Deus' obsession with the size of his phallus, typical of an exhibitionist and alluded to only verbally in the trilogy, receives comic images in *Le bassin de John Wayne* (*The Hips of John Wayne*, 1997) and *Vai e vem*, both starring Monteiro using variations of his heteronyms, such as 'João, o Obscuro' (John, the Obscure) and 'João Vuvu' (Quarrelsome John).

What differentiates the trilogy from the improvisation and incompleteness of the family film is the ritualistic, even sacred character conferred by Monteiro on such minor, daily acts. The ritual of washing and bathing, one of his favourite activities, leads to the revelation of the plain beauty of the teenagers' hands, naked bodies and bare faces. The close-ups, at these points, constitute epiphanic moments which neutralise any sense of perversion or ridicule. In *The Spousals of God*, a long close-up of Joaninha's face, capturing the moment when her eye produces a tear, recalls Carl Theodor Dreyer's famous close-ups in *La passion de Jeanne d'Arc* (*The Passion of Joan of Arc*, 1928), showing the tears spouting out of Maria Falconetti's eyes and rolling down her plain face.

But because everything in Monteiro's work receives a dialectical counterpoint, the purifying, epiphanic bath finds its complement in the eulogy of dirt, an essential component of the erotic act. In *God's Comedy*, detail shots are devoted to the bloody hands of the brutish butcher, who has just removed the skin of a lamb hanging upside down, which also merits a close-up. At the sight of the poor dead animal, João de Deus paraphrases the Bible: 'This is how the sins of the world are taken away.' The recipes minutely prepared by him for his nymphets are part of the erotic ritual, which includes, on his part, the swallowing of pubic hair and the use of the bath milk in the preparation of the ice-cream *paraíso* (paradise), the flavour which made his parlour famous. This is conveniently served to Joaninha in a blue dish in the shape of a vagina.

Despite its documentary techniques and family home-movie characteristics, Monteiro's trilogy cannot be classified simply as realistic. In fact, the use of realist dogmas is aimed at giving credibility to the director's cinephile fantasies, which include, as among the *nouvelle vague* directors, his love for literature, painting and classical music. His films are replete with citations, from Dante to *The Arabian Nights*, from Camões to Jorge de Sena, from Dreyer to Godard. The character of João de Deus draws on autobiographical data as much as on one of the most famous characters of film history: Count Dracula, or Nosferatu, played by the actor

Max Schreck in *Nosferatu – eine Symphonie des Grauens* (*Nosferatu the Vampire*, F. W. Murnau, 1922), an early milestone of the vampire genre. In the trilogy, the presence of *Nosferatu* is so strong that the films acquire fantastic overtones. At the end of *Recollections of the Yellow House*, after escaping from the mental hospital, João de Deus reappears, shrouded in a cloud of dry ice, from inside a trapdoor in the street inadvertently opened by passing kids, just like the vampire emerging from inside the ghost-ship in Murnau's film. In *God's Comedy*, the name of the actor himself is given as Max Monteiro, in an allusion to Max Schreck.

As an actor, Monteiro goes out of his way to resemble Nosferatu. Naturally thin, with a big skull, a huge aquiline nose, deep-set eyes and jug ears, just like Schreck in Murnau's film, he often walks with short, ballet-like steps, with his hands turned down and raised like the vampire's. And like the vampire, he is often shot against the light, especially when he is preparing an assault on one of his nymphets. Thanks to his resemblance to the vampire, the unattractive João de Deus becomes a convincing kind of Don Juan. Indeed, only the irresistible charm of such a supernatural being can explain the fact that so many lovely girls, in the flower of their youth, would be willing to participate in his strange erotic rituals, which include, besides the constant baths and hand washings, eating ice-creams and sweets to saturation point and then sitting on and smashing a big cone full of raw eggs.

However, to counterbalance the fantastic effect, the films always offer a second version of the facts, which radically differ from the one shown from João's ritualistic and intimate point of view. For example, in *God's Comedy*, although Rosarinho looks entirely satisfied after the somewhat painful sex she has just had with Mr João, and enjoys the spicy rice he prepared for her, João is in the end accused by Judite of having 'torn the ass' of her best employee. The same is true of Joaninha, who, after joyfully going through all the stages of the bath and ice-cream rituals with Mr João, probably tells a very different story to her butcher father, who subsequently slashes the hero's face and sends him dying to hospital.

In the police's version of the events, presented in *The Spousals of God*, João is a psychopath, already identifiable from the shape of his skull, who had been sent to the mental hospital for having exposed his genitals to a seven-year-old girl in a public garden. João's former boss in the ice-cream parlour, Judite, is accused of recruiting under-age girls for prostitution. As João does not defend himself from such accusations, arguing instead that his only misfortune was 'to have been born in Portugal', it is up to the spectator to make up his/her mind.

The double perspective works, to a great extent, as social criticism. In *God's Comedy*, João's frauds are nothing more than the mirror of an entire society living off illegal activities.

The innocent Rosarinho lives in a miserable district called Cambodja, where children sell pictures of crimes to the press – and also of Rosarinho naked. The owner of the ice-cream parlour not only trades in girls, but sells her own body to foreign businessmen. The moralist butcher who slashes João's face sells black market meat, falsifying the health inspection stamp with the help of his wife and daughters. Compared to that, João's little sins do not look so terrible.

In conclusion then, Monteiro bequeathed an invaluable contribution to Portuguese and world film history. His originality derives from his courage to express with absolute freedom his obsessive imagination, through which he visited and redefined various genres, among them, the documentary, the comedy, the family movie and the fantastic film. Insisting on his role as an *auteur*, which left little room for creative work on the part of his collaborators, Monteiro immortalised, in his trilogy *Recollections of the Yellow House*, *God's Comedy* and *The Spousals of God*, the character of João de Deus, played by himself as the supreme creator. But the use of comedy and parody relativises the character's pretensions, as they stress his human fallibility.*

* I would like to thank Lisa Shaw, Teixeira Coelho and Stephen Shennan for their useful suggestions to this chapter.

Lúcia Nagib

REFERENCES

Monteiro, João César (1973) 'Minha certidão', *Revista & ETC* (30 April), 8.

Odin, Roger (1995) 'Le film de famille dans l'instituition familiale', in Roger Odin (ed.) *Le film de famille – usage privé, usage public*. Paris: Meridiens Klincksieck, 27–41.

BELLE EPOQUE

FERNANDO TRUEBA, SPAIN, 1992

1992 was a watershed year for Spain's place in the international cultural scene. The Barcelona Olympic games, the International Seville Exhibition and the events taking place in Madrid, European capital for culture, all contributed to consolidate the image of modernity the Socialist government had been trying hard to establish since the early 1980s. If one regards the Spanish Transition as a process of outgrowing the cultural structures of Francoism and building up a new image of the country, it is only at this point that the process is fully completed. In terms of popularity and critical reception, *Belle Epoque* (1992) is one of the key Spanish films of the 1990s and can be studied as the cinematic counterpart of the year's celebrations: it came as a confirmation of the power of the Spanish cultural industry and a sign of change in the approach to film. Not only was the film a healthy box-office hit (it cost 300 million pesetas, and by the end of 1993 it had made almost 700 million, approximately 4,200,000 Euro), it also suggested a new attitude to the past that definitely left behind memories of the Civil War.

The film's exhibition cycle was as long as it was sucessful. It opened in December 1992, to almost unanimous praise (only Tomás Fernández Valenti in the monthly *Dirigido por...* expressed doubts, and it becomes clear from the review this is due to a failure to engage with the film). Ángel Fernández-Santos' review in *El País*, for instance, was mostly a love letter to director Fernando Trueba, in which he poured compliments on Trueba's cinematic skills and regarded the film as perfection itself. Eutiquiano Rodríguez Marchante, the *ABC* newspaper critic, also praised the 'perfection' of the film, underlining the sense of joy it communicated. The film critic of Valencia's listings magazine *Cartelera Turia* dwelled on the libertarianism of the film and on the marked contrast with the 'civil war' films of the 1980s. The reviewer said *Belle Epoque* could convince audiences that the past was not as dark as had been portrayed in the previous decade; that Spanish history had, in fact, usable traits to strengthen a libertarian tradition. In general, critics were generous (some would say excessively so) with the performances, the cinematography and the script (the words 'genius' and 'masterpiece' recur slightly too much). Even if in most instances the film is regarded as a simple assertion of the joys of life, one cannot help reading a political subtext in considering this the path to be followed for new Spanish film, particularly in the way it dealt with early twentieth-century political issues.

Its success was confirmed abroad. The film was subsequently presented at the London Film Festival in November 1993 and then went on to open in the United States. It was Spain's candidate for the 1993 Oscars, was nominated in January by the Academy and won the Best Foreign Film Award in March 1994. Trueba's acceptance speech about not believing in any other god than Billy Wilder and therefore thanking the director of *The Apartment*, was widely covered by the press. He was placing himself *with* old Hollywood and *against* the values of the new Hollywood. Commentators back in Spain tended to underline that the Oscar meant international recognition of Spanish cinema. Trueba's film represented the great white hope for Spanish cinema in contrast with Pedro Almodóvar's *Kika* which had a famously harsh reception in 1993 from the same critical establishment.

As reviewers pointed out, one of the reasons that *Belle Epoque* is important in the context of Spanish film history was the shift it represented in the cinematic treatment of the years preceding the Spanish Civil War. Such a re-apprasial was long overdue and one can feel the reviewers' relief that it had come at last. The encouragment given to literary adaptations in the mid-1980s meant that a number of filmmakers sought to secure funding with adaptations from novels taking place during the years leading up to the war, the war itself and the early 1940s, with strong emphasis on the corruption of the times and the unhappiness of the Spanish people.

Belle Epoque was not the first film to adopt an ironic perspective to deal with periods of strife in Spanish history, but it was the first time that audiences were encouraged to move forward, leaving behind all resentment for the past. Actually, this move away from historical reflection has been criticised by observers abroad: even if one could perceive that the old ways of representing the past were repetitive, this did not mean that one could altogether avoid engaging with Spain's problematic history and escape into arcadia.

The film's title seems to designate a historical period, but it actually refers to a particular time in the lives of the protagonists. The film was set in 1931, rather than in the actual *belle epoque*, the pre-1914 years, when Spain was about to enter a period of relative prosperity and feel for the first time the winds of progress and modernity. In the first instance, Trueba had intended to set his film in 1917, so that the echoes of the Soviet Revolution would be the background to the events, coinciding with the first wave of modernity in Spain. However, the decision to settle for the hopes of the Second Republic actually proved an apt one. In this way, events were brought closer to the audiences, on the threshold of a more recognisable sequence of events, that would end in the Civil War (thus making the film darker in its implications). This has been regarded as a time of hope for the future by left-wing historians. In this way, the title actually refers to the 'beautiful time' in which the potential for personal freedom contributed to a few magical days for the characters in a village, while the echoes of change in the capital suggested that the past could now be left behind.

Trueba has insisted that 'the narrative takes liberties', in the sense that he did not plan to take a straightforward story with a beginning and a clear closure. Although it does appear to be a young man's story, it takes a number of detours and introduces different threads, to the point that the group portrait becomes more important than the arguably sketchy central thread.

Fernando (Jorge Sanz), an ex-seminarist, has deserted from the army in the early days of 1931, seduced by the libertarian ideals of the period. He wanders into the country house of Manolo, an old libertarian painter and intellectual (Fernando Fernán Gómez). The older man represents an open attitude towards politics and sex (he has a *zarzuela* actress-singer wife who is happily living with her lover and only visits once a year). The old stoic and the young man become good friends, but when the arrival of Manolo's daughters is announced, he tries to convince Fernando to leave; as soon as he sees them getting off the train, the young man decides to stay. From this moment, the script shifts focus to the daughters. Having been brought up by Manolo and his eccentric wife, they represent distinct types of 'new' womanhood: Clara (Miriam Díaz-Aroca) is a young and still attractive widow who only misses her husband as a sex object; Violeta (Ariadna Gil) is veterinarian characterised in terms of a dry wit and sober dress-sense; Rocío (Maribel Verdú) is sensual and frivoluous; and Luz (Penélope Cruz), the youngest, a curious and innocent nymphet. Although intended as instances of 'liberated women', they are constructed to a large extent as the projections of a male heterosexual gaze, rather than autonomous characters. The women are as interested in handsome Fernando as the boy is excited by all of them. One narrative thread of the film will be precisely to show Fernando being seduced in turn by each of the women.

Other characters contribute to a rich frieze in which several motives typical of the historical period the film is set in are represented. For instance, the narrative includes Don Luis (Agustín González), a liberal priest who likes to play cards and is obsessed by food, but who is also a man with intellectual leanings, who has exchanged epistolary correspondence with such luminaries as Miguel de Unamuno. He will grow disappointed in the new historical period and commits suicide at the end of the film, under the inflence of Unamuno's bleak essay *El sentimiento trágico de la vida.* Another strand of the plot concerns Juanito (Gabino Diego) who is in love (or in lust) with Rocío. He belongs to a wealthy and strongly traditional family in the village, and is constantly nagged by his mother (Chus Lampreave). Juanito will renounce his beliefs in order to be accepted by Manolo's daughter, but is rejected when he suggests to Rocío that, given that the Republic is approaching, they can practice 'free love'. Eventually, it transpires that Rocío has been using Fernando to make Juanito jealous, although she does intend to marry the latter.

Towards the end of the film, Amalia (Mary Carmen Ramírez), the young women's mother, arrives with her lover (Michel Galabru), waking up the household with a beautiful *zarzuela* aria (from Pablo Sorozábal's *La tabernera del puerto*). After having sex with her husband, thus being unfaithful to the lover (a whimsical instance of the 'world upside down' motive) she shares a few days with her daughters and shows interest in their sex lives, insisting that Clara should marry again and that Violeta should find a woman who loves her. The holiday will come to an end when she leaves for America on an artistic tour (financed by her lover), taking with her Luz and Fernando. The latter has, by now, decided to marry the youngest daughter.

In an interview with Luis Alegre, Trueba has focused on the melancholy ending: 'Both [Fernando and Manolo] know each other and are quite honest. They know that actually the ending is a compromise, that it is a conventional solution, the "logical" ending of the situation. They don't rebel, they accept it, but don't quite believe in it'. Such compromise is developed in the script: we have just seen Don Luis' body hanging at the end of the rope; as Manolo and Fernando part, the former tells the young man that in getting a son-in-law he is losing a friend as if nostalgic for the homosocial bonding the film shows in the early scenes; as they say goodbye to the women, Luz keeps a watchful eye on her sisters, as if to make sure there will not be any more fun with them. It is certainly a return to a harsher reality and the start of a life of responsibility. The 'beautiful days' are definitely over. Clearly now Fernando will have to commit to one woman, enter a life of responsibility and earn a living.

Although there is a strong element of fable in the world as portrayed in the film ('a fairy-tale country' is the name of the aria sung by Amalia), bold traces of history are all too obvious across the canvas, and it does not take much to see how they would subsequently affect the fate of the country. Tensions regarding religion, and between supporters of monarchy and republicans, are constantly acknowledged, although their actual impact is only shown at the beginning and at the end, in an attempt to put brackets of harsh reality to a lighthearted narrative. The film opens with a civil guard killing his father-in-law over a difference of opinion on what to do with the deserter, Fernando, and then committing suicide; near the conclusion, the priest's suicide leaves a bitter taste. Between the opening and the closure, however, Trueba created his own personal world where the seeds of fratricide violence dissolve in the sun-drenched countryside. He has claimed not to be greatly interested in the ideological landscape of the time other than as background to the characters' stories.

Actually, the implications of actual events are somehow softened. One clear instance is the burning of the church early in the film. Church-burning was one of the main causes for friction between right and left in Spain on the eve of the Civil War. The symbolic force of arson together with the desecration of a temple, was deployed by the Catholic Church to illustrate the evil in 'communists and anarchists', who were held responsible. Historical evidence has suggested that personal motivations were as important as political ones in such acts, and in Trueba's film, a sexton burns the church just because Don Luis would not give him a raise: instead of a strong ideological cause, we find a disagreement on salaries and a vindictive employee of the same persuasion as the priest.

Otherwise, José Luis Alcaine's cinematography contributes to represent the house and its surroundings as an amber-coloured world isolated from the pressures of historical process. Camera movements work in a similar fashion. Long takes and group framings insist on the pleasures of the situation. The script has plenty of time for family gatherings, including a picnic by the river, a hunting expedition, several communal meals and popular festivities. Most characters prominently share libertarian politics with a joyful approach to sex. Fernando Trueba has defended this notion of personal freedom as the real target of any politics: 'Characters in the film are not very political, militant or activists. They are just people who represent civilisation in its more concrete sense. They are people without ideologies to sell, who only belive in individual freedom and they exercise it. They are what I understand normality should be like.'

Spanish audiences are aware such hopes were soon to be crushed, but still the film lingers in the optimism of the time. One pertinent image to describe the main body of the narrative is that of the arcadia, the imaginary setting where one can let desire wander without taking hold of any particular object and with no painful consequences. Examples of such arcadias are the imaginary worlds of such plays as Shakespeare's *A Midsummer Night's Dream*, Lewis Carroll's Alice's books and Oscar Wilde's *The Importance of Being Earnest*, where fancy reigns and any threat is easily deflected. Couples are made and broken easily in such surroundings (Fernando claims to have 'fallen in love' after each sexual encounter). In particular, Trueba explains, his inspiration for this particular film comes from Renoir's 1936 *Une Partie de Campagne* in its emphasis on the joys of surface and rejection of psychologism. In doing this, he claims to be moving away from the old ways of approaching history as trauma and shock (as, to some extent, he had done in *El año de las luces* [*The Year of Awakening*, 1986]): the ending may be melancholy but it does not necessarily entail a catastrophe in the lives of the protagonists. His dénouement does not attempt to convince audiences of the need to be more understanding. And he steers clear of any suggestion of preachiness.

The film therefore recreates a point in time that is in many ways unreal. In fact, his arcadia comes across as an alternative to actual events as they actually ensued: it invites the viewer to wonder what if the potential of the period had been realised, rather than interrupted by political tension and the Civil War. The seeds for concord and pleasantness, for mutual tolerance and pacific coexistence were, after all, there, and it is a heritage that he seeks to recover. Trueba deals with the social atmosphere of the time. The presence of carlists, the Church, army deserters, women's emancipation, local elections, anarchism, communism and burning of churches are all alluded to in the film. But there seems to be an effort on the side of screenwriter Rafael Azcona to take out some edge from those issues. In the case of Juanito's mother, who does not share libertarian convictions, the script presents her in such broad strokes as to render her harmless: somewhat awkwardly she will welcome the Republic out of her hate for the Bourbon dynasty. Manolo's family represents a generation of Spaniards who were prepared to carry out such change.

Characters may have diverging allegiances, but these are never deep enough to erupt into violence. In order to articulate this idea, the Trueba trivialises political differences in a way that brings some elements of the script close to Wildean frivolity. Don Luis, the priest, uses rhetoric to advocate tolerance, in a reversal of the consolidated image of the Catholic Church according to liberal discourse. Even more clearly, Juanito will change political allegiances for lust: he starts out as a catholic Carlista under his mother's influence, but his love for Rocío pushes him to renounce religion and reactionary politics, only to return to them once more when Rocío kicks him out of her bed. Political beliefs are something precarious that one can put on or take off as pertinent. The effect is that individuals triumph over ideals.

If politics dominates the film's background, sex is a prominent element in the motivation for characters' actions. Plot parallelisms with Trueba's *The Year of Awakening*, in which the sexual initiation of an adolescent had more tragic undertones, are clear enough. However, the whole attitude is different here. Characters are allowed to gleefully seek sexual satisfaction and they are not punished for it. If anything, sex elicits envy. On the one hand the film follows a 'Rites of Passage' motive: a young man (and it is often a man) discovers sex and desire. In other films dealing with the Civil War years (or the immediate post-war) such transit was often painful, as it had to deal with repression and fear. *Belle Epoque*, on the other hand, celebrates the joys of promiscuity. Trueba has declared that he wanted to recover some idea of 'animality' in the film's view of sex, and this is clearly articulated in the images. Sex is natural and unmediated by social discourse. This is a recurrent motive in the script, perfectly underlined in the *mise-en-scène*. When Manolo asks Fernando to read to him from the Bible, the passage he happens to pick by chance is one in Ecclesiastes that proposes that animals and humans are the same and share the same fate. Trueba shot sex scenes as passionate rubbing of flesh. One of them has the couple embracing in the mud. There is an awareness of sexual repression, but, as in the Arcadia, the perfumed air of the film's location seems to counterbalance any qualms. Again, attitudes toward sex are precarious: Rocío flirts and blithely has sex with handsome Fernando, but will play virgin with unattractive Juanito. The same element of whimsy when representing politics is reflected in sexual matters. Rocío is both coy and sexually agressive, plays around with the idea of virginity but really wants to have it both ways.

Such animality and triviality, however, has its limits in Trueba's worldview, just as the political arcadia could not help but be limited by actual historical events. The force of desire seems to be expressed within the (narrow) boundaries of the heterosexual matrix.

Actually, the film seems to find the idea of homosexuality uncomfortable and does not make any attempt to understand it, even when it represents sexual dissidence. First, in an early sequence, when Manolo invites Fernando to spend the night in the same bed as himself, the young man shows signs of homosexual panic: 'You are not a faggot, are you?' But if the thought of male homosexuality elicits phobic attitudes, the presence of lesbianism needs to be mediated by heterosexist positions. Ariadna Gil's performance as Violeta (a forename that signifies her fate, as violets were a symbol for lesbianism at the time) is sensitive, but the script deals with her sexual orientation in terms of cliché: she is a working woman, who can pull a punch when necessary, likes hunting, dresses with elegance and chops wood; her sister explains she became a lesbian because their mother dressed her as a boy when she was still a child and (even more absurdly) in confession the priest told her about touching her genitals. She has been praised as a character that is accepted by everybody (although Manolo's joy when the possibility of her becoming straight appears speaks volumes of the more traditional attitudes underlying the script). Still, Trueba's treatment of the character is clumsy. A fine example of this is the 'seduction' scene at the carnival. In the original script, revelation of the actual identity of the soldier and the maid is gradual, and Azcona insists on ambiguity: audiences are not supposed to know who these people are, taking them as a real maid and a real soldier during the carnival scene. But in the film several things have changed. Jorge Sanz's awkward embarrassment make it impossible for anybody to imagine him as anything else than a clumsy boy dressed as a maid. But also Trueba has added a prelude to the party that undercuts any possible ambiguity. The scene is problematic because it uses a lesbian character to seek identification with male hetero-sexual audiences.

When Trueba was asked about the slippery representation of gender politics, he did nothing but assert his heterosexuality and claim that 'the only possible fantasies are male fantasies and female fantasies', which denotes a limited view of the possibilities of desire. His attitude is corroborated by the way he deals with what could be an intriguing scene. Violeta fantasises about Fernando being a girl, and seems to be perfectly fooled by the disguise, whereas Fernando is aroused by Violeta because he knows the truth about her sex. Naturally, such distribution of knowledge makes audiences identify with Fernando, whereas Violeta appears to be just fooling herself. Actually, audiences are assured that she might be a heterosexual woman at heart. The film does not even attempt to build a female gaze, even if such desires are articulated in the script. Fernando is presented as the innocent who plays the hunter but in each case is hunted by the women. However, acknowledgement of women's sexual desire in the narrative does not mean that their gaze is articulated in the *mise-en-scène*. Although they all appreciate Fernando's looks, the camera is uninterested in portraying him as an object of desire. The script suggests that desire is mutual, but the cinematic point of view is clearly masculine. Before Rocío has sex with Fernando, we are shown a close-up of her throbbing buttocks, which invite identification with the boy's gaze. There are no equivalents to present Fernando as an object of desire. This in spite of the fact that the plot turns around the idea of women actively desiring handsome men and not men in general (Juanito is not an object of desire in the narrative). We find voyeuristic representations of femaleness without male equivalent.

For all the claims of animality, then, attitudes toward sex are more conventional than libertarian. In the treatment of female characters as desiring subjects, the film seems to offer a feminist agenda. In the diegetic context, these women were at the forefront of sexual liberation. Still, Azcona presents them as victims of misoginistic and sexphobic attitudes. Although they can recognise their own desire (something women at that time were only seldom portrayed as doing), they cannot always act on it without some pretense. One example is the scene by the river when Clara seduces Fernando: in order to have sex with him, she has first to push him into the river.

Belle Epoque undoubtedly carved a new path for historical representation in Spanish cinema, but as Paul Julian Smith suggested in his *Sight and Sound* review, some distinctiveness was being lost: 'It is Trueba's achievement to have shown that a Spaniard can direct a period picture as polished and inoffensive as any in European cinema.' On the verge of globalisation, Spanish cinema was successful and available to all. The new path seemed actually to be the path of least resistance.

Alberto Mira

REFERENCES

Alegre, Luis (1992) 'Entrevista con Fernando trueba', *Dirigido por...*, 208, 38–42.

Fernández-Santos, Ángel (1992) 'Síntomas de maestría', *El país*, 13 December.

Fernández Valenti, Tomás (1992) 'La españa soñada', *Dirigido por...*, 208, 34–7.

Rodríguez Marchante, Eutiquiano (1992) '*Belle Epoque:* Fernando Trueba apunta, dispara y da de lleno en la comedia', *ABC*, 5 December.

Smith, Paul Julian (1994) 'Belle Epoque', *Sight and Sound*, 4, 4, 38.

Trueba, Fernando (1995) 'Entrevista', *El periódico*, 26 March.

Vanaclocha, José (1992) *Cartelera Turia*, 14 December.

VIAGEM AO PRINCÍPIO DO MUNDO JOURNEY TO THE BEGINNING OF THE WORLD

MANOEL DE OLIVEIRA, PORTUGAL, 1997

In Manoel de Oliveira's *Viagem ao princípio do mundo* (*Journey to the Beginning of the World*, 1997), an aging film director and three younger actors travel across northern Portugal. Through reminiscences, stops at places known in the past and a visit to an isolated village, their journey traverses, in a sort of metaphorical time travel, multiple personal and national temporalities. Rather than 'real' time travel, as one might find in science fiction, Oliveira's journey to the beginning of the world involves travel to a time of identity formation, seen in both retrospective and prospective terms. It is a film of return, reminiscence and *le temps perdu* as the director moves inexorably toward the end of his life. At the same time, it is a film of discovery, hope and transformation as one of the actors connects with his roots and begins to understand his own identity in a way that he never had before.

The film is deceptively simple. The director Manoel, played by Marcello Mastroianni (1924–96) in his last screen role, and his companions, who are making a film in Portugal, have embarked on a journey so Afonso (Jean-Yves Gautier) – a French actor of Portuguese descent – can visit places his father, who left Portugal during the Spanish Civil War, had told him about, but that he himself had never seen. In particular, he wants to meet his father's sister, Maria Afonso (Isabel de Castro), who still lives in Lugar do Teso, near Castro Laboreiro in the extreme north of the country. Accompanying Manoel and Afonso are Judite and Duarte, played by Oliveira regulars Leonor Silveira and Diogo Dória, respectively. Along the way, the actors learn that Manoel also intends to revisit some of the places of his youth. Manoel de Oliveira himself is the driver. Although he does not appear frequently, and he does not speak, his appearances are sufficient for the spectator to draw the appropriate connection between him and his alter ego, the fictional director played by Mastroianni. They have the same first name, they wear similar floppy brimmed hats, and at some points the *mise-en-scène* aligns them in such a way to make it seem as if one is the shadow or visual echo of the other (Manuel Cintra Ferreira writes that at such moments Mastroianni, in the foreground, seems like an 'amplification' of Oliveira, who remains discretely in the background).

The journey thus develops two distinct but closely related dramatic lines. The first, which goes from the beginning of the film until the group's arrival in Lugar do Teso, involves Manoel's nostalgic return, as along the way he reminisces about the people and places of his youth: the Jesuit boarding school across the river from Caminha, the statue of Pedro Macau, and the Grand Hotel de Pezo, where Manoel would go with his brothers when he was an adolescent. The second part, which takes place largely in Lugar do Teso, focuses not on physical travel, but rather on the (re)establishment of family ties and the transformation of identity. Afonso's journey is not precisely the same as Manoel's, even though they are on the road together. The actor had never been to Portugal before, although his father, who had fled the harshness of the area in his youth, had told him much about it. His desire was to go to Lugar do Teso, and to meet what was left of his father's family. Whereas Manoel's trip is characterised by return, on the one hand, and distance and impossibility, on the other, Afonso's is one of discovery, increasing proximity and hopeful possibility.

The film is based loosely on true stories: Manoel de Oliveira's youth in northern Portugal, and the experience of actor Yves Afonso, the son of a Portuguese emigrant to France, who traveled to Portugal in 1987 to participate in a Franco-Portuguese film production, Paulo Rocha's *O Desejado-As Montanhas da Lua* (*Les Montagnes de la Lune, Mountains of the Moon*, 1987). A strikingly profound variation on the road movie, *Journey to the Beginning of the World* has little concern with showing the beautiful landscapes its characters traverse. Its focus, rather, is on the interactions among the characters themselves and on questions of memory, aging, time and identity. Sequences frequently take place within the confined space of their car, and when they do stop along the way, the emphasis is on dialogue – mostly in French – rather than action. This is in tune with Oliveira's conception of the cinema, in which language is as important as image. Both are constructed discourses, *representations* of the 'real' world, and both are essential cinematic elements, although one may have precedence over the other in specific sequences.

Also in tune with his notion of the cinema, with very few exceptions Oliveira's camera is static. This does not mean that the film itself is static, for it most certainly is not. Movement takes multiple forms in *Journey to the Beginning of the World*: shots from a fixed camera looking out the back window of the moving car, the movement of objects or people in the frame, cuts from one shot to another and, perhaps most importantly, the movement of language and ideas. The film is replete with historical and literary references, providing a historical density that allows it to go beyond the existential issues confronting its personages to a broader focus on questions involving language and the nation.

The film opens with a recurring visual motif: a shot looking out from the back window of the car. In this case the shot – a dizzying 71 seconds – focuses on the highway. No scenery, just the gray pavement divided by single or double white stripes, with an occasional arrow indicating a turn lane, and the wheels of other cars going in the other direction. Similar shots provide transitions between the film's narrative blocks, as the car moves forward and the highway and countryside recede. Accompanied by the atonal music of Emmanuel Nunes, these transitions provide a distancing affect, as if the automobile and its passengers were in fact traveling into the past. In the words of Stephen Holden, 'As the car glides through the countryside, the camera is always pointed back, and the pictures of the world literally receding have a piercing poignancy.'

With the camera still focused on the road, the initial dialogue begins *in media res*, presenting some of the film's major themes: age and ageing, death, memory, *saudade*, atavism, and identity. The dialogue foregrounds the question of age, as Judite and Manoel talk about age differences. Their divergent attitudes concerning the matter reflect their respective ages. Manoel insists on the impact of ageing because he experiences it daily. He walks with a cane, he feels the deterioration of the body, even if his mind remains strong, and he knows that death is not far away. Despite the fact that he is a respected film director ('a respected *old* director', in his words), he also knows that age and illness keep people apart, and that the young prefer the company of the young, leaving the old behind. The question of age and death is made much more poignant by the fact that Mastroianni died not long after filming *Journey to the Beginning of the World*, which is dedicated to him.

Judite, on the other hand, attempts to dismiss the issue of age, perhaps because it does not yet affect her directly. Young, intelligent and beautiful, she can look optimistically toward the future, and she therefore has the freedom to be ironic, sarcastic and even sexually suggestive, as well as to make light of Manoel's concerns. Even her clothes – a white and blue outfit with a sailor's motif – express a rather ironic perspective on the journey. Her mildly and playfully seductive attitude leads Duarte, who often provides his companions with the historical or cultural context of what they are seeing or saying, to compare her somewhat hyperbolically to the Biblical Judith, who charmed and murdered the Assyrian general Holofernes. Fortunately, the director Manoel keeps his head.

Closely related to age is the question of memory. Jonathan Romney has referred to *Journey to the Beginning of the World* as perhaps the 'most Proustian' film ever made. It deals with some of the phantasms of the past which have left significant traces in the present, but which are never completely attainable. In Romney's words, this 'intensely philosophical film … could only have been made by a director old enough to know memory not as an abstraction but as a reality laden with a lifetime's existential weight'. Manoel's return to places he had known in the past is impossible, and not only because of the inexistence of 'real' time travel. Things and places have changed or are out of reach. The boarding school he had attended is on the far side of the river, and it can only be seen clearly with binoculars. The statue of Pedro Macau is not where he remembers it being, and it has lost an arm to vandals. The Grand Hotel in Pezo, where he had vacationed when he was an adolescent, is now a crumbling ruin.

The first stop along the road is in Caminha, across the Minho River from the Spanish city of La Guardia, where Mastroianni's Manoel – and Manoel de Oliveira – studied in a Jesuit boarding school at the age of 10 or 11. Reminiscing about certain formative moments of his past, Manoel recalls the harsh conditions of the school, the discipline and punishment to which he and the other students were subjected (the Jesuits were 'merciless', he says), sin or sinful thoughts and confession. As the camera accompanies a crew team rowing smoothly across the water, Manoel talks about the fear he felt when he had to cross the river in a small boat in order to return home for the holidays. The waves made them feel as if they were at sea, and he feared drowning. The boatman, however, was calm. In Manoel's words, he was 'small and tough, thin and dry', but he seemed like a giant.

In addition to elements of Manoel's past and his interactions with his traveling companion, this initial sequence also begins to lay the groundwork for a historical reading, although the film has no pretense of elaborating a full-blown allegorical perspective. In the course of the conversation, however, are references to the Portuguese monarchy, the Republic, the Jesuits (who were expelled in 1910, shortly after the beginning of the Republic) and, somewhat implicitly, Portugal's relations with Spain. It is no coincidence that one of the travelers is named 'Duarte', perhaps after Portugal's philosopher-king who ruled from 1433–38 and who supported the expeditions of his brother, Prince Henry the Navigator (1394–1460), who, acting like a human giant, led the ships of a 'small and tough, thin and dry' country on some of the most important navigations of European history.

The following transitional sequence, with the fixed camera again focusing out of the back window of the car, transpires initially in silence, with neither dialogue nor music, as the vehicle and its occupants drive through the gates and passageways of the citadel in Valença do Minho. The silence represents a signal for the spectator to focus on the image, which gives an even greater sense of travel into the past. It is only after they have passed the citadel that Duarte provides contextual information, saying that it has been dated to a fortified camp from early Roman times. When Judite affirms 'those days are gone', Duarte responds by saying, 'Between eras, there lies a time which becomes the present', referring both to the inexorability of time and to the simultaneous existence of diverse temporalities, or at least remnants thereof.

As they continue on their journey, Manoel remembers a statue he had once seen along the road when traveling with his father and brothers. The statue is of a figure called Pedro Macau, a man on one knee supporting a huge log on his shoulders. As indicated above, the statue is not precisely where Manoel remembers it to be, and it has changed: it has lost an arm, and the trellis that once existed on top of the log is no longer there. A local woman tells them a poem about Pedro Macau, who is in perpetual 'exile' because he cannot put the log down. Critics tend to see the statue as a symbol of the human condition, human suffering or for the inability to escape one's past or destiny. Stephen Holden, however, interprets it as a 'symbol of the aged director himself carrying on in a world that barely seems to notice'.

Given the film's proclivity for historical suggestion, one might venture to add yet another layer of interpretation. At one point in the conversation with the local woman, Manoel associates Pedro Macau with both his father and the 'small and tough' boatman who would ferry him across the Minho River, as well as with Afonso's father, about whom we know little at this point. Afonso suggests that they are all 'as tough as giants'. Duarte then asks the woman why he is called Pedro Macau, which serves as an invitation for the spectator to reflect on the episode. One might reasonably see the name in historical and geographical terms associated with Portuguese navigations to the Far East, for they used what is now known as Macau as a staging area as early as 1516, and they set up more permanent settlement in 1557. The expansion of the Portuguese empire in the Age of Navigation contrasts mightily with its rather marginal position in today's Europe, almost as if it is exiled from its own past.

The film's most poignant sequence takes place outside what is left of the Grande Hotel de Pezo. This is the first sequence in which Oliveira's camera becomes autonomous, so to speak. Up to this point, it had either been fixed, or had moved in point-of-view shots, such as when Duarte or Judite look through binoculars at the boarding school in La Guardia. As they drive through Pezo toward the hotel, Manoel's facial expression reveals a certain air of restrained excitement, but when the car moves through its gates the image becomes darker, presumably because the car is driving under trees. The shift from light to dark, however, is metaphorical, anticipating the sequence that is about to begin and expressing the long but inexorable transition from youth to old age.

When the car stops and the passengers exit, the camera is at a distance. As the group begins to move away from the car, Emmanuel Nunes' plaintive piano begins to accompany the scene. The camera tracks as they walk slowly across the shaded grounds, with Oliveira hovering silently in the background. The camera then takes off on its own in a low-angle traveling shot to the left along the hotel's decaying walls. After shifting back to the group walking along silently, it then travels back to the right, offering yet another perspective on the decay. Manoel then walks off by himself. He sees a flower on the branch of a small tree, and he tries to reach it but is unable to do so. A well-worn metaphor for youth, his inability to reach the flower visually represents the impossibility of return. When he walks back to his traveling companion, he appears even frailer than before, saying simply, '*Que désolation*.' One can only wonder if he is obviously referring to the hotel, and probably to himself as well. The ruins, he says, are 'the future of a heady past'. But he is also referring to the modern world, with its destructive tendencies.

He recalls the groans of a boy with typhoid fever who had once been at the hotel. Now, the hotel is no more – its garden is gone, there are no more doors or windows – and all he can remember are the groans, which are engraved in his heart. The illness, however, is the illness of the modern world, which allows such destruction to happen. When Judite suggests that they are simply ruins to those who did not know the hotel, but not for Manoel since he can remember, he objects, implying that the pain is much worse for those who can compare the past and the present. Manoel knows that for him it is the end of the road; no matter how hard he tries, he cannot relive the past. The visit to the Grande Hotel also represents the end of his centrality in the film, which shifts its attention to Afonso.

Afonso's story begins in earnest only after the group leaves Pezo, where he tells Manoel that the past they had been discussing was his (Manoel's) and that it has nothing to do with him, since it is not his father's past. Although Afonso tells his companions his father's story – his departure from Portugal, his arrest in Spain, his escape to France, his hardship and successes, his early death – the narrative shift takes place only after the group stops at a bridge between Castro Laboreiro and Lugar do Teso. In this sequence, not a word is spoken. After they get out of the car, Manoel and his driver stand side by side – for the first time in the film – on the bridge by which they stopped, while Afonso, Duarte and Judite walk from the bridge, which is relatively modern, to a much older, more primitive bridge a few yards away. The sequence's final shot – looking through the old bridge to the more modern one – is again metaphorical, representing not only transition, but also coexistent or superimposed temporalities. 'Between eras, there lies a time which becomes the present.'

Lugar do Teso is an extremely isolated village that seems to have stopped in time. Indeed, within the context of the film, it is the 'beginning of the world'. There, Afonso and his fellow travelers meet his aunt, Maria Afonso, who, according to Stéphane Bouquet, is a veritable phantasm, 'carrying with her the mystery of the origins'. Toughened by a hard life, she seems to belong to an earlier, almost pre-modern age, at the beginning of the nation and the inception of the family. One should remember that the word *princípio* in Portuguese has at least two meanings: 'beginning' and 'principle'. Maria Afonso represents both the beginning and the fundamental or underlying principle of the world through and to which Afonso and the others travel.

Their initial encounter takes place in the house of Maria Afonso's daughter-in-law, Cristine (Cécile Sanz de Alba), a young French woman who had married Maria Afonso's son, and Afonso's cousin, Joaquim. The encounter is marked by suspicion and difficulty in communication, since Afonso does not speak Portuguese, and Maria Afonso repeatedly asks, '*Por que não fala nossa fala?*' ('Why can't he speak our language'). They can only communicate indirectly and imperfectly, through translation. Finally, unable to convince her that he is in fact her nephew, Afonso stands, takes off his coat, walks over to his aunt, asks her to put her hand on his arm, and tells her that what matters is blood, not language, and that they have the same blood in their veins.

The following sequence takes us to the very origins of the Portuguese nation, to the beginning and principle of the world. Afonso asks to go to the cemetery to see where his ancestors are buried. Maria Afonso wants to change clothes before she goes, so the group goes up the hill to her house. As they walk, Duarte asks José, Maria Afonso's husband, why all of the mailboxes have the name Afonso on them. He replies that they are all descendents of Afonso Henrique the founder of Portugal. In the ensuing conversation, which takes place in a dark house without electricity, Maria Afonso and José recognise that when they die, there will be nothing left, since the young people have left and are not interested in the kind of life they lead.

Language, ancestry and nation are traditionally seen as the pillars of identity. But are things really that simple? Despite Afonso's successful encounter with his aunt, *Journey to the Beginning of the World* in fact problematises the question of identity, particularly through a number of references to contemporaneous wars in Bosnia and Croatia, where conflicts generated by deep-seated ethnic identities resulted in the hundreds of thousands of deaths and the horrendous resurgence of ethnic cleansing. Atavism can clearly have a positive side, as Afonso's journey to his roots, but it can also be much, much darker. In the film's initial sequence, Manoel's reference to Sarajevo leads Duarte, who is looking directly into the camera, to say simply 'apocalypse now', in an explicit reference to Francis Ford Coppola's 1979 film. Later, when contemplating the ruins of the Grande Hotel do Pezo and discussing the perhaps fatal illness of the modern world, Duarte compares the situation to 'Sarajevo without the bullets'. Even Maria Afonso, who reveals an abiding concern with the negative impact of war, refers to the situation in Croatia.

And what about the question of language and the nation? Jonathan Romney suggests that *Journey to the Beginning of the World* is 'an entirely unsentimental enquiry into endangered national identity, by a director who has made a speciality of being linguistically and culturally polyglot. [It] has mainly French dialogue, with most of the Portuguese translated back into French for Afonso's benefit.' In this sense, the historical subtext that runs throughout the film – with references to events ranging from the nation's founding to the European Union – becomes even more significant, especially when seen in relation to comments, made at certain moments of the film, that Portuguese is not important in France and that 'nobody cares about us', or references, starting with Afonso's father, to emigration to other countries.

Although it raises all of these issues, at least tangentially, *Journey to the Beginning of the World* is not a political film *per se*. It focuses on personal and existential issues related to the passing of time, aging and death. Manoel's journey to the beginning of the world is a journey toward death, a fact made painfully clear in one of the final sequences in the film, which takes place in a cemetery. As Afonso and his aunt Maria Afonso kneel together, their hands clasped, Manoel walks off by himself. In a long shot, the camera focuses on him surrounded by gravestones. As he slowly walks off-screen, back toward the rest of the group, all that is left are the gravestones. Oliveira's film, however, does not end on this sombre note. Rather, it recognises death as the last act of life, which is characterised by multiple and constant transformations and modulations around a core whose roots are deeper than one might realise.

Randal Johnson

REFERENCES

Bouquet, Stéphane (1997) 'Histoire de fantômes portugais', *Cahiers du cinéma*, 514, June, 72–3.
Ferreira, Manuel Cintra (1998) 'Viagem ao Princípio do Mundo (1997)', Lisboa: Cinemateca Portuguesa. Ciclo Manoel de Oliveira: 90 Anos, 18 December, Textos Cinemateca Portuguesa, 59.

Holden, Stephen (1998) '*Journey to the Beginning of the World*: Fading in a World That Seemed Eternal', *The New York Times*, 26 June.

Romney, Jonathan (1998) 'Eye Travel', *Sight and Sound*, 7, July, 34–5.

TORRENTE: EL BRAZO TONTO DE LA LEY TORRENTE: THE DUMB ARM OF THE LAW / TORRENTE 2: MISIÓN EN MARBELLA TORRENTE 2: MISSION IN MARBELLA

SANTIAGO SEGURA, SPAIN, 1998/2001

What would be the (popular) appeal of a fascist, racist, sexist and alcoholic protagonist for Spanish audiences? Of a 'filthy, petty, loathsome, despicable' character'? Such is the character of José Luis Torrente, or simply Torrente, a Spanish ex-policeman, created and played by the film's director Santiago Segura. And not only once but twice since both *Torrente, el brazo tonto de la ley* (*Torrente: The Dumb Arm of the Law*, 1998) and *Torrente 2: misión en Marbella* (*Torrente 2: Mission in Marbella*, 2001) were phenomenal successes. The question is: how can one account for this filmic character becoming a phenomenon in times of political correctness and Hollywood blockbusters? Perhaps some of the answers lie, as we shall see, with Santiago Segura whose persona became a symbol in and through popular discourse and whose work has succeeded in addressing a broad popular Spanish audience.

Torrente introduces us to a grubby, disreputable ex-detective preying on African immigrants, unaware of the real crimes (committed by white youths) affecting the streets of Madrid. Lecher that he is, it is not long before he is chasing after his new neighbour, Amparito (Neus Asensi); Torrente wants to get closer to Amparito and enlists her nerdy cousin Rafi (Javier Cámara) as his sidekick. Torrente accidentally finds himself infiltrating a drug ring that is being operated from a Chinese restaurant. By sheer luck he lands the booty and runs off with the money to Torremolinos. *Torrente 2* moves from the urban setting of Madrid to the glamour of sunny Marbella where our hero, in tacky Sonny Crockett clothing, is living the Miami-Vice-style high life with his illicit gains, though an unfortunate spin of the casino wheel sees him down on his luck. He creates a detective agency, 'Investigaciones Torrente', to rebuild his career. This time the plot has the private eye and his new goofy sidekick Cuco (Gabino Diego) unknowingly spoiling the plans of Spinelli (José Luis Moreno), a villainous international terrorist who wants to destroy Marbella in 48 hours.

Segura's directorial début broke box-office records for a Spanish film in the first weeks of release in March 1998 ('*Torrente*, box-office record for Spanish cinema with 1,505 million pesetas', announced *El País*), and throughout its record-breaking run. It became Spain's highest grossing film, grossing 11 million Euro; more than 2.5 million spectators went to see the comic activities of Segura. Its international projection should not be underestimated either: it was successful in Turkey, Italy, Russia, Central and Eastern Europe, and the Low Countries, as well as screening in festivals such as Cannes and Sorrento. Economically, the returns for the producers (Rocabruno España and Andrés Vicente Gómez with 75 per cent, Cartel S.A. with 25 per cent) yielded significant profits, especially given the relatively small budget at Segura's disposal, a mere 375 million pesetas. Professionally, Segura's first feature film was also recognised by the Spanish Academy of Film Arts and Sciences who awarded him the Goya for best new director and rewarded the forgotten 1960s comedy actor Tony Leblanc's work as best supporting actor. The sequel, *Torrente 2*, surpassed all commercial calculations and expectations, becoming once again the biggest-ever domestic hit. *Screen International* (Spain) followed Segura's second venture throughout 2001 grossing 3.5 million euro over its first weekend. In order to give an idea of the scale of Segura's second consecutive success, Jennifer Green resorted to name-dropping: '*Torrente* currently holds the title as the biggest domestic hit ever, and is fourth on the list of all-time top-grossers in Spain behind Fox's *Titanic*, Buena Vista's *The Sixth Sense* and Fox's *Star Wars: Episode I – The Phantom's Menace*.' Segura could by now 'open' a film at the box office and he certainly capitalised on his media profile: his second film wowed cinemagoers (more than five million), and in comparison with its predecessor it significantly increased its box-office takings (over 22 million Euro), this time to be shared by Segura's own production company, Amiguetes Entertainment SL, and Andrés Vicente Gómez's Lolafilms.

In *Hollywood, Hype and Audiences: Selling and Watching Popular Film in the 1990s*, Thomas Austin provides us with a useful term derived from the film industry to explain the phenomenal success of certain Hollywood products: the 'event' film. This term 'is used by the industry to designate the small number of films in any one year which achieve huge commercial success by attracting occasional cinemagoers as well as more frequent viewers'. Austin's study focuses on the relationships between Hollywood, popular media and audiences, as well as the circulation of Hollywood films in Great Britain, in particular *Basic Instinct* (Paul Verhoeven, 1992), *Bram Stoker's Dracula* (Francis Ford Coppola, 1992) and *Natural Born Killers* (Oliver Stone, 1994). Any comparison between Segura and Hollywood is unsustainable in terms of mass appeal and economic muscle. What is of interest is the marketing and self-promotion strategies exploited by the director in the weeks leading up to the release of his films, particularly his 'multiple invitations-to-view to a number of taste publics'. During the marketing blitz leading to *Torrente's* première Segura appeared almost daily in television spots and the press, with his thumbs up and a speech bubble which read: 'This is working, *amiguetes!*' – who these '*amiguetes*' (chums) are and Segura's target audience will soon become clear… Torrente was hailed as a new hero by popular cinema magazines and in national newspapers. The weekend supplement of *El País*, *El País de la tentaciones*, announced his arrival thus: 'Ladies and Gentlemen, Spain has found its new hero: a '*casposo*' [trashy] character typifying the times in which we live.' The coverage in popular film magazines and weekly cultural supplements before its general release was extensive, producing multiple avenues of access to the film. His comeback in *Torrente 2* consolidated his heroic status: '*El héroe español ha vuelto*' ('The Spanish hero is back') as the promotional poster reminded viewers; *Torrente 2*, of course, reaped the benefits based on the familiarity of audiences and the built-in marketing looks of the first film.

The films themselves respond to what Barbara Klinger refers to as the 'dispersible text' in these terms: 'One of the chief activities of commodification … is to pry open the insularity of the text as object and to disperse it into an assortment of elements that can be turned into capital.' Among the filmic elements subject to commodification, she includes characters and stars, subject matter and genre, and style. Austin elaborates upon Klinger's notion and describes it as 'a package designed to achieve commercial, cultural and social reach, by both facilitating and benefiting from promotional and conversational processes of fragmentation, elaboration and diffusion.' Indeed, Segura's vocation for commercial success confirmed his effective publicity and advertising campaigns, and was backed by the word of mouth of the many '*amiguetes*' who watched the film. Moreover, he nurtured this relationship in media appearances and in face-to-face encounters with his fans in his tours of Spain.

Segura is at home in his relationship with popular media and audiences; he is acutely aware of the fundamental aesthetic and economic axioms by which Hollywood operates and is aware too of the impossibility of understanding popular film without reference to the laws of the market – '*la taquilla es la vida*' Segura *dixit*. The popularity of his films earned him enough critical kudos among Spanish film industry circles, the Spanish Academy of Film Arts and Sciences and its official publication *Academia: Revista del Cine Español*, to be invited to write an article entitled '*El cine español no existe*' ('Spanish cinema does not exist'); controversial as it sounds, the article merely emphasised the challenges faced by the Spanish film industry and the need to sell and promote Spanish films in order to compete with Hollywood products. Like many other contemporary Spanish filmmakers, Segura comes across as someone who will try to fuse the commercial appeal of Hollywood aesthetics with Spanish aesthetics. Indeed, the late 1990s and the early 2000s have witnessed a number of 'event films' in Spanish cinema, the most recent being *La gran aventura de Mortadelo y Filemón* (*Mortadelo & Filemon: The Big Adventure*, Javier Fesser, 2003), a film version of the beloved Spanish comic strip heroes of the same name which tapped into the popular tastes of different generations, and *Airbag* (Juanma Bajo Ulloa, 1997), a tongue-in-cheek comedy-cum-thriller, whose political incorrectness caught the eye of Spanish audiences. These are hits that have broken through the hegemony of Hollywood and responded to shifts in audience responses to popular Spanish films. A new generation of Spanish directors (Alex de la Iglesia, Alejandro Amenábar, Icíar Bollaín to name but a few) have been changing the face of Spanish cinema both at home and abroad. Their success has had a significant effect on the willingness of producers and directors to chance their arm in areas traditionally monopolised by Hollywood cinema.

One of America's leading specialist film magazines, *Cineaste*, in collaboration with the Spanish Ministry of Culture's Institute of Cinema and Audiovisual Arts, recently devoted a supplement to contemporary Spanish cinema. *Torrente* is mentioned implicitly in the editorial and reappears in a more explicit manner in a debate between various Spanish filmmakers ('Spanish Filmmakers' Forum'). The editorial's concluding paragraph reads as follows: 'Like all national cinemas, however, the Spanish film industry faces many serious challenges. Hollywood interests dominate national exhibition and distribution, and the production sector has an uneasy relationship with television. Many young Spanish viewers attend the movies nowadays mainly to see neo-vulgar comedies, some of which star a not-too-bright cop who is a self-proclaimed fascist, male-chauvinist and racist.'

Torrente – alluded to, yet not specifically mentioned – is the representative of a contemporary trend of Spanish cinema of neo-vulgar comedies (a term coined by Núria Triana-Toribio) which arguably responds to the (coarse, vulgar) tastes of 'young Spanish viewers', many would say a young male spectatorship. Interestingly, this popular hero is appropriated by an international specialised film magazine, working within the bounds of so-called respectable journalism, to frame a discussion on the current situation of Spanish cinema. The section 'Spanish Filmmakers' Forum' nevertheless poses crucial questions about the commercial success of popular film: 'What problems exist for Spanish cinema in this time of globalisation? For example, is Spanish cinema losing its national character? Is there a "Europeanisation" or "Hollywoodisation" of national production? Is the notable commercial success of "neo-vulgar" comedies such as *Airbag* and *Torrente 2* negatively affecting cinematic production of a more artistic nature?' For the purposes of this chapter, we can focus on the last question, since the cultural stakes underpinning it display not only significant and value-laden suppositions about popular and art cinema but also frame the discussion in terms of what might or might not constitute a legitimate Spanish cinema. An implicit rejection of the 'popular aesthetic' –'negatively affecting cinematic production of a more artistic nature' – follows on from the editorial's reference to the simple and vulgar taste formations of those watching Segura's films. Popular cinema and popular tastes are rendered illegitimate; a 'cinematic production of a more artistic nature' would, on the other hand, represent a legitimate film culture. Such notions of legitimate or illegitimate culture are constructed through a cultural logic of taste, as Pierre Bordieu reminded us in *Distinction: A Social Critique of the Judgement of Taste*. The apparently disinterested realm of a specialist film magazine such as *Cineaste*, therefore, raises issues of taste, aesthetics and canon formation. Whilst aesthetic values are always open to debate, the ironic and self-deprecating publicity tagline run by Segura for the marketing and promotion of *Torrente*, 'Just when you thought Spanish cinema was getting better...' hints not only unabashedly at issues of taste but also at that type of criticism that rejects popular cultural forms on aesthetic grounds. Shifts in audience response to popular Spanish films are bringing with them shifts in the cultural status of cinema and changes in established canons of taste and categorisation.

In the wake of the phenomenal success of *Torrente*, it is no coincidence that Segura pays parodic tribute to the Bond phenomenon by sending up the 007 films in the opening credits of *Torrente 2*. A savvy choice on the part of Segura since Bond, the popular hero *par excellence* and resilient cultural icon of popular film, has been throughout the decades a highly profitable brand name. However, our detective is not 'a guru of male style, an emblem of glamour ... a loaded symbol of sex and violence', as Agent 007 is described in the first pages of *The James Bond Phenomenon: A Critical Reader*. Nonetheless, Torrente has become a cultural icon of Spanish popular film. In fact, the James Bond over-the-top spoof resonates beyond the screen image and allows an analysis of the 'Torrente phenomenon' along the lines of Tony Bennett and Janet Woollacott's seminal work on the 'Bond phenomenon' in *Bond and Beyond: The Political Career of a Popular Hero*, in which the focus is on contextual issues such as the cultural significance of the Bond films and novels, their sociological dimension and the investment of the readers and spectators in screen characters. The Bond figure is grotesquely re-shaped (or mis-shaped) and re-worked in the rotund figure of Torrente; it becomes a playful appropriation and vengeful re-deployment of the received screen popular image.

Fanzines, comic books and porn magazines, television games and variety shows all formed a central part of Santiago Segura's growing artistic experiences. One can turn to

Torrente: The Book and the website of the Santiago Segura Official Friends Club (SSOFC) in order to trace his emergence throughout the 1990s. Segura's three shorts, together with *Relatos de la medianoche* (*The Midnight Tales*, 1989), which have gained cult status, are collected in a box-set limited edition of 666 copies entitled *History: Santiago Segura – Corto Greatest Hits*. Evilio, Segura's first character and protagonist of two of these low-budget shorts (*Evilio* [1992] and *El Purificador [Evilio vuelve]* [*Vigilante (Evilio Returns)*], 1994), as well as the Goya-winning *Perturbado* (*Insane*, 1993), came out in subcultural society in the pages of underground publications such as the fanzines *2000 Maniacos*, *Quatermass*, *Zineshock*, *Mondo Brutto*, youth culture publications devoted to music (*Ruta 66, Subterfuge*), comics, as well as other circuits of exhibition and reception like the horror film festivals of San Sebastián and Sitges. The first half of the 1990s made Segura the standard-bearer of 'Iberian trash cinema' in the eyes of horror fans. His first shorts already anticipate the use of a personal take on gore and splatter generic codes and conventions, black humour and *mise-en-scène* as fundamental aspects of his cinematic culture. Segura references American horror classics such as *Psycho* (Alfred Hitchcock, 1960), *The Texas Chainsaw Massacre* (Tobe Hooper, 1974), *Halloween* (John Carpenter, 1978) and *Friday the 13th* (Sean Cunningham, 1980), as well as the Spanish horror products of the late 1960s and early 1970s. As Núria Triana-Toribio and Andrew Willis have each argued, in these shorts Segura is rejecting certain value judgements and aesthetic criteria underpinning the tastes of mainstream and specialised film critics through his use of the horror genre. In Willis' words, 'Segura uses the horror genre, and an excessive take on its codes and conventions, as a way of celebrating that rejection and indeed opposition to the critical establishment sense of "good taste".' Triana-Toribio would say that Segura is 'self-consciously rejecting the Miró legislation model of "good films"'.

Segura had by the mid-1990s established his subcultural reputation and his fandom profile was up-and-coming. His work tapped into specific taste publics, into social groups organised around shared cultural interests, preferences and practices, that is, into subcultures. Alex de la Iglesia's first two films also showed a distinct fan-sensibility and contributed to establish the cinematic pedigree of Segura; *Acción mutante* (*Mutant Action*, 1993) transformed Segura into a desirable supporting actor and *El día de la bestia* (*The Day of the Beast*, 1995) meant his coming of age as a protagonist, as well as being recognised as the best newcomer by the Spanish film industry in 1996. By the end of the 1990s Segura had become a popular figure. The success of *Torrente* transcended the expected spectatorship of the (male) '*amiguetes*' circle, millions by now, and his films moved into mainstream, commercial cinema. Along the way, Segura succeeded in aggregating several specific markets to his group of friends.

Meritxell Esquirol and Josep Lluís Fecé have defined Segura's films as the first Spanish blockbusters and as multimedia products, that is, a product of contemporary cultural industries, which should be analysed in terms of the role it plays 'in the audience's everyday life and its links with other forms of entertainment'. In other words, films like *Torrente* and *Torrente 2* acknowledge the importance of consumption practices, of how audiences use and make meanings from the commodities they consume. The interactive play between the films and the spectator is further promoted and exploited via the merchandising of the 'Torrente' brand: the movie book, VHS, DVD, videogames, Internet and fan sites. Both the movie book and the DVD offer film enthusiasts the possibility to acquire exclusive extra-textual information about the world of *Torrente*. Computer-mediated communications and the interactive nature of the Internet were well exploited by Segura and his production company Amiguetes Entertainment SL for the launching of *Torrente 2*.

The SSOFC website, to which almost 1000 users are subscribed at present, was created in August 2002 as a result of the fusion of its namesake and '*La página no oficial de Santiago Segura*' ('The Unofficial Santiago Segura Page'). It is not the intention here to study this fan community (age, gender, reasons, motivations) but rather to consider briefly a fan-produced text – the SSOFC fanzine – since it provides a specific scenario of reception in which a fragmented community of self-confessed fans actively exchange responses to their favourite text. The electronic fanzine is the electronic equivalent of the underground printed publications typical of subcultures, with which Santiago Segura himself was, and still is, well acquainted.

The fanzines were posted by SSOFC on March 2001, October 2001 and May 2002. Like any other marginal publication, its frequency, dependent as it is on the individual tastes, predilections and self-management of the authors, occurs at irregular intervals. Issue 1, for instance, is mainly a tie-in to *Torrente 2*; apart from publicising Santiago Segura's second directorial venture, the fanzine reviews other commercial spin-offs such as the films' soundtracks. Regular sections display information about Segura which will be complemented in future issues, editorials, collaborations from fans (in this particular issue an Argentinean fan reports on the success of Segura overseas), related links, quizzes, letters to the editor, and '*el rincón de Evilio*' (a column in which the eponymous psycho-killer expresses his opinions on popular topical issues). The editorial of the October 2001 issue provides the fans with a sense of belonging to the Santiago Segura virtual community in true fannish rhetoric: 'Belonging to the SSOFC is to be congenial to art, culture, humour and fraudulent feelings. *Amiguetes*, you should never forget that behind a *cutre* [vulgar] and *casposo* [trashy] Torrente there is a knowing Santiago Segura full of eccentric nonsense'.

The cultural impact of Santiago Segura and his creation 'Torrente', however, is undeniable. The twenty-first century cultural phenomenon of Torrente was commented upon in the daily national press: *El Mundo* acknowledged that its extraordinary success had 'transformed its protagonist into a *fin-de-siècle* media celebrity'; *El País* included a profile of Segura to account for the unclassifiable and excessive personality of this '"alternative" sociological model: mordant, scatological, randy, nonsensical and lucid'. The box-office pull of the films made Segura a bankable name for the industry, placing him, as the mainstream film magazine *Cinerama* observed in its summer issue, amongst the fifty most powerful people in the contemporary world of Spanish film. Shortly after the first weeks of its success, the phenomenon of Torrente generated a new critical and popular vocabulary: from the self-explanatory '*torrentemanía*' and box-office oriented '*torrentazo*', to adjectives denoting a cinematic style, '*torrentiano*'. Critics, audiences and fans have also generated a lexicon around the persona of Santiago Segura himself – '*santiagoseguril*', '*segurismo*'. Cultural studies commentators have turned their attention to the persona of Santiago Segura who, according to Triana-Toribio, 'is possibly the most ubiquitous figure in contemporary Spanish culture; a celebrity to whom all generations have been exposed in both Spain and Spanish-speaking Latin America, particularly in the last seven years via television, the internet and cinemas'. *Torrente* and *Torrente 2* have certainly made their mark in the contemporary canon of Spanish cinema. As cultural landmarks of the turn of the twenty-first century, the two Santiago Segura vehicles invite us to engage with other ways of judging the cultural significance of a film, and to be more open in our understanding of the pleasures of popular forms and of audience investments in specific texts.

Antonio Lázaro-Reboll

REFERENCES

Austin, Thomas (2002) *Hollywood, Hype and Audiences: Selling and Watching Popular Film in the 1990s*. Manchester: Manchester University Press.

Bennett, Tony and Janet Woollacott (1987) *Bond and Beyond: The Political Career of a Popular Hero*. Basingstoke: Macmillan.

Bourdieu, Pierre (1984) *Distinction: A Social Critique of the Judgement of Taste*. London:

Routledge.

Cinerama (2000) 'Los 50 más poderosos del cine español', 93, July/August, 36–46.

El mundo (1999) 'Las mejores películas nacionales de los noventa', December 24, 17.

El país (1998) 'Torrente, récord de recaudación del cine español con 1.505 millones', www. elpais.es/p/d/19981117/cultura/torren.htm (accessed 17 November).

Esquirol, Meritxell and Josep Lluís Fecé (2001) 'Un freak en el parque de atracciones: *Torrente, el brazo tonto de la ley*', *Archivos de la filmoteca*, 39, October, 27–39.

Green, Jennifer (2001) '*Torrente 2: Mission in Marbella*', *Screen International*, April 6–12, 1303, 312.

Klinger, Barbara (1989) 'Digressions at the Cinema: Reception and Mass Culture', *Cinema Journal*, 28, 4, 3–19.

Lindner, Christoph (ed.) (2003) *The James Bond Phenomenon: A Critical Reader*. Manchester: Manchester University Press.

Triana-Toribio, Núria (2003) *Spanish National Cinema*. London: Routledge.

Willis, Andrew (2004) 'From the margins to the mainstream: trends in recent Spanish horror cinema', in Antonio Lázaro-Reboll and Andrew Willis (eds) *Spanish Popular Cinema*. Manchester: Manchester University Press.

TODO SOBRE MI MADRE ALL ABOUT MY MOTHER 23

PEDRO ALMODÓVAR, SPAIN, 1999

Regarded by many as Pedro Almodóvar's finest film, *Todo sobre mi madre* (*All About My Mother*, 1999) won the Oscar for best foreign language film in March 2000. In many ways, the film represents a culmination, and perhaps a distillation, of Almodóvar's directorial style, and of themes addressed repeatedly in his work as a whole. Where some of the earlier films clearly reflect Almodóvar's learning curve in cinematic technique, be it the amateurish inventiveness in his first film, *Pepi, Luci, Bom y otras chicas del montón* (*Pepi, Luci, Bom*, 1981), or the high-gloss aesthetic of *Mujeres al borde de un ataque de nervios* (*Women on the Verge of a Nervous Breakdown*, 1988), here the directing is perfectly balanced, each shot and each choice in the *mise-en-scène* appearing the most natural and appropriate. Almodóvar's debt to Hollywood genre films remains apparent in *All About My Mother* which transcribes classic melodrama into a European, contemporary, post-feminist version, where friends replace family, and the world of drug-addicts and transsexuals substitutes home and housewife. Moreover, Almodóvar's melodrama is coloured by the fact that it was produced subsequent to the recuperation of the genre by feminist and neo-Marxist academics and critics, as a form that could be read for its ideological contradictions. A knowing, self-conscious use of film melodrama combines with the foregrounding of theatrical elements to turn *All About My Mother*, in common with many previous Almodóvar films, into an interrogation of performance itself.

Peter Brooks has characterised melodrama as the 'theatrical impulse itself: the impulse towards dramatisation, heightening, expression, acting out'. While other mainstream film genres concentrated on external conflicts protagonised by males (westerns, gangster movies, and so on), melodrama became the vehicle for the exploration of internal, often moral conflicts, frequently involving female protagonists, often in the role of victim. Melodramatic plots involved omniscient narration and, frequently, flashbacks (a result of the need for dramatic action but without the sense of movement or progression that characterises other, more dynamic genres).

The content of *All About My Mother* is certainly melodramatic: a mother loses her son and goes in search of the long-lost father to inform him; the father is a transsexual, a drug addict and HIV-positive; in her search she encounters old and new friends who quickly grow to need her. With a cast made up almost entirely of females, the characters' dramas involve the moral conflicts typical of melodrama: Manuela (Cecilia Roth) follows her dead son's donated organs in a desperate attempt to be close to him, then determines to let the father know, despite the certain pain of a reunion; Agrado (Antonia Sanjuán) gives up prostitution; Nina (Candela Peña) gives up drugs; Huma (Marisa Paredes) gives up Nina; Rosa (Penélope Cruz) gives birth to a baby who will be HIV-positive like her; and Rosa's mother (Rosa Maria Sardá) must decide whether to accept or reject the baby.

The story unfolds using omniscient narration and simple linear time (one event after another in chronological order). There are only two flashbacks, both diegetically motivated (in that they represent the memories of the protagonists themselves): Manuela, on returning to the performance of Tennessee Williams' *A Streetcar Named Desire*, which she had seen with her son the night he was killed, remembers how he looked as he waited for her opposite the theatre; and when she tells actress Huma about her son, Huma also recalls the night, and remembers seeing the boy's face through the taxi window asking her for an autograph. The story is dependent on coincidences and sudden twists, as is characteristically the case in classic melodrama. It is chance that brings Rosa into contact with Esteban-Lola, so that she ends up having his second child (his first being Manuela's dead son). Coincidence also brings Manuela into contact with Huma and Nina, a meeting which changes all their lives. In another stroke of melodramatic fate, Rosa dies in childbirth, leaving Manuela to bring up her husband's second child.

Feminist theorists from the 1970s onwards have seen melodrama as an antidote to, in the words of Laura Mulvey, the 'overvaluation of virility under patriarchy', as a genre whose simultaneous aims were to allow the exploration of female-orientated issues, and to 'soften' sexual difference, making the domestic sphere acceptable to men. What interested these feminist critics was the extent to which melodrama could be understood as conservative, educating women to accept the constraints of the patriarchal order, or conversely, the extent to which it might be opened up to more subversive readings (exposing and exploding the myths of patriarchy). Almodóvar's world – partly a reflection of a post-feminist reality and partly an idealisation or fantasy, in fact represents a disavowal of patriarchy. The domestic sphere in *All About My Mother* is entirely female, even to the extent that the biologically male father, Esteban, has become a transsexual. Male characters remain tangential to the dramatic action, and they determine neither the suffering of the females nor the resolution of that suffering. Consequently, unlike classic melodramas in which, according to Ann Kaplan, 'events are never reconciled at the end in a way which is beneficial to women', *All About My Mother* offers a happy ending, in which single motherhood and female friendship have replaced the conventional patriarchal family unit.

Parallel to the re-assessment of gender representations in melodrama came the re-evaluation of the formal style associated with the genre. Working at the same time, albeit independently, in the literary and cinematic fields, academics questioned why melodrama had been considered a less important dramatic form (less important than tragedy in the theatre, less important than westerns or gangster films in cinema). The way in which melodrama tends to be constrained by the dictates of realism or verisimilitude provides the key to understanding both its previous undervaluation, and its subsequent recuperation. Christine Gledhill explains: 'Whereas the realist-humanist tradition had privileged aesthetic coherence as the embodiment of authorial vision, the neo-Marxist perspective looked to stylistic "excess" and narrative disjuncture for their exposure of contradictions between a mainstream film's aesthetic and ideological programmes. Formal contradiction became a new source of critical value because it allowed apparently ideologically complicit films to be read "against the grain" for their overt critique of the represented status quo.'

The notion of melodramatic 'excess', a term coined by Geoffrey Nowell-Smith, requires clarification. He characterises 'excess' as 'undischarged emotion which cannot be accommodated within the action' and therefore has to be expressed in the music and the *mise-en-scène*. Nowell-Smith points out that the music and *mise-en-scène* do not merely heighten the emotionality of melodrama, but, 'to some extent they substitute for it'. This is particularly relevant to Almodóvar. Whereas in some of his earlier films such as *Tacones lejanos* (*High Heels*, 1991) characters frequently resort to the histrionic, in *All About My Mother* the emotions are often conveyed as much through *mise-en-scène* and music as through dialogue. Though not subject to the institutional constraints of a defensively patriarchal and socially conservative Hollywood, and consequently not constrained in terms of what he can depict on film (hence the self-sufficient women, transexuality, lesbianism, drugs, AIDS), Almodóvar does not abandon the compensatory use of classic melodramatic *mise-en-scène*.

In his pioneering article, Thomas Elsaesser described Hollywood melodrama as 'the most highly elaborated, complex mode of cinematic signification that the American cinema has ever produced, because of the restricted scope for external action determined by the subject, and because everything, as Sirk said, happens "inside"'. Douglas Sirk, himself a European working in the USA, was the acknowledged master of this compensatory *mise-en-scène*. His 1950s melodramas are rich in examples of what Elsaesser refers to as 'the contrasting emotional qualities of textures and materials'. Surfaces, furniture and above all, objects, take on metaphorical significance, enhancing or even carrying the full weight of the emotional dynamics of the drama.

The very first images of *All About My Mother*, which accompany the title sequence, are an eloquent visualisation of its themes of life, death and care for others. Rather than an establishing shot of a patient surrounded by medical staff who are explaining to relatives the hopelessness of the circumstances, Almodóvar makes the materials in the *mise-en-scène* express the harsh realities of the intensive care unit. We see the blurred hospital blinds in the background and the clear plastic of the drip bag. The titles, in life-blood red, appear blurred, gradually coming into focus, their instability a metaphor for the life and death situation depicted. The camera follows the drip of the saline along the plastic tube as far as the hospital machinery which is keeping this body alive. No human tissue is visible and the man-made materials testify to the artificiality of a life preserved clinically. Eventually the camera tilts upwards revealing nurse Manuela, thus linking her with the medical and pastoral care of victims.

Extreme close-ups of objects in the *mise-en-scène* are used as a kind of shorthand, quickly expressing the relationships of characters to the world around them. As Manuela and her son Esteban sit down to watch *All About Eve*, he writes in his notebook a potential title for his next piece: 'All About My Mother'. His relationship with words, as intense as his relationship with his mother, is metaphorically embodied in the shot composition by means of a shot/reverse shot (normally reserved for dialogue between two people): we see his point of view on a close-up of his pencil, followed by a reverse shot from the point of view of the notebook itself, the camera filming from underneath the translucent paper. When Esteban asks to see a photograph of his mother as an amateur actress, Manuela presents him with only half a photograph. Esteban runs his finger along the rough edge of the photo, its very texture indicating an untidy rupture rather than a clean break. Esteban subsequently writes in his notebook that this photograph symbolises the half of his existence which he feels is always missing – his father. Esteban's relationship to his writing and to the drama he loves is illustrated by an extreme close-up of the larger-than-life eyes of his idol, actress Huma Rojo, in a poster which occupies the whole theatre wall. So magnified is this close-up that the individual dots which make up the image are clearly visible.

All About My Mother exploits the versatility of the camera and *mise-en-scène* to seek out the intimate suffering and joys of the protagonists, but in such a way as to make each shot decision seem like the most natural of all possible choices. The perfect example of Almodóvar's capacity to mobilise exactly the right amount of technique and technology, in a perfect economy of directing, is the road accident of Manuela's son, Esteban. This scene is, to date, the most powerfully dramatic in all of Almodóvar's work. The situation is not particularly original: an impressionable young man runs after his idol in pursuit of an autograph; in the pouring rain he is hit by a car and left unconscious in the road, his mother witnessing it all then running to her son's side. A more conventional director, in an action film with a large special effects budget, might film such a scene something like this: a close-up of the young man as he sees his chance, then cut to a full shot as he runs after the departing taxi; a long shot of another car going far too fast and then a cut to a close-up of the driver's shocked face as he slams on the brakes; slow motion begins as we see a choreographed crash (using at least two stuntmen), and the young man is thrown high into the air and lands face down on the road; cut to a close-up of his mother raising her hands to her face with a terrified scream before a final full shot of the boy prostrate in the road, a pool of blood beside his head. Such a *mise-en-scène* would entail an expensive take, exploiting action-sequence conventions used in hundreds of similar moments on film. Almodóvar's version is much more restrained, economic (both in showy technique and in financial terms): as Esteban sets off towards Huma, a shot tracking rapidly away from Manuela indicates the speed of her son's pursuit of the taxi (the camera movement is itself dramatic); there is no shot of the other car, but a very blurred long shot of the road indicates the poor visibility; the impact of the car hitting Esteban is heard, the only image being the broken glass of the windscreen which fills the frame in close-up; cut to a subjective shot, the camera, masterfully, appearing to take the point of view of the victim: we do not see the moment of impact as the car hits Esteban; indeed, we do not see Esteban at all. Instead, the camera appears to flail around as it falls towards the ground and remains in a dislocated roll position as the distant (and out of focus) Manuela runs in slow motion towards the camera, shouting 'my son' repeatedly. The soundtrack intensifies the trauma of the accident. The sudden suspension of the music coincides with the impact of the car. The soundtrack void is filled not by the explosion of metal and glass which in action films passes for verisimilitude, but rather, by an internal, subjective sound (Manuela's audio point-of-view or, perhaps even, Esteban's). The continuing rain is heard, but as if inside an echo chamber, magnified along with Manuela's breathing. When she reaches her dying son, her face (still out of focus and blurred by the rain) comes right up against the camera in an extreme close-up. The slow motion images as she continues to shout 'my son' are not synchronised with her voice on the soundtrack, this disjunction suggesting that the physical qualities of her anguished cries, are more important than the words themselves.

Finally, a small camera movement indicates an apparent fall to a resting place in an extreme close-up of the wet road, suggesting Esteban's point of view as he loses consciousness.

Such examples of directorial economy and restraint in *All About My Mother* are to some extent made possible by the 'siphoning off' – to use a phrase from Nowell-Smith – of excess emotionality into the stage performances included in the film. This diversion of theatricality into the 'safely theatrical' space of the stage also contributes to a general thematisation of performance itself.

Even at its most 'excessive' or metaphorical, narrative cinema must stay within certain limits dictated by verisimilitude (what is 'realistic' or 'believable' for audiences). To escape such constraints, a director can turn to distancing devices, which foreground the constructed nature of cinema itself. In many of his earlier films, Almodóvar uses self-reflexive or *mise-en-abîme* techniques, including films within films, theatrical or even camp performances, clearly meant to emphasise how *unrealistic* they are. Parodies, such as the spoof adverts in the early films, make for good comedy. But in his serious dramas, Almodóvar often finds a more metaphorical mode of address (less restricted by verisimilitude), by using the theatre. As well as offering Almodóvar a more abstract, metaphorical *mise-en-scène*, the world of the theatre permits the introduction of a further thematic element, that of acting, performance and, by extension, the 'performativity' of life itself.

The idea for *All About My Mother* originated from a performance at the start of Almodóvar's eleventh film, *La flor de mi secreto* (*The Flower of My Secret*, 1995). Nurse Manuela volunteers as an actress in simulations designed to train doctors in the art of soliciting from newly-bereaved relatives the consent for organ donations. Manuela plays a grieving mother in this video-recorded simulation in the earlier film. The character re-appears as the main protagonist in *All About My Mother*, in which life dramatically imitates the simulation when her own son is killed and she enacts the grieving mother for real. The title is a homage to Joseph L. Mankiewicz's 1950 film classic, *All About Eve*. A scene from this film is watched by the impressionable writer Esteban and his mother Manuela, and it inspires the young man to wait outside the theatre for his idol, the actress Huma Rojo, just as Eve Harrington waits for actress Margo in *All About Eve*. Esteban dies whilst pursuing Huma in search of an autograph after her performance in *A Streetcar Named Desire*. Thus, Manuela's obsession with a play, which in her words 'has marked her life' is two-fold: she met her husband in a production of the play years before, and now she loses her son after another performance. Unable to keep her life separate from the play, she encounters the actresses who play Blanche and Stella, and eventually plays the role of

Stella for the second time in her life. Just as in *All About Eve*, Manuela first becomes an assistant to the diva and then an understudy, though in her case without calculation. Manuela also has to 'perform' surrogate motherhood twice in the film, and maintain the pretence of strength despite overwhelming grief for her lost son. By making Manuela both a stand-in actress and a stand-in mother, Almodóvar makes explicit how much the roles have in common. So when Almodóvar dedicates the film to all those actresses who have played actresses on the stage or in films, it is a dedication which colours the entire film (and many of his other films). More than the obvious theatrical context, Manuela represents the actress in all women, a point made by Almodóvar in the press book of the film: 'My idea at first was to make a film about the acting abilities of certain people who aren't actors. As a child I remember seeing this quality among the women in my family. They pretended much better than the men. Through these lies they were able to avoid more than one tragedy.'

In this film, motherhood, and even gender, is equated with performance. Almodóvar's long list of all types of actresses on the stage and in life, in the dedication which concludes the film, includes men who 'perform' as women. Performing gender is a theme that runs throughout Almodóvar's work. In *All About My Mother*, the theme is embodied in the character of Agrado.

Agrado spends all her time performing womanhood. She is a prostitute and a half-operated transsexual: she has breasts but has not had her penis removed because her male clients like their women 'well-hung'. But she abandons prostitution when she re-encounters Manuela, and begins to work for Huma in the equally performative world of the stage. This culminates in a veritable (indeed quite literal) *coup de théâtre* which is the most humorous sequence in the film. When Huma and Nina have come to blows and are unable to act, Agrado takes to the stage to explain why the play has been cancelled. In a sublime episode, she offers the audience the story of her life. But what follows is the story of her body and its relationship to plastic surgery and silicone. Part by part, she explains how much it has cost her, much to the amusement of the theatre audience. But this theatrical price list culminates in a small piece of Agrado's own philosophy: 'The more you become like what you have dreamed for yourself, the more authentic you are.' Agrado's impromptu performance on the Barcelona stage (which Almodóvar based on a real event, involving the famous Spanish theatre actress Lola Membrives), asserts that authenticity – in her case womanhood – is achieved as much through desire as through biological or essential nature. Her maxim is close to Baudrillard's example of 'the play of femininity' which he sees in transvestism: 'What transvestites love is this game of signs, what excites them is to seduce the signs themselves. With them everything is makeup, theatre and seduction. They appear obsessed with games of sex, but they are obsessed, first of all, with play itself; and if their lives appear more sexually endowed than our own, it is because they make sex into a total, gestural, sensual and ritual game, an exalted but ironic invocation.'

The wit of Almodóvar's transvestite and transsexual characters is part of the 'game' of playing the woman, and humour is often a protective mechanism against potentially hostile reactions. Joan Riviere's early psychoanalytic study of 'womanliness as masquerade' equates playing the role of the feminine with the need 'to avert anxiety and the retribution feared from men' by women who aspire to masculinity. Almodóvar's films typify the assertion – made by Judith Butler in *Gender Trouble* – that all gender is 'performatively constituted'.

Here too, *All About My Mother* represents a distillation of themes in previous films. In the earliest films, gender role-playing is often 'camply' self-conscious, a parody of gender. The drag queens who populate Almodóvar's early films reflect the licentious and carnivalesque *movida* (the *movida* was the explosion of pop and youth subcultures centred on Madrid which followed the death of the dictator Franco and the consequent liberalisation of legal and social restrictions in Spain), and provide a theatrical element of comedy. In *Laberinto de pasiones* (*Labyrinth of Passions*, 1983) Almodóvar himself appears in drag and is far from convincing as a woman. By the time of *High Heels*, a fully developed transvestite character appears in the shape of Letal, who, for Paul Julian Smith, represents 'the primacy of voluntarism, the freedom of the subject to place him/herself on either side of the sexual divide'. Alejandro Yarza sees the transvestite as a metaphor for the radical 'restructuring of traditional binary gender oppositions' which characterises all Almodóvar's films.

In *All About My Mother*, as in many of Almodóvar's films, the exposure of the mechanisms which construct gender roles in film, which usually *represent* but also *reinforce* patriarchy, amounts to what Laura Mulvey refers to as destroying the pleasure of the 'invisible guest', (the mythical 'fly on the wall' who sees everything in a film but without being seen). This, for Mulvey, is one way 'to strike a blow against the monolithic accumulation of patriarchal film conventions'. In Almodóvar, the self-conscious foregrounding of gender constructions forms part of a more generally self-conscious mode of representation that lays bare the 'constructed' nature of all art and, perhaps, of social identity. Perhaps the key to the success of *All About My Mother* lies in its combination of two different worlds and two different modes of address in a creative, mutually-enhancing tension. The arch-conservative world of 1950s America is replaced by the arch-permissive and diverse world of post-Franco Spain. And the subtle art of the superficially conservative yet highly metaphorical Hollywood melodrama, is combined with the knowing irony of a post-feminist, European auteur.

Mark Allinson

REFERENCES

Allinson, Mark (2001) *A Spanish Labyrinth: The Films of Pedro Almodóvar*. London and New York: I B Tauris.

Baudrillard, Jean (1990) *Seduction*, trans. Brian Singer. London: Macmillan.

Brooks, Peter (1976) *The Melodramatic Imagination*. New Haven and London: Yale University Press.

Butler, Judith (1990) *Gender Trouble*. London: Routledge.

Elsaesser, Thomas (1972) 'Tales of Sound and Fury: Observations on the Family Melodrama', *Monogram*, 4, 2–15.

Gledhill, Christine (ed). (1987) *Home is Where the Heart Is: Studies in Melodrama and the Woman's Film*. London: BFI.

Kaplan, Ann (1983) *Women and Film: Both Sides of the Camera*. London: Routledge.

Mulvey, Laura (1989) *Visual and Other Pleasures*. London: Macmillan.

Nowell-Smith, Geoffrey (1977) 'Minelli and melodrama', *Screen*, 18, 2, 113–18.

Riviere, Joan (1986) 'Womanliness as Masquerade', in Victor Burgin, James Donald and Cora Kaplan (eds) *Formations of Fantasy*. London: Methuen, 35–44.

Smith, Paul Julian (2000) *Desire Unlimited*, 2nd edn. London: Verso.

Yarza, Alejandro (1999) *Un caníbal en Madrid. La sensibilidad camp y el reciclaje de la historia en el cine de Pedro Almodóvar*. Madrid: Libertarias.

LUCÍA Y EL SEXO SEX AND LUCÍA

JULIO MEDEM, SPAIN, 2001

Lucía y el sexo (*Sex and Lucía*, 2001), the fifth feature by Julio Medem, is something of an anomaly. Medem is known as a cold, even cerebral director, who trained as a surgeon and a film critic before turning to filmmaking. Although the formalism of his work has not always pleased academics and journalists in Spain, Medem has the reputation of being the one true *auteur* to emerge in the 1990s. He is thus contrasted with both Hollywood, whose films remain dominant in the Spanish market, and the crudely commercial local comedies which also became massively popular in that decade. Medem is also known in Spain as a 'Basque' director, or yet more precisely a *donostiarra* (native of San Sebastián). Beginning with *Vacas* (*Cows*, 1992) his earlier films had obliquely explored the complexities of Basque identity and history. *Sex and Lucía* would seem to go against all these stereotypes. Far from being intellectual, the film boasted graphic sex scenes which soon became notorious. Breaking out of the art-house circuit, it was massively popular at the box office, with an audience of 1,258,919 in Spain and a healthy 269,488 in the US, in spite of an 'R' certificate which restricted exhibition. Finally, *Sex and Lucía* was set and shot in the central capital of Madrid, much resented by Basque nationalists, and the parched and sun-bleached Balearic island of Formentera, the antipodes of the damp and frigid Basque country.

It is perhaps not surprising, then, that the word most used about the film is *huida* (flight). Lucía (Paz Vega), a waitress in a Madrid restaurant, flees to an unknown island when she believes her writer-boyfriend Lorenzo (Tristán Ulloa) has died. Medem said that he also fled to the Mediterranean after the rigours of his previous feature, the chilly and tragic *Los amantes del círculo polar* (*Lovers of the Arctic Circle*, 1998). A flight into light, *Sex and Lucía* also marks an escape from the rigours and restrictions of conventional movie production; it was highly innovative as the first Spanish feature to be shot on high definition digital video. This enabled Medem to have an extended period of rehearsal with his actors (the leads had little film experience) and a lengthy shooting period of eighteen weeks on location, all for a modest budget of $3,000,000.

Following a new trend for Hollywood majors to fund European production in local languages, *Sex and Lucía* was made under the umbrella of Warner Bros.' Spanish arm by Sogecine, a respected Spanish producer which has specialised in young *auteurs* such as Alejandro Amenábar and Daniel Calparsoro. Again, the US connection was something of an anomaly, as Medem has been outspoken in attacking Hollywood's dominance over distribution in Spain. Indeed, when *Sex and Lucía* had its UK premiere at the London Film Festival he spoke at a round table debate significantly titled 'European cinema's enemy at the gates'. Nominated for no fewer than twelve Goya awards, *Sex and Lucía* was rewarded with two: Paz Vega won for best new actress and Alberto Iglesias, Medem's constant collaborator and composer for the recent Almodóvar films, for original score. Medem's (and Warner Sogecine's) risky venture thus paid off both commercially and critically.

Innovative in its production context, *Sex and Lucía* was also unusual in its distribution. While the poster remained the same in all territories (a seductively tousle-haired Lucía on a motor scooter with a lighthouse looming in the background), the trailers are significantly different. The Spanish trailer (included on the UK DVD) seems to feature three different films: a fast-paced thriller (a running man, a screaming child); a slow erotic drama (Lucía strips and submits); and a romance (Lucía, fully clothed, stares moodily out to sea at sunset). The plot is impossible to piece together and the only credit, reinforcing the *auteur*'s signature, is 'A film by Julio Medem'. The US trailer, available through IMDb, is much more accessible. Beginning once more with the authorial imprimatur ('From the internationally acclaimed director...') and the film's selection for the independent festivals of Sundance, Toronto and Rotterdam, the trailer breaks down the complex story and multiple characters into a more familiar quest format and love triangle. Intertitles read: 'a dreamer looking for adventure' (Lucía); 'a writer looking for material' (Lorenzo); and 'a stranger looking for trouble' (Belén, the young babysitter with whom Lorenzo will become obsessed). The trailer also helpfully spells out the implications of the title with the tagline: 'Sex is risk ... romance ... obsession ... passion ... lust.'

While the US trailer is noticeably less graphic than the Spanish, which boasts abundant nudity, English-language distributors clearly sold the film on its erotic content to audiences who, unlike Spaniards, were less likely to be familiar with Medem's auteurist track record. This is seen most obviously in the reversal of the Spanish title (*Lucía y el sexo* becomes *Sex and Lucía*). The change makes no sense in the context of the film itself, which is divided into two sections in the original order. Given the extreme difficulty for foreign language films to make a mark in English-speaking territories, the distributors could hardly be blamed for this populism. Indeed one attraction of European art movies has long been that they have tended to feature a more graphic sexual content than that allowed by Hollywood.

In spite of its 'flight' from the past, then, *Sex and Lucía*'s plot is as opaque as Medem's previous art-house hits. The official synopsis is written by Medem himself:

> Lucía is a young waitress in a restaurant in the centre of Madrid. After the loss of her long-time boyfriend, a writer, she seeks refuge on a quiet, secluded Mediterranean island. There, bathed in an atmosphere of fresh air and dazzling sun, Lucía begins to discover the dark corners of her past relationship, as if they were forbidden passages of a novel which the author now, from afar, allows her to read.

What is fascinating here is that Medem is clearly as interested in atmosphere and location as in character and plot. The list of IMDb keywords (submitted by viewers) gives a very different and considerably more dramatic impression of the film: male frontal nudity, animal attack, coma, dog, full moon, infidelity, internet chat, island, love at first sight, mermaid, motor scooter, scuba diving, striptease, writer's block, writer. While the audience was clearly struck by concrete motifs, Medem is more concerned with abstract relations: between city and island, past and present, reader and writer. Medem's own account of the writing process is of a journey on which he let himself go with a vague idea of sex as the motive force for the plot. Working on each character separately (the flight to the island was originally unconnected to the love story in Madrid), Medem only found a solution to the structural problems in the plot when he projected his 'creative confusion' onto Lorenzo, who turned into a writer at a late stage in the creative process. A stand-in for the director, Lorenzo became the 'hand which moves the destiny of the characters' and the whole film turned into an allegory of the relation between the writer and reader of fiction: a relation, Medem says, of intimacy, freedom and protection, all at once.

The *New York Times* wrote suggestively that Medem's screenplays are 'a damp tangle, as wet and mixed-up as a headful of summer hair'. Yet, like Medem's own metaphor of the aimless journey whose destination cannot be predicted, this belies the artistry and industry Medem puts into constructing a plot. *Sex and Lucía* is full of symmetries and formal patterns. Most obvious is the circle. Just as the moon and sun are frequently shown in gorgeously degraded images of digital video, so the plot is articulated by cycles in time and place. Lorenzo makes love with Elena (Najwa Nimri) in the sea on his birthday and under a full moon. It is also on his birthday that he will be told of the existence of the daughter conceived on the same night years earlier. Inevitably, the child will be called Luna. The tiniest details recur. When Lucía first confesses her love to Lorenzo we inexplicably see a dog attack on the television in the bar where they are sitting (much later Luna will be killed by an identical dog). Elena, who is like most of *Sex and Lucía*'s principles a keen cook, claims to be a specialist in paella, the dish which Lucía will order when she arrives on the island. Through repetition the circle links up with the double: 'Carlos' (played by Daniel Freire) is a mysterious diver on the island, gifted with an unusually large penis. But he is also 'Antonio', the lover of Belén's mother back in Madrid. Through the internet, characters adopt new names and new characters at will. Elena will be cured of her grief over the death of her child by an electronic story sent to her by 'the lighthouse man' (Lorenzo's chat room pseudonym).

Nonetheless, and in spite of frequent flashbacks, the plot seems to move slowly in relatively linear fashion towards a definitive conclusion: Lorenzo, who has survived a coma, returns to the island to be reconciled with both Elena, the mother of his lost daughter, and Lucía, his fugitive lover. Yet Medem immediately, playfully, returns us to the middle of the story for a final scene: Elena is shown taking a photo of Luna in the Madrid square above which Lorenzo composes his novel with a happy Lucía in attendance. As Lorenzo says of his own fiction, this is clearly 'a story with many advantages', not the least of which is its combination of the simple and the complex, the free and the constrained.

In his notes to the UK DVD Robert Stone writes that the theme of all Medem's films is 'fantasy made real because of the emotions invested in it'. Certainly, this holds true for the motif of writing, which is as pervasive in the film as sex. It remains unclear at the end of the film how much of the subplot of babysitter Belén, louche lover Carlos, and dead child Luna has been invented by Lorenzo. But if he is the puppet master, pulling the other characters' strings, then they too fictionalise their experience. Lucía has been stalking Lorenzo before they meet and narrates their future in the bar in some detail. She correctly predicts that they will move in together and he will fall in love with her as she already has with him. At this point, as elsewhere, Lucía is clearly in control of her own story. Belén, who imitates the moves of her porn star mother as she watches her on screen, is encouraged by Lorenzo to sleep with Carlos. Instead she seduces Lorenzo himself with a delicious meal and kinky black lingerie. It is a pornographic scenario which will have tragic consequences.

The theme of literature thus links up with that of sex. Lucía and Lorenzo's love-making, plotted in advance by Lucía, is distinctly literary, or at least cinematic. Medem seems to cite such unlikely Hollywood sources as *9½ Weeks* (blindfold tasting) and *Basic Instinct* (public panty removal). The two lovers are soon taking polaroids of their love-making and Medem crosscuts between the act itself and their later voyeuristic or exhibitionistic viewing of the photos. Typically self-conscious, Medem makes us aware of how voyeurism and fiction can be part of our most intimate experiences. Sex is by no means straightforward, not just a basic instinct.

However, there is an imbalance here. While IMDb correspondents were obviously struck by the male nudity, female bodies are much more blatantly displayed for the audience's pleasure. On their first night together, a drunken Lucía is disrobed by Lorenzo, splayed naked over the bed (he removes his own clothes more quickly and standing up). Lucía later performs a practised striptease for her boyfriend, pealing off her leather mini skirt; Lorenzo's strip is played for laughs as he jumps up and down to remove his trousers. In a brief shot of an erect penis manipulated by a female hand, the two leads are substituted by body doubles (these are the same actors who perform in the porn video by Belén's mother which we glimpse on a television screen). This adds another small twist to the 'damp tangle' of sexual role-play in the film. It could be argued that men are as fetishised as women in *Sex and Lucía*. Carlos may smear Lucía's naked body with mud on the beach, but he is objectified himself, reduced to the huge (prosthetic?) penis. The latter is exploited by Elena as a source of sex without intimacy. The island's topography is likewise reduced to two features, each as parodic or portentous as the other: the phallic lighthouse to which Lucía is constantly drawn and the vaginal hole down which she falls to the sea. Where once Medem affectionately parodied Basque identities (a bug exterminator in *Tierra* [1986] is named after Urtzi, the god of thunder), here he cites, celebrates and playfully undermines more familiar gender stereotypes. It is no accident that there is also a windmill on the island; *Sex and Lucía*'s characters are quixotic in their ambitions and their creator's irony is teasingly Cervantine.

The themes of storytelling and sex are not just explored in the screenplay. They are also played out in the film's technique in ways which do not always coincide with the surface narrative. The art design is meticulously planned. The lamp in Lucía's first bedroom has a stylised sun design (Medem cuts in the next shot to her swimming in the dazzling light). Luna's bedroom, which receives a separate design credit, is dedicated to the sea where she was conceived. It contains a toy aquarium, a little mermaid doll and fish painted on the blue walls (when she dies she will be embraced underwater by her mother as siren). The fashionable wardrobe is credited to, amongst others, Sybilla and Amaya Arzuaga, two of Spain's most respected designers. The high definition digital video brings an unusual look to familiar locations, exaggerating differences. A nocturnal Madrid is dark and brown (although Lucía's restaurant, in a typical tiny premonition, promises 'Mediterranean cuisine' long before she thinks of fleeing the capital). The sun-drenched island is bled of almost all colour. But at night the huge moon, which first hung over Madrid, does not fail to appear. In the opening sequence the moon is made to rhyme with Paz Vega's round, luminous face and much later with a button, another small detail which Medem tempts us to endow with significance.

Taking advantage of the mobility of the small electronic camera, Medem's cinematography is also unusually flexible. We get in very close to the principals (or their doubles) in the sex scenes, with body parts (a nipple, an erect penis) shown in extreme close-up. The camera alternates between high and low angles as Lucía stalks the beach, often naked, or Lorenzo talks in the city square to his little daughter Luna. In the opening sequence once more, when Lucía returns to the flat and fears Lorenzo is dead, the camera whirls from side to side and up and down and chases after her though the empty city streets. But elsewhere the camera can be static. Lucía and Elena are shot from within the black hole by the lighthouse, their looming figures framed by darkness against the blue Mediterranean sky streaked with white clouds. This is the closest Medem comes to the showy subjective shots from the perspective of animals (as in *Cows* and in *La ardilla roja* [*The Red Squirrel*, 1993]) that brought him so much criticism from Spanish reviewers.

Significantly, although Lorenzo is said to control the narrative (one reviewer said the film should have been called *Sex and Lorenzo*), Lucía is generally granted the point of view. On the morning after she is first drunkenly disrobed, Lucía strolls through Lorenzo's attic apartment, taking possession of this new space: we see the kitchen, furniture and computer all from her perspective. Elsewhere the camera wobbles sympathetically to imitate her drunkenness or seasickness (we are told that the island floats giddily on top of the sea). Medem uses reflections to complicate and qualify the individual's sense of self. Lorenzo is often shown reflected in the computer screen as he writes, at one with his words; but so is Elena, as she receives the healing narrative from the 'lighthouse man'. The visual here coincides with the textual, cinematography with screenplay.

Editing is more complex. Already noted is the use of graphic matches (moons, buttons and faces) that serve to link, suggestively and obscurely, different times, places and characters. Elsewhere Medem uses a fade to white to link sequences in an equally ambiguous way. This can almost be read as a visual pun. Lucía, happy with Lorenzo in Madrid, sings the cheesy 1960s pop song '*Un rayo de sol*' ('A sunbeam'). As if on cue the screen soon flares up into blinding light and we flash-forward to Lucía, now riding her motor scooter on the island after the supposed death of her boyfriend. Sound bridges serve a similar purpose. Lucía's orgasmic groans as she has sex with Lorenzo fade into Elena's screams as she gives birth to his daughter Luna in hospital. Clearly sex can have unintended consequences.

But if different scenes are brought together by sound and image, the same scene can also be split apart. Twice Medem cranes up from the city square (Elena plays with Luna) to the attic (Lorenzo writes with Lucía). The two couples coincide in time and space, but neither is aware of the other. Cross-cutting makes some sequences difficult to read: Lorenzo sees himself in bed with Belén even as he fantasises that she is sleeping with Carlos, her mother's boyfriend. Other scenes are disrupted by jump cuts. When Lucía and Lorenzo first make love (a scene comically delayed by Lucía's earlier drunkenness), the jump cuts prevent us from smoothly visualising the whole scene and enjoying that fullness of vision required for pornographic pleasure. The young couple's lovemaking is often accompanied by Alberto Iglesias' main string and flute theme, an unmistakeably romantic waltz. Lorenzo's kinky soirée with Belén (which results in the child's death) is set rather to ominous electronic drones. Medem shows us through his mastery of cinematic technique that the familiar scene of love-making can be shot and felt in an infinite number of ways.

If the technique is often showy (and Medem has often been attacked for excessive formalism), it can also be unusually economical. Lucía's flight to the island is a case in point. First, she runs desperately through the night streets, pursued by Medem's steadycam. There is the briefest shot of the façade of Madrid's historic Atocha station. We then see the sunrise reflected in the window of a train and Lucía's shadow cast on the white wake of a ship. And while incidental details loom large on screen (the button, the lampshade), vital plot points are entirely omitted. When Luna is killed by the dog we see only babysitter Belén sinking stunned to the floor in her black fetish underwear; the broken window from which, we assume, Lorenzo has thrown himself in despair; and the lyrical fantasy sequence of the child returning to the watery embrace of her mermaid-mother. The audience might well wonder what exactly has happened. Once again, Medem shows that he is more concerned with atmosphere and location than with character and plot.

At one point Lucía asks Lorenzo if he would prefer wild sex with a stranger or sex with a steady partner who is wildly in love with him. He does not reply. Lorenzo clearly has difficulty choosing between domesticity and adventure, obsessed with his one night stand with Elena and tempted by perverse babysitter Belén (the similarity of the two women's names is also typical of Medem). Medem's appeal in *Sex and Lucía* to graphic sexual content, comparable to then recent French films such as François Ozon's *Sitcom* (1998) and Cathérine Breillat's *A ma sœur* (2001), might seem uncharacteristic. But *Sex and Lucía* retains that formal, even cerebral, interest that is characteristic of the director. Like his writer hero, then, Medem could be seen as torn between two extremes. It is significant that in *Tierra* the main character also has to choose between a domestic goddess and a sex genius.

We have also seen that the marketing of *Sex and Lucía* insisted on the auteurist credentials of its 'internationally acclaimed' director as well as on the film's sexual content. Even in Spain, actors Paz Vega and Tristán Ulloa were hardly box-office draws, known as they were mainly for television drama. This, then, was another flight from the familiar, in which the domesticated Vega, known for *7 Vidas* (a *Friends*-like sitcom) was transformed into a big-screen sex symbol. While Medem himself had claimed that *Sex and Lucía* was an antidote to the tragic *Lovers of the Arctic Circle*, in which the central couple were ultimately separated by death, it is not clear that *Sex and Lucía*'s ending achieves the emotional payoff that he was evidently aiming for. As in the previous film, the pace lags dangerously in the final act. And Medem's minute formalism, his insistence on tiny details of screenplay and *mise-en-scène*, serves once more to distance the viewer, even as the director coaxes fiercely emotional performances from his inexperienced leads. In spite of these reservations, *Sex and Lucía* is still a brave departure for a gifted filmmaker who is unafraid to innovate in both form and content. While it remains to be seen if, as Medem predicted at the London Film Festival, digital video will save European cinema from the Hollywood enemy at its gates, *Sex and Lucía* is a prime example of an unapologetically auteurist project that achieved resounding commercial success.

Paul Julian Smith

FILMOGRAPHY

LA ALDEA MALDITA THE CURSED VILLAGE 1930
Director: Florián Rey
Production Pedro Larrañaga and Florián Rey
Screeenplay: Florián Rey
Photography: Alberto Arroyo
Art Direction: Paulino Méndez
Music: Rafael Martínez
Cast: Pedro Larrañaga (Juan), Carmen Viance (Acacia), Pedro Pastor (Grandfather), Amelia Muñoz (Magdalena), Pilar Torres (Fuensantica), Ramón Meca (Tío Lucas)
Running time: 58 mins.

A CANÇÃO DE LISBOA SONG OF LISBON 1933
Director: José Cottinelli Telmo
Producer: João Ortigao Ramos
Screenplay: José Cottinelli Telmo
Photography: Henri Barreyre, César de Sá
Editors: Tonka Taldy, José Cottinelli Telmo, José Gomes Ferreira
Music: René Bohet, Raul Ferrão, Raúl Portela, Jaime Silva Filho
Sound: Hans-Cristof Wohlrab, Paulo de Brito Aranha
Cast: Vasco Santana (Vasco Leitao), Beatriz Costa (Alice), António Silva (Caetano), Teresa Gomes (Aunt), Sofía Santos (Aunt), Manoel de Oliveira (Vasco's Friend)
Running time: 85 mins.

LA VERBENA DE LA PALOMA FAIR OF THE DOVE 1935
Director: Benito Perojo
Production: Benito Perojo, for CIFESA
Screenplay: Benito Perojo, based on the libretto by Ricardo de la Vega; additional dialogue by Pedro de Répide
Photography: Fred Mandel
Editor: H. Taverna
Art Direction: Fernando Mignoni
Music: Tomás Bretón; lyrics by Ricardo de la Vega
Sound: León Lucas de la Peña
Cast: Miguel Ligero (Don Hilarión), Roberto Rey (Julián), Raquel Rodrigo (Susana), Sélica Pérez Carpio (Señá Rita), Dolores Cortés (Aunt Antonia), Charito Leonís (Casta), Enrique Salvador (Don Sebastián)
Running time: 78 mins.

ANIKI-BÓBÓ 1942
Director: Manoel de Oliveira
Producer: Fernando Garcia
Screenplay: João Rodrigues de Freitas, Manoel de Oliveira, Nascimento Fernandes, António Lopes Ribeiro, Manuel Matos; based on the novel *Meninos* by Manoel de Oliveira
Photography: Antonio Mendes

Editors: Manoel de Oliveira and Vieira de Sousa
Art Direction: José Porto
Music: Jaime Silva Filho
Sound: Louis Sousa Santos
Cast: Nascimento Fernandes (shop owner), Fernanda Matos (Teresinha), Horacio Silva (Carlitos), Antonio Santos (Eduardito), Américo Botelho (Estrelas), Feliciano David (Pompeu), Manuel de Azevedo (street singer), Rafael Mota (Rafael)
Running time: 102 mins.

LOS ÚLTIMOS DE FILIPINAS LAST STAND IN THE PHILIPPINES 1945
Director: Antonio Román
Producer: Pedro de Juan Pinzones
Screenplay: Pedro de Juan Pinzones and Antonio Román; based on *El fuerte de Baler* by Enrique Alfonso Barcones and Rafael Sánchez, and *Los héroes de Baler* by Enrique Llovet Sánchez
Photography: Enrique Guerner
Editor: Bienvenida Sanz
Art Direction: Sigfrido Burmann and Francisco Canet
Music: Jorge Halpern
Sound: Antonio Alonso Ciller
Cast: Armando Calvo (Teniente Martín Cerezo), José Nieto (Capitán Enrique de las Morenas), Guillermo Marín (Doctor Rogelio Vigil), Manolo Morán (Pedro Vila), Juan Calvo (Cabo Olivares), Fernando Rey (Juan Chamizo), Manuel Kayser (Fray Cándido), Carlos Muñoz (Santamaría), José Miguel Rupert (Moisés), Nani Fernández (Tala)
Running time: 99 mins.

LOLA LA PICONERA LOLA THE COALGIRL 1951
Director: Luis Lucia
Producer: Juan Manuel de Rada for Cifesa
Screenplay: Luis Lucia; adapted by Ricardo Blasco and José Luis Colina from the play *Cuando las Cortes de Cádiz* by José María Pemán
Photography: Theodore J. Pahle
Editor: Juan Serra
Art Direction: Sigfrido Burmann
Music: Manuel L. Quiroga; lyrics by Rafael de León and Juan Quintero
Sound: Antonio Alonso Ciller
Cast: Juanita Reina (Lola), Virgilio Teixeira (Cpt. Gustavo), Manuel Luna (Field Marshall Víctor), Félix Dafauce (Juan de Acuña), Fernando Nogueras (Rafael Otero), Fernando Fernández de Córdoba (General Alburquerque), Alberto Romea (Salazar), Valeriano Andrés (Lt. Jouvert), José Guardiola (Gallardo), Ana Esmeralda (dancer), José Toledano (dancer)
Running time: 89 mins.

MARCELINO PAN Y VINO THE MIRACLE OF MARCELINO 1954
Director: Ladislao Vajda
Producer: Vicente Sempere for Chamartín Films
Screenplay: José María Sánchez Silva and Ladislao Vajda; based on a story by José María Sánchez Silva
Photography: Heinrich Gärtner
Editor: Julio Peña
Art Direction: Antonio Simont
Music: Pablo Sorozábal

Sound: Alfonso Carvajal and Jesús Moreno

Cast: Pablito Calvo (Marcelino), Rafael Rivelles (Brother Superior), Juan Calvo (Brother Papilla), Antonio Vico (Brother Puerta), José Nieto (blacksmith), Juanjo Menéndez (Brother Gil), Fernando Rey (Narrator), Mariano Azaña (Brother Malo), Carmen Carbonell (Alfonsa), Joaquín Roa (Brother Talán), Rafael Calvo (Don Emilio)

Running time: 91 mins.

CALLE MAYOR MAIN STREET 1956

Director: Juan Antonio Bardem

Producers: Manuel J. Goyanes and Samuel Menkes for Cesáreo González

Screenplay: Juan Antonio Bardem; inspired by the play *La señorita de Trévelez* by Carlos Arniches

Photography: Michel Kelber

Editor: Margarita de Ochoa

Art Direction: Enrique Alarcón

Music: Joseph Kosma and Isidro B. Maiztegui

Sound: Fernando Bernáldez

Cast: Betsy Blair (Isabel), José Suárez (Juan), Yves Massard (Federico), Dora Doll (Tonia), Luis Peña (Luis), Alfonso Goda (Calvo), Manuel Alexandre (Luciano), María Gámez (Madre), Lila Kedrova (Pepita)

Running time: 99 mins.

EL ÚLTIMO CUPLÉ THE LAST TORCH SONG 1957

Director: Juan de Orduña

Producer: Juan de Orduña

Screenplay: Jesús María de Arozamena and Antonio Mas Guindal

Photography: José F. Aguayo

Editor: Antonio Cánovas

Art Direction: Sigfrido Burmann

Original Music: Juan Solano

Sound: Enrique Larriva

Cast: Sara Montiel (Maria Luján), Armando Calvo (Juan), Enrique Vera (Pepe Molina), Julia Martínez (Trini), Matilde Muñoz Sampedro (Paca), José Moreno (Cándido), Laly del Amo (Luisa), Aurora García Alonso (Micaela), Alfredo Mayo (Prince Wladimiro)

Running time: 110 mins.

VIRIDIANA 1961

Director: Luis Buñuel

Producers: Gustavo Alatriste, Ricardo Muñoz Suay and Pere Portabella

Screenplay: Julio Alejandro and Luis Buñuel

Photography: José F. Aguayo

Editor: Pedro del Rey

Art Direction: Francisco Canet

Music: Gustavo Pittaluga

Sound: Aurelio García Tijeras

Cast: Silvia Pinal (Viridiana), Francisco Rabal (Jorge), Fernando Rey (Don Jaime), Margarita Lozano (Ramona), José Calvo (beggar), José Manuel Martín (beggar), Victoria Zinny (Lucia), Luis Heredia (beggar), Teresa Rabal (Rita)

Running time: 90 mins.

EL VERDUGO THE EXECUTIONER 1963

Director: Luis García Berlanga

Producers: Nazario Belmar and José Manuel M. Herrero for Naga Films-Zebra Films
Screenplay: Rafael Azcona and Luis García Berlanga, with Ennio Flaiano
Photography: Tonino delli Colli
Editor: Alfonso Santacana
Art Direction: Luís Argüello and José Antonio de la Guerra
Music: Miguel Asins Arbó
Sound: Felipe Fernández
Cast: Nino Manfredi (José Luis Rodríguez), Emma Penella (Carmen), José Isbert (Amadeo), José Luis López Vázquez (Antonio), Ángel Álvarez (Álvarez), Guido Alberti (Director de la prisión), María Luisa Ponte (Estefanía), María Isbert (Ignacia)
Running time: 90 mins.

EL EXTRAÑO VIAJE STRANGE JOURNEY 1964
Director: Fernando Fernán Gómez
Producers: Antonio López Moreno and Francisco Molero
Screenplay: Pedro Beltrán; based on a story by Manuel Ruiz Castillo and Pedro Beltrán
Photography: José F. Aguayo
Editor: Rosa G. Salgado
Art Direction: Sigfrido Burmann
Music: Cristóbal Halffter
Sound: Felipe Fernández and Jesús Ocaña
Cast: Carlos Larrañaga (Fernando), Tota Alba (Ignacia Vidal), Lina Canalejas (Beatriz), Sara Lezana (Angelines), Rafaela Aparicio (Paquita Vidal), Jesus Franco (Venancio Vidal), María Luisa Ponte (Mercera)
Running time: 92 mins.

LA NOCHE DE WALPURGIS SHADOW OF THE WEREWOLF 1971
Director: León Klimovsky
Producer: Salvadore Romero
Screenplay: Jacinto Molina and Hans Munkel
Photography: Leopoldo Villaseñor
Editor: Antonio Gimeno
Art Direction: Ludwig Orny
Music: Antón García Abril
Sound: Sanmateo
Cast: Paul Naschy (Waldemar Daninsky), Gaby Fuchs (Elvira), Barbara Capell (Genevieve Bennett), Patty Shepard (Countess Wandessa d'Arville de Nadasdy), Andrés Resino (Inspector Marcel), Yelena Samarina (Elizabeth Daninsky)
Running time: 85 mins.

EL ESPÍRITU DE LA COLMENA SPIRIT OF THE BEEHIVE 1973
Director: Víctor Erice
Producer: Elías Querejeta
Screenplay: Víctor Erice and Ángel Fernández Santos
Photography: Luis Cuadrado
Editor: Pablo del Amo
Art Direction: Jaime Chávarri
Music: Luis de Pablo
Sound: Luis Rodríguez and Eduardo Fernández

Cast: Fernando Fernán Gómez (Fernando), Teresa Gimpera (Teresa), Ana Torrent (Ana), Isabel Tellería (Isabel), José Villasante (The Frankenstein Monster), Juan Francisco Margallo (The Fugitive), Laly Soldevila (The Teacher)
Running time: 97 mins.

CRIA CUERVOS RAISE RAVENS 1975
Director: Carlos Saura
Producer: Elías Querejeta
Screenplay: Carlos Saura
Photography: Teodoro Escamilla
Editor: Pablo González del Amo
Art Direction: Rafael Palmero
Music: Federico Mompou and José L. Perales
Sound: Bernardo Menz and Miguel Ángel Polo
Cast: Geraldine Chaplin (Ana – The Mother), Mónica Randall (Paulina), Florinda Chico (Rosa), Ana Torrent (Ana), Héctor Alterio (Anselmo), Germán Cobos (Nicolás Garontes), Mirta Miller (Amelia Garontes), Josefina Díaz (Grandmother)
Running time: 107 mins.

EL DIPUTADO CONFESSIONS OF A CONGRESSMAN 1978
Director: Eloy de la Iglesia
Producer: José Antonio Pérez Giner
Screenplay: Gonzalo Goicoechea and Eloy de la Iglesia
Photography: Antonio Cuevas
Editor: Julio Peña
Art Direction: Lorenzo Collado
Sound: Jacinto Cora
Cast: José Sacristán (Roberto Orbea), María Luisa San José (Carmen Orbea), José Luis Alonso (Juanito), Enrique Vivó (Morena Pastrana), Agustín González (Carres), Queta Claver (Juanito's Mother), Ángel Pardo (Nes), Juan Antonio Bardem (Himself)
Running time: 110 mins.

ARREBATO RAPTURE 1979
Director: Iván Zulueta
Producer: Nicolás Astiárraga
Screenplay: Iván Zulueta
Photography: Ángel Luis Fernández
Editors: José Luis Peláez, José Pérez Luna and María Elena Sáinz de Rozas
Art Direction: Iván Zulueta, Carlos Astiárraga and Eduardo Eznarriaga
Music: Negativo and Iván Zulueta
Sound: Miguel Ángel Polo
Cast: Eusebio Poncela (José Sirgado), Will More (Pedro P.), Cecilia Roth (Ana), Marta Fernández Muro (Marta), Carmen Giralt (Tía Carmen), Helena Fernán Gómez (Gloria), Antonio Gasset (Editor)
Running time: 110 mins.

LOS SANTOS INOCENTES THE HOLY INNOCENTS 1984
Director: Mario Camus
Producer: Julián Mateos for Ganesh S.A.
Screenplay: Antonio Larreta, Manuel Matji and Mario Camus; based on the novel by Miguel Delibes

Photography: Hans Burman
Editor: José María Biurrun
Art Direction: Rafael Palmero
Music: Antón García Abril
Sound: Carlos Faruelo and Eduardo Fernández
Cast: Alfredo Landa (Paco, El Bajo), Terele Pávez (Régula), Francisco Rabal (Azarías), Belén Ballesteros (Nieves), Juan Sánchez (Quirce), Juan Diego (Señorito Iván), Ágata Lys (Doña Pura), Agustín González (Don Pedro), Mary Carrillo (Señora Marquesa), Maribel Martín (Miriam)
Running time: 107 mins.

TRILOGIA DE JOÃO DE DEUS as below
Director: João César Monteiro
Screenplay: João César Monteiro

RECORDAÇÕES DA CASA AMARELA RECOLLECTIONS OF THE YELLOW HOUSE 1989
Producers: Joaquim Pinto and João Pedro Bénard
Photography: José António Loureiro
Editors: Helena Alves and Claudio Martínez
Art Direction: Luís Monteiro
Sound: Vasco Pimentel
Cast: João César Monteiro (João de Deus), Manuela de Freitas (Dona Violeta), Ruy Furtado (Senhor Armando), Teresa Calado (Menina Julieta), Duarte de Almeida (Ferdinando), António Terrinha (Doctor)
Running time: 122 mins.

A COMEDIA DE DEUS GOD'S COMEDY 1995
Producer: Joaquim Pinto
Photography: Mário Barroso
Editor: Carla Bogalheiro
Art Direction: Emmanuel de Chauvigny
Sound: Rolly Belhassen
Cast: Cláudia Teixeira (Joaninha), João César Monteiro (Max Monteiro as João de Deus), Manuela de Freitas (Judite), Raquel Ascensão (Rosarinho), Gracinda Nave (Felícia), Patrícia Abreu (Alexandra), Saraiva Serrano (Sr. Tomé), Maria João Ribeiro (Carmen), Bruno Sousa (Bruno)
Running time: 170 mins.

AS BODAS DE DEUS THE SPOUSALS OF GOD 1998
Producer: Paulo Branco
Photography: Mario Barroso
Editor: Joaquim Pinto
Art Direction: Alfredo Furiga
Sound: Joaquim Pinto
Cast: João César Monteiro (João de Deus), José Airosa (Omar Raschid), Luís Miguel Cintra (God's Messenger), Manuela de Freitas (Sister Bernarda), Jean Douchet (Bardamu), Rita Durão (Joana de Deus), João Listz (Sparafucile), Ana Velazquez (Leonor)
Running time: 150 mins.

BELLE EPOQUE 1992
Director Fernando Trueba

Producer: Andrés Vicente Gómez
Screenplay: Rafael Azcona
Photography: José Luis Alcaine for Lolafilms
Editor: Carmen Frías
Art Direction: Juan Botella
Music: Antoine Duhamel
Sound: Georges Prat
Cast: Jorge Sanz (Fernando), Fernando Fernán Gómez (Manolo), Penélope Cruz (Luz), Maribel Verdú (Rocío),
Ariadna Gil (Violeta), Miriam Díaz Aroca (Clara), Gabino Diego (Juanito), Chus Lampreave (Juanito's Mother),
Agustín González (Priest), Mary Carmen Ramírez (Amalia), Michel Galabru (Danglard)
Running time: 108 mins.

VIAGEM AO PRINCÍPIO DO MUNDO JOURNEY TO THE BEGINNING OF THE WORLD 1997
Director: Manoel de Oliveira
Producer: Paulo Branco
Screenplay: Manoel de Oliveira
Photography: Renato Berta
Editor: Valérie Loiseleux
Music: Emmanuel Nuñes
Sound: Jean-Paul Mugel
Cast: Marcello Mastroianni (Manoel), Jean-Yves Gautier (Afonso), Leonor Silveira (Judite), Diogo Dória (Duarte),
Isabel de Castro (Maria Afonso), Cécile Sanz de Alba (Christina), José Pinto (José Afonso), Adelaide Teixeira
(Senhora)
Running time: 95 mins.

TORRENTE/TORRENTE 2 as below
Director: Santiago Segura
Screenplay: Santiago Segura

TORRENTE: EL BRAZO TONTO DE LA LEY TORRENTE: THE DUMB ARM OF THE LAW 1998
Producers: Andrés Vicente Gómez and Fernando Trueba
Photography: José Luis Alcaine
Editor: Carmen Frías
Art Direction: Juan Botella
Music: Antoine Duhamel
Sound: Georges Prat
Cast: Santiago Segura (Torrente), Tony Leblanc (Padre), Javier Cámara (Rafi), Neus Asensi (Amparito), Chus
Lampreave (Reme), Julio Sanjuán (Malaguita), Jaime Barnatán (Toneti), Darío Paso (Bombilla), Espartaco Santoni
(Mendoza)
Running time: 97 mins.

TORRENTE 2: MISIÓN EN MARBELLA TORRENTE: MISSION IN MARBELLA 2001
Producers: Juan Dakas and Andrés Vicente Gómez
Photography: Guillermo Granillo
Editors: Fidel Collado
Art Direction: José Luis Arrizabalaga and Biaffra
Music: Roque Baños
Cast: Santiago Segura (Torrente), Tony Leblanc (Padre), Javier Cámara (Rafi), Neus Asensi (Amparito), Chus

Lampreave (Reme), Gabino Diego (Cuco), José Luis Moreno (Espinelli), Inés Sastre (Singer), José Luis López Vázquez (Guijarro), Juanito Navarro (Mayor of Marbella)
Running time: 99 mins.

TODO SOBRE MI MADRE ALL ABOUT MY MOTHER 1999
Director: Pedro Almodóvar
Producer: Agustín Almodóvar for El Deseo
Screenplay: Pedro Almodóvar
Photography: Affonso Beatto
Editor: José Salcedo
Art Direction: Antxón Gómez
Music: Alberto Iglesias
Sound: Miguel Rejas
Cast: Cecilia Roth (Manuela), Marisa Paredes (Huma Rojo), Antonia Sanjuán (Agrado), Penélope Cruz (María Rosa), Candela Peña (Nina), Rosa María Sardá (Mother), Toni Cantó (Lola), Eloy Azorín (Esteban), Fernando Fernán Gómez (Father), Carlos Lozano (Mario)
Running time: 101 mins.

LUCÍA Y EL SEXO SEX AND LUCIA 2001
Director: Julio Medem
Producers: Fernando Bovaira and Enrique López Lavigne
Screenplay: Julio Medem
Photography: Kiko de la Rica
Editors: Iván Aledo
Art Direction: Montse Sanz
Music: Alberto Iglesias
Sound: Agustín Peinado
Cast: Paz Vega (Lucía), Tristán Ulloa (Lorenzo), Nawja Nimri (Elena), Daniel Freire (Carlos/Antonio), Elena Anaya (Belén), Silvia Llanos (Luna), Diana Suárez (Madre de Belén), Javier Cámara (Pepe)
Running time: 128 mins.

BIBLIOGRAPHY

GENERAL HISTORIES AND REFERENCE

Bernaola, Carmelo (1986) *Evolución de la banda sonora en España*. Madrid: Festival de cine de Alcalá de Henares.

Borau, José Luis (ed.) *Diccionario del cine español*. Madrid: Alianza Editorial.

Camporesi, Valeria (1994) *Para grandes y chicos: un cine para los españoles (1940–1990)*. Madrid: Ediciones Turfán.

Caparrós Lera, José María (1999) *Historia crítica del cine español (desde 1897 hasta hoy)*. Barcelona: Ariel.

D'Lugo, Marvin (1997) *Guide to the Cinema of Spain*. Westport, CT: Greenwood Press.

Delgado Casado, Juan (1993) *La bibliografía cinematográfica española: aproximación histórica*. Madrid: Arco/Libros S.L.

Evans, Peter William (ed.) (1999) *Spanish Cinema: The Auteurist Tradition*. Oxford: Oxford University Press.

España, Rafael de (1994) *Directory of Spanish and Portuguese Film Makers and Films*. Trowbridge: Flicks Books

García Fernández, Emilio Carlos (1985) *Historia del cine en Galicia (1896–1994)* La Coruña: La Voz de Galicia.

González Requena, Jesús (1988) 'Apuntes para una historia de lo rural en el cine español', in *El campo en el cine español*. Madrid: Banco de Crédito Agrícola/Filmoteca Española.

Gubern, Román, José Enrique Monterde, Julio Pérez Perucha, Esteve Riambau, Casimiro Torreiro (1995) *Historia del cine español*. Madrid: Cátedra.

Leitão Ramos, Jorge (1989) *Diccionàrio do cinema português 1962–1988*. Lisbon: Camino.

Manzanera, María (1992) *El cine de animación en España: Largometrajes 1945–1985*. Murcia: Universidad de Murcia.

Matos-Cruz, José (1989) *Prontuário do cinema português 1896–1989*. Lisbon: Cinemateca Portuguesa.

Méndez Leite, Fernando (1965) *Historia del cine español* (2 vols.). Madrid: Rialp.

Oltra i Costa, Romà (1990) *Seixanta anys de cinema català (1930–1990)*. Barcelona: Institut del Cinema Català.

Passek, Jean Loup (ed.) (1982) *Le cinema Portugais*. Paris: L'equerre.

Pérez Perucha, Julio (ed.) (1997) *Antología crítica del cine español 1906–1995*. Madrid: Cátedra/Filmoteca española.

Pina, Luis de (1986) *História do cinema português*, Lisbon: Publicações Europa-América.

Porter i Moix, Miguel (1992) *Història del cinema a Catalunya (1895–1990)*. Barcelona: Departament de Cultura de la Generalitat de Catalunya.

Rosa, Emilio de la and Hipólito Vivar (1993) *Breve Historia del cine de animación en España*. Teruel: Animateruel.

Schwartz, Ronald (1986) *The Spanish Film Directors, 1950–1985*. Metuchen, NJ and London: Scarecrow Press.

_____ (1991) *The Great Spanish Films: 1950–1990*. Metuchen, NJ and London: Scarecrow Press.

Stone, Rob (2002) *Spanish Cinema*. Harlow: Longman.

Torres, Augusto M. (1989) *Cine español 1896–1988*. Madrid: Ministerio de Cultura.

_____ (2004) *Directores españoles malditos*. Madrid: Huerga y Fierro.

Triana-Toribio, Nuria (2003) *Spanish National Cinema*. London and New York: Routledge.

Vallés Copeiro del Villar, Antonio (1992) *Historia de la política de fomento del cine español*. Valencia: Filmoteca de la Generalitat Valenciana.

HISTORICAL: PRE-1975 CINEMA

Álvarez Berciano, Rosa, and Ramón Sala Noguer (2000) *El cine en la zona nacional (1936–1939)*. Madrid: Ediciones Mensajero.

Amo, Alfonso del (1996) *Catálogo general del cine de la Guerra Civil*. Madrid: Filmoteca Nacional.

António, Lauro (1978) *Cinema e Censura em Portugal: 1926–1974*. Lisbon: Arcádia.

Azevedo, Manuel de (1945) *Ambições e Limites do cinema Português*. Lisbon: Seara Nova.

Azevedo, Cândido (1999) *A censura de Salazar e Marcelo Caetano*. Lisbon: Caminho.

Besas, Peter (1985) *Behind the Spanish Lens: Spanish Cinema under Fascism and Democracy*. Denver: Arden.

Bosch, A. and F. del Rincón (1998) 'Franco and Hollywood, 1939–56', *New Left Review*, 232, 112–27.

Bussière-Perrin, Annie and Perrin Sánchez Biosca (eds) (1997) *Co-textes n. 36. El Verdugo-Le Bourreau de Luis García Berlanga*. Paris: Centre d'Etudes et de Recherches Sociocritiques.

Camporesi, Valeria (1999) 'Imágenes de la televisión en el cine español de los sesenta: Fragmentos de una historia de la representación', *Archivos de la Filmoteca*, 32, 148–62.

Caparrós Lera, José María (1981) *Arte y política en el cine de la República*. Barcelona: Ediciones de la Universidad.

Castro, Antonio (1974) *El cine español en el banquillo*. Valencia: Fernando Torres.

Castro de Paz, José Luis (2002) *Un cinema herido. Los turbios años cuarenta en el cine español (1939–1950)*. Barcelona: Paidós.

Cheikh, Slim Ben (1998) 'Aniki-Bóbó', *L'art du cinéma*, 21–3, 15–21.

Costa, Henrique Alves (1954) *Breve História de Imprensa Cinematográfica Portuguesa*. Porto: Cineclube do Porto.

_____ (1978) *Breve História do Cinema Português: 1896–1962*. Lisbon: Instituto de Cultura e Língua Portuguesa.

Costa, João Bernardo da (1996) *O Cinema Português nunca Existiu*. Lisbon: CTT.

Elena, Alberto (1997) 'La llamada de África: una aproximación al cine colonial español', in Román Gubern (ed.) *Un siglo de cine español*. Madrid: Academia de las Artes y Ciencias Cinematográficas de España.

Equipo cartelera turia (1974) *Cine español: cine de subgéneros*. Valencia: Fernando Torres.

_____ (1975) *Siete trabajos sobre cine español*. Valencia: Fernando Torres.

Estivill Pérez, José (1999) 'La industria española del cine y el impacto de la obligatoriedad del doblaje en 1941', *Hispania* 202, 677–91.

Evans, Peter William (1996) 'Cifesa and authoritarian aesthetics', in Helen Graham and Jo Labanyi (eds) *Spanish Cultural Studies: An Introduction*. Oxford: Oxford University Press, 215–22.

Fanés, Félix (1989) *El cas Cifesa: Vint anys de cine espanyol (1932–1951)*. Valencia: Ediciones de la Filmoteca.

Fernández Cuenca, Carlos (1972) *La guerra de España y el cine* (2 vols.). Madrid: Editora Nacional.

Fonseca, M. S. (1988) 'Aniki-Bóbó (1942)' Lisboa: Textos Cinemateca Portuguesa, Pasta 39.

Franco, Josep (2000) *Cifesa, mite i modernitat. Els anys de la República*. Valencia: L'Eixam.

Freitas, Rodrigues de Freitas (1993) 'Menino milionários na sala de aula', *Presença*, 4, 2, 2–3, Lisbon: Contexto.

Galán, Diego (1974) *Venturas y desventuras de La prima Angélica*. Valencia: Fernando Torres.

González Ballesteros, Teodoro (1981) *Aspectos jurídicos de la censura cinematográfica en españa con especial referencia al período 1936-1977*. Madrid: Editora de la Universidad Complutense de Madrid.

García Escudero, José María (1962) *Cine español*. Madrid: Ediciones Rialp.

González López, Palmira (1987) *Els anys daurats del cinema classic a Barcelona (1906–1923)*. Barcelona: Edicions 62.

González-Medina, José Luis (1997) 'E. G. Maroto's *Canelita en rama* (1943)', *Tesserae: Journal of Iberian and Latin American Studies*, 3, 1, 15–29.

Granja, Paulo Jorge (2001) 'A Comédia à Portuguesa, ou a Máquina de Sonhos a Preto e Branco do Estado Novo', in Luís Reis Torgal (ed.) *O Cinema sob o Olhar de Salazar*. Lisbon: Temas e Debates, 194–233.

Gubern, Román (1976) *Cine español del exilio*. Barcelona: Editorial Lumen.

_____ (1981) *La censura. Función política y ordenamiento jurídico bajo el franquismo (1936–1975)*. Barcelona: Península.

_____ (1991) *Melodrama en el cine español (1930–1960)*. Buenos Aires: Ya Fue Producciones.

Heredero, Carlos F. (1993) *Las huellas del tiempo. Cine español 1951–1961*. Valencia: Ediciones de la Filmoteca.

Heredero, Carlos F. and José Enrique Monterde (2003) *Los 'Nuevos cines' en España. Ilusiones y desencanto de los años sesenta*. Valencia: Institut Valenciá de Cinematografia.

Hernández, Marta (1976) *El aparato cinematográfico español*. Madrid: Akal.

Higginbotham, Virginia (1988) *Spanish Film Under Franco*. Austin: University of Texas Press.

Jolivet, Anne-Marie (2003) *La pantalla subliminal: Marcelino Pan y Vino según Vajda*. Valencia: IVAC.

Labanyi, Jo (1997) 'Race, gender and disavowal in Spanish cinema of the early Franco period: the missionary film and the folkloric musical', *Screen*, 38, 3, 215–31.

_____ (2000) 'Feminizing the nation: women, subordination and subversion in post Civil War Spanish cinema' in Ulrike

Sieglohr (ed.) *Heroines Without Heroes: Reconstructing Female and National Identities in European Cinema, 1941–1951*. London: Cassell, 163–82.

Lomillos, Miguel Ángel (1998) 'El discurso familiar en *El espíritu de la colmena*: La separación de los padres', *Banda Aparte*, 9/10, 57–70.

Lopes, João [n.d.] *Aniki-Bobó*. Lisboa: Secretaria de Estado da Reforma Educativa.

Marías, Miguel (1970) 'El extraño caso de *El extraño viaje*', *Nuestro cine*, 94, 54–6.

Martínez, Josefina (1992) *Los primeros veinticinco años de cine en Madrid 1896–1920*. Madrid: Filmoteca española.

Martínez Bretón, Juan Antonio (1988) *Influencia de la Iglesia católica en la cinematografía española (1951–1962)*. Madrid: Harofarma.

Matos-Cruz, José (1999) *O Cais do Olhar. O cinema português de longa metragem e a ficção muda*. Lisbon: Cinemateca Portuguesa.

Minguet, Joan M. and Julio Pérez Perucha (eds) (1994) *El paso del mudo al sonoro en el cine español* (2 vols). Madrid: AEHC.

Mira, Alberto (1999) 'Al cine por razón de estado: estética y política en *Alba de América*', *Bulletin of Hispanic Studies*, lxxvi, 1, 124–38.

_____ (2000) 'Transformations of the Urban Landscape in Spanish Film Noir', in Myrto Konstantarakos (ed.) *Spaces in European Cinema*. Exeter: Intellect, 124–37.

_____ (2004) 'Spectacular Metaphors: the rhetoric of historical representation in CIFESA epics', in Antonio Lázaro Reboll and Andrew Willis (eds) *Spanish Popular Cinema*. Manchester: Manchester University Press, 60–75.

Moix, Terenci (1993) *Suspiros de España: la copla y el cine de nuestro recuerdo*. Barcelona: Plaza & Janés.

Paulo, Heloisa (2000) 'A colónia portuguesa do Brasil e o cinema no Estado Novo', in Luís Reis Torgal (ed.) *O cinema sob o olhar de Salazar*. Coimbra: Círculo de Leitores, 117–37.

Pérez Bowie, José Antonio (1996) *Materiales para un sueño: en torno a la recepción del cine en España (1896–1936)*. Salamanca: Librería Cervantes.

Pérez Merinero, Carlos and David Pérez Merinero (1975) *Del cinema como arma de clase: Antología de nuestro cinema (1932–1935)*. Valencia: Fernando Torres.

Pina, Luis de (1977) *A aventura do cinema português*. Lisbon: Editorial Vega.

_____ (1994) *A comédia clásica portuguesa*. A Corunha: Xunta de Galicia.

Pozo Arenas, Santiago (1984) *La industria del cine en España. Legislación y aspectos económicos (1896–1970)*. Barcelona: Publicacions i edicions de la Universitat de Barcelona.

Rey, Florián (2003) *La aldea maldita. Guión original 1942*. La Almunia de Doña Godina: Asociación Cultural 'Florián Rey'.

Ribeiro, M. Félix (1983) *Filmes, Figuras e factos da história do cinema português 1896–1949*. Lisboa: Cinemateca Portuguesa.

Roberts, Stephen (1999) 'In Search of a New Spanish Realism: Bardem's *Calle Mayor*', in Peter William Evans (ed.) *Spanish Cinema: The Auteurist Tradition*. Oxford: Oxford University Press, 19–37.

Roma Torres, António (1974) *Cinema Português. Ano Gulbenkian*. Lisbon: Zero.

Ros, Xon de (1999) 'Innocence Lost: Sound and Silence in *El espíritu de la colmena*', *Bulletin of Hispanic Studies*, lxxvi, 27-37.

Sánchez-Biosca, Vicente (1997) 'Un realismo a la española: *El verdugo* entre humor negro y modernidad', *Contextes*, 36, 79-90.

Sánchez Vidal, Agustín (1994) *Los Jimeno y los orígenes del cine en Zaragoza*. Zaragoza: Patronato Municipal de las Artes Escénicas y de la Imagen.

Seguin, Jean-Claude (ed.) (1977) *Le Bourreau (El Verdugo)*, *L'Avant-Scène Cinéma*, 465.

Smith, Paul Julian (1999) 'Between Metaphysics and Scienticism: Rehistoricising Victor Erice's *El espíritu de la colmena* (1973)', in Peter William Evans (ed.) *Spanish Cinema: The Auteurist Tradition*. Oxford and New York: Oxford University Press, 93–114.

Taléns, Jenaro (1986) *El ojo tachado. Lectura de "Un chien andalou" de Luis Buñuel*. Madrid: Cátedra.

Torgal, Luís Reis (ed.) (2000) *O cinema Sob o Olhar de Salazar*. Lisbon: Autores e temas e debates.

Tubau, Iván (1983) *Crítica cinematográfica Española: Bazin contra Aristarco, la gran controversia de los años sesenta.* Barcelona: Edicions de la Universitat.

Various Authors (1973) *The Portuguese Cinema.* Lisbon: Office of the Secretary of State for Information and Tourism.

____ (1985) *Cinema Novo Portugues (1960–1974).* Lisbon: Cinemateca Portuguesa.

Vernon, Katherine (1986) 'Reviewing the Spanish Civil War: Franco's film *Raza*', *Film and History*, 16, 2, 26–34.

Woods, Eva (2004) 'From Rags to Riches: the ideology of stardom in folkloric musical comedy films of the late 1930s and 1940s', in Antonio Lázaro Reboll and Andrew Willis (eds) *Spanish Popular Cinema.* Manchester: Manchester University Press.

HISTORICAL: POST-1975 CINEMA

Aguilar, Carlos (ed.) (1999) *Cine fantástico y de terror español.* San Sebastián: Donostia Kultura.

Arroyo, José (1992) '*La ley del deseo*: a gay seduction', in Richard Dyer and Ginnette Vincendeau (eds) *European Popular Cinema.* London: Routledge.

Ballesteros, Isolina (2001) *Cine (ins)urgente: textos fílmicos y contextos culturales de la españa postfranquista.* Madrid: Editorial Fundamentos.

Bassa, Joan and Ramón Freixas (1996) *Expediente S: Softcore, sexploitation, cine S.* Barcelona: Futura Ediciones.

Bouquet, Stéphane (1997) 'Histoire de fantômes portugais', *Cahiers du cinéma*, 514, June, 72–3.

Caparrós Lera, José María (1992) *El cine español de la democracia: de la muerte de Franco al cambio socialista (1975–1989).* Barcelona: Editorial Anthropos.

D'Lugo, Marvin (1991) 'Catalan Cinema: Historical Experience and Cinematic Practice', *Quarterly Review of Film and Video*, 13, 1–3, 131–47.

Deleyto, Celestino (1994) 'Rewriting Spain: Metafiction and Intertextuality in Saura's *Carmen*', in *Journal of Hispanic Research*, 2, 237–47.

____ (1999) 'Motherland: Space, Femininity and Spanishness in *Jamón jamón*', in Peter William Evans (ed.) *Spanish Cinema: The Auteurist Tradition.* Oxford: Oxford University Press.

Desothale, Duleep C. (1992) 'Sex, Society and Oppression in post-Franco Cinema: The Homosexual Statement in Iglesia's *El Diputado*', in George Cabello-Castellet, Juame Marti-Olivella and Guy H. Wood (eds) *Cine-Lit*: *Essays on Peninsular Film and Fiction.* Corvallis, OR.: Portland State University; Oregon State University; Reed College.

Deveny, Thomas G. (1993) *Cain On Screen: Contemporary Spanish Cinema.* London: Scarecrow Press.

Evans, Peter William (1982) '*El espíritu de la colmena*: The Monster, The Place of the Father, and Growing Up in the Dictatorship', *Vida Hispánica*, 31, 3.

____ (1996) *Women on the Verge of a Nervous Breakdown.* London: British Film Institute.

____ (1999) '*Furtivos*: My Mother, My Lover', in Peter William Evans (ed.) *Spanish Cinema: The Auteurist Tradition.* Oxford: Oxford University Press.

Ferreira, Manuel Cintra (1998) '*Viagem ao Princípio do Mundo* (1997)', Lisboa: Cinemateca Portuguesa. Ciclo Manoel de Oliveira: 90 Anos, 18 December, Textos Cinemateca Portuguesa, Pasta 59.

Fiddian, Robin and Peter William Evans (1989) *Challenges to Authority: Fiction and Film in Contemporary Spain.* London: Tamesis.

Fouz Fernández, Santiago and Christopher G. Perriam (2000) 'Beyond Almodóvar: Homosexuality in Spanish Cinema of the 1990s', in David Alderson and Linda Anderson (eds) *Territories of Desire in Queer Culture: Refiguring Contemporary Boundaries.* Manchester: Manchester University Press.

Gamez-Fuentes, M.-J. (2001) 'Maternidad y ausencia en *Cría cuervos* de Carlos Saura', *Hispanic Research Journal*, 2, 2, 153–64.

García Fernández, Emilio C. (1992) *El cine español contemporáneo.* Barcelona: CILEH.

Godsland, Shelley and Anne M. White (eds) (2002) *Cultura Popular: Studies in Spanish and Latin American Popular Culture.* Bern: Peter Lang.

Gómez Benítez de Castro, Ramiro (1998) *La producción cinematográfica española de la transición a la democracia (1976–1986).* Bilbao: Mensajero.

Heredero, Carlos F. (1997) *Espejo de miradas: Entrevistas con nuevos directores del cine español de los años noventa.*

Alcalá de Henares: Festival de cine de Alcalá de Henares.

Heredero, Carlos F. and Antonio Santamarina (2002) *Semillas de futuro. Cine Español 1990–2001*. Madrid: Academia de Artes y Ciencias Cinematográficas de España.

Hopewell, John (1986) *Out of the Past: Spanish Cinema after Franco*. London: British Film Institute.

Hurtado, José A. and Francisco Picó (eds) *Escritos sobre cine español 1973–1987*. Valencia: Filmoteca de la Generalitat Valenciana.

Insdorf, Annette (1983) 'Soñar con tus ojos: Carlos Saura's Melodic Cinema', *Quarterly Review of Film Studies*, 8, 2, 49–53.

Jordan, Barry (2000a) 'How Spanish is it? Spanish Cinema and National Identity', in Barry Jordan and Rikki Morgan Tamosunas (eds) *Contemporary Spanish Cultural Studies*. London: Arnold, 68–78.

____ (2000b) 'The Spanish Film Industry in the 1980s and 1990s', in Barry Jordan and Rikki Morgan Tamosunas (eds) *Contemporary Spanish Cultural Studies*. London: Arnold, 179–92.

____ (2003) 'Spain's new cinema of the 1990s: Santiago Segura and the Torrente phenomenon', *New Cinemas: Journal of Contemporary Film*, 1, 3, 191–207.

Jordan, Barry and Rikki Morgan-Tamosunas (1998) *Contemporary Spanish Cinema*. Manchester: Manchester University Press.

Kinder, Marsha (1993) *Blood Cinema: The Reconstruction of National Identity in Spain*. Berkeley, Los Angeles, London: University of California Press.

____ (1997) *Refiguring Spain: Cinema/Media/Representation*. Durham: Duke University Press.

Lázaro Reboll, Antonio (2002) 'Exploitation in the Cinema of Klimovsky and Franco', in Shelley Godsland and Anne M. White (eds) *Cultura Popular: Studies in Spanish and Latin American Popular Culture*. Bern: Peter Lang, 83–95.

Llorens, Antonio (1988) *El cine negro español*. Valladolid: Semana de Cine de Valladolid.

López Echevarrieta, Alberto (1984) *El cine vasco: De ayer a hoy*. Bilbao: Mensajero.

Losilla, Carlos (1989) 'Legislación, industria y escritura', in José A. Hurtado and Francisco Picó (eds) *Escritos sobre cine español 1973–1987*. Valencia: Filmoteca de la Generalitat Valenciana, 33–43.

Martín Márquez, Susan (1999) *Feminist Discourse and Spanish Cinema: Sight Unseen*. Oxford and New York: Oxford University Press.

Martínez Torres, Augusto (2002) 'Prólogo', in *Arrebato. Guión cinematográfico de Iván Zulueta*. Madrid: Ocho y medio, 7–21.

Martin-Márquez, Susan L. (1991) 'La óptica del optimismo en *Los santos inocentes* de Mario Camus', *Romance Languages Annual*, 3, 500–4.

____ (1999) *Feminist Discourse and Spanish Cinema: Sight Unseen*. Oxford: Oxford University Press.

Molina Foix, Vicente (1985) 'La guerra detrás de la ventana', *Revista de Occidente*, 53, 112–18.

____ (1977) *New Cinema in Spain*. London: British Film Institute.

Monterde, José Enrique (1989) 'El cine histórico durante la transición política', in José A. Hurtado and Francisco Picó (eds) *Escritos sobre cine español 1973–1987*. Valencia: Filmoteca de la Generalitat Valenciana, 45–63.

____ (1993) *Veinte años de cine español (1973–1992)*. Barcelona: Paidós.

Moreiras, Cristina (2002) *Cultura herida: Literatura y cine en la España democrática*. Madrid: Ediciones Libertarias.

Pavlović, Tatjana (2003) *Despotic Bodies and Transgressive Bodies: Spanish Culture from Francisco Franco to Jesús Franco*. New York: SUNY Press.

Pérez Niño, Tomás and Joe Krankol (1996) *España erótica: historia del cine clasificado S*. Madrid: T&B Ediciones.

Rabalska, Carmen (2000) 'A canon of disability: deformity, illness and transgression in Spanish Cinema', *Tesserae: International Journal of Iberian Studies*, 13, 1, 25–33.

Sánchez-Biosca, Vicente (1995) *Una cultura de la fragmentación. Pastiche, relato y cuerpo en el cine y la televisión*, Valencia: Ediciones de la Filmoteca.

Santaolalla, Isabel (1999) 'Julio Medem's *Vacas* (1991): historicising the forest', in Peter William Evans (ed.) *Spanish Cinema: The Auteurist Tradition*. Oxford: Oxford University Press, 310–24.

Santoro, Patricia J. (1996) *Novel into Film: The Case of La familia de Pascual Duarte and Los santos inocentes*. Newark: University of Delaware Press; London: Associated University Presses.

Saz, S. M. (1996) 'Society and Film in Post-Franco Spain: *Confessions of a Congressman* as a Quirk of Tradition', *Cinefocus*, 4, 64–71.

Smith, Paul Julian (1992) *Laws of Desire: Questions of Homosexuality in Spanish Writing and Film 1960–1990*. Oxford: Clarendon.

____ (1996)*Vision Machines: Cinema, Literature and Sexuality in Spain and Cuba*. London: Verso.

____ (2003) *Contemporary Spanish Culture: TV, Fashion, Art and Film*. Cambridge: Polity.

Stone, Rob (2001) 'Through a Glass Darkly: Ritual and Transition in Carlos Saura's *Bodas de sangre*', in *Bulletin of Hispanic Studies*, 78, 199–215.

Taléns, Jenaro and Santos Zunzunegui (eds) (1998) *Modes of Representation in Spanish Cinema*. Minneapolis: University of Minnesota Press.

Tjersland, Todd (2003) 'Cinema of the doomed: the tragic horror of Paul Naschy', in Steven Jay Schneider (ed.) *Fear Without Frontiers: Horror Cinema Across the Globe*. Godalming: FAB Press.

Trenzado Romero, Manuel (1999) *Cultura de masas y cambio político: el cine español de la transición*. Madrid: Siglo XXI.

Van-Liew, Maria (1998) '*Cría cuervos*: The Process of Self-Discovery', in George Cabello-Castellet, Juame Marti-Olivella and Guy H. Wood (eds) *Cine-Lit, III: Essays on Hispanic Film and Fiction*. Corvallis, OR: Oregon State University.

Varela, Antonio (1989) 'Reading and Viewing *Los santos inocentes*', *Romance Languages Annual*, 1, 639–44.

Vernon, Katherine (1993) 'Melodrama Against Itself: Pedro Almodóvar's *What Have I Done to Deserve This?*', *Film Quarterly*, 46, 3, 28–40.

____ (1998) 'Scripting a social imaginary: Hollywood in/and Spanish cinema', in Jenaro Taléns and Santos Zunzunegui (eds) *Modes of Representation in Spanish Cinema*. Minneapolis: University of Minnesota Press, 319–29.

Vernon, Katherine and Barbara Morris (eds) (1995) *Post-Franco, Postmodern: The Films of Pedro Almodóvar*. London: Greenwood.

Willis, Andrew (2004) 'From the margins to the mainstream: trends in recent Spanish horror cinema', in Antonio Lázaro Reboll and Andrew Willis (eds) *Spanish Popular Cinema*. Manchester: Manchester University Press, 237–49.

Zunzunegui, Santos (1986) *El cine en el País Vasco: La aventura de una cinematografía periférica*. Murcia: Filmoteca Regional de Murcia.

FILMMAKERS

Aguilar, Carlos (1992) *El cine español en sus intérpretes*, Madrid: Verdoux.

Aguilar, Carlos, Dolores Devesa, Francisco Llinás, Carlos Losilla, José Luis Marqués, Alicia Potes, Casimiro Torreiro (1996) *Conocer a Eloy de la Iglesia*. San Sebastian: Filmoteca Vasca.

Alfaya, Javier (1971) *Sara Montiel*. Barcelona: Dopesa.

Allinson, Mark (2001) *A Spanish Labyrinth: The Films of Pedro Almodóvar*. London and New York: I. B. Tauris.

Angulo, Jesús and Francisco Llinás (eds) (1993) *Fernando Fernán Gómez. El hombre que quiso ser Jackie Cooper*. San Sebastián: Patronato Municipal de Cultura.

Angulo, Jesús, Carlos Fernández Heredero and José Luis Rebordinos (1995) *Javier Aguirresarobe. En el umbral de la oscuridad*. San Sebastián: Filmoteca Vasca/Fundación Caja Vital Kutxa.

Aranda, J. Fransisco (1976) *Luis Buñuel: A Critical Biography*. New York: Da Capo.

Arocena, Carmen (1996) *Víctor Erice*. Madrid: Cátedra.

Balbo, Lucas, Peter Blumenstock and Christian Kessler (eds) (1993) *Obsession: The Films of Jess Franco*. Berlin: Graf Haufer und Frank Trebbin.

Bardem, Juan Antonio (2002) *Y todavía sigue*. Barcelona: Ediciones B.

Barreira, Domingo F. (1968) *Biografía de Florián Rey*. Madrid: ASDREC.

Brasó, Enrique (2002) *Conversaciones con Fernando Fernán Gómez*. Madrid: Espasa-Calpe.

Buñuel, Luis (1983) *My Last Breath*. London: Flamingo.

Cañeque, Carlos and Maite Grani (1993) *¡Bienvenido Míster Berlanga!* Barcelona: Destino.

Caparrós Lera, José María (ed.) (1992) *Memoria de dos pioneros: Fructuós Gelabert/Francisco Elías*. Madrid: Cineclub

Orbis/Círculo de escritores cinematográficos.

Cerón Gómez, Juan Francisco (1998) *El cine de Juan Antonio Bardem*. Murcia: Universidad de Murcia.

Costa, João Bénard da (1981) 'O cinema é um vício', in *Manoel de Oliveira*. Lisboa: Cinemateca Portuguesa, 5–12.

D'Allones, Fabrice Revault (ed.) (2004) *Pour João César Monteiro*. Paris: Yellow Now.

D'Lugo, Marvin (1983) 'Carlos Saura: Constructive Imagination in Post-Franco Cinema', *Quarterly Review of Film Studies*, 8, 2, 35–47.

____ (1991a) *Carlos Saura: The Practice of Seeing*. Princeton, NJ: Princeton University Press.

____ (1991b) 'Almodóvar's City of Desire', *Quarterly Review of Film and Video*, 13, 4, 47–66.

De Baecque, Antoine and Parsi Jacques (1999) *Conversas com Manoel de Oliveira*, trans. Henrique Cunha. Porto: Campos das Letras.

Donapetry, María (2000) 'Conversación con Sara Montiel: "Trátame de tú"', *Arizona Journal of Hispanic Cultural Studies*, 4, 225–33.

Edwards, Gwynne (1995) *Indecent Exposures: Buñuel, Saura, Erice and Almodóvar*. London: Marion Boyars.

Espelt, Ramón (1989) *Mirada al Món de Bigas Luna*. Barcelona: Laertes.

Evans, Peter William (1995) *The Films of Luis Buñuel: Subjectivity and Desire*. Oxford: Clarendon.

Evans, Peter William and Isabel Santaolalla (eds) (2004) *Luis Buñuel: New Readings*. London: British Film Institute.

Fernández Cuenca, Carlos (1962) *Recuerdo y presencia de Florián Rey*. San Sebastián: X Festival Internacional de Cine.

____ (1972) *Segundo de Chomón (maestro de la fantasía y de la técnica)*. Madrid: Editora Nacional.

Frugone, Juan Carlos (1984) *Oficio de gente humilde... Mario Camus*. Valladolid: Semana Internacional de Cine de Valladolid.

Frugone, Juan Carlos (1987) *Rafael Azcona: Atrapados por la vida*. Valladolid: Semana Internacional de Cine.

Galán, Diego and Antonio Llorens (1984) *Fernando Fernán Gómez: apasionadas andanzas de un señor muy pelirrojo*, Valencia: Fernando Torres/Fundación Municipal de Cine.

García de León, Maria Antonia and Teresa Maldonado (1989) *Pedro Almodóvar, la otra España cañí*. Ciudad Real: Biblioteca de Autores Manchegos.

Gómez Rufo, Antonio (1990) *Berlanga contra el poder y la gloria*. Madrid: Temas de Hoy.

Guarner, José Luis and Peter Besas (1985) *El inquietante cine de Vicente Aranda*. Madrid: Imagfic.

Gubern, Román (1994) *Benito Perojo. Pionerismo y supervivencia*. Madrid: Ediciones de la Filmoteca.

Heredero, Carlos F. (1989), *Iván Zulueta. La vanguardia frente al espejo*, Alcalá de Henares: Festival de cine de Alcalá de Henares.

____ (1990) *José Luis Borau: Teoría y práctica de un cineasta*. Madrid: Filmoteca Española.

____ (1994) *El lenguaje de la luz. Entrevistas con directores de fotografía del cine español*. Alcalá de Henares: Festival de Cine.

____ (1999) *20 nuevos directores del cine español*. Madrid: Alianza Editorial.

Hernández Les, Juan (1986) *El cine de Elías Querejeta, un productor singular*. Bilbao: Ediciones Mensajero.

Hernández Les, Juan and Manuel Hidalgo (1981) *El último austrohúngaro: Conversaciones con Berlanga*. Barcelona: Anagrama.

Hidalgo, Manuel (1981) *Carlos Saura*. Madrid: Ediciones JC.

Kinder, Marsha (1987) 'Pleasure and the New Spanish Mentality: A Conversation with Pedro Almodóvar', *Film Quarterly*, Fall, 33–44.

Lasa, Joan Francesc de (1988) *El món de Fructuós Gelabert*. Barcelona: Departament de Cultura de la Generalitat de Catalunya.

Lardeau, Yann, Philippe Tancelin and Jacques Parsi (eds) (1988) *Manoel de Oliveira*. París: Dis, Voir.

Lizalde, E. (1962) *Juan Antonio Bardem*. México: UNAM.

Llinás, Francisco (1989) *Directores de fotografía del cine español*. Madrid: Filmoteca Española.

____ (1995) *José Antonio Nieves Conde*. Valladolid: Semana Internacional de Cine.

Llopis, Juan Manuel (1988) *Juan Piqueras: El "Delluc" español*. Valencia: Filmoteca de la Generalitat Valenciana.

Marías, Miguel (1990) *Manuel Mur Oti. Las raíces del Drama*. Lisboa: Cinemateca Portuguesa/Filmoteca Española.

Matos-Cruz, José de (ed.) (1982) *J. Leitão de Barros*. Lisbon: Cinemateca Portuguesa.

_____ (1983) *António Lopes Ribeiro*. Lisbon: Cinemateca Portuguesa.

_____ (1984) *Jorge Brum do Canto*. Lisbon: Cinemateca Portuguesa.

Méndez Leite, Fernando (1987) *La noche de Juan Antonio Bardem*. Madrid: ICAA.

Molina, Jacinto (1997) *Paul Naschy. Memorias de un hombre lobo*, Madrid: Alberto Santos.

Monteiro, João César (1973) 'Minha certidão', in *Revista & ETC* (30 April), 8.

Montiel, Sara (2001) *Memorias: Vivir es un placer*. Barcelona: Plaza y Janés.

Oliveira, Manoel de (2001) 'Parole et cinéma', *Cahiers du cinéma*, 555, March, 42–5.

Parsi, Jacques (2002) *Manoel de Oliveira*. Paris: Fundação Calouste Gulbenkian.

Payán, Miguel Juan and José Luis López (1985) *Manuel Gutiérrez Aragón*. Madrid: Ediciones JC.

Pérez Millán, Juan Antonio (1992) *Pilar Miró. Directora de cine*. Valladolid: Semana Internacional de Cine.

Pérez Perucha, Julio (ed.) (1984) *El cine de José Isbert*. Valencia: Ayuntamiento de Valencia.

Porter i Moix, Miquel (1985) *Adrià Gual i el cinema primitiu a Catalunya*. Barcelona: Universitat de Barcelona.

Riambau, Esteve (ed.) (1990) *Antes del Apocalipsis. El cine de Marco Ferreri*. Valencia/Madrid: Mostra del Mediterrani/ Cátedra.

Romaguera i Ramio, Joaquim (1987) *Un mecenatge cinematogràfic. Vida i obra de Delmiro de Caralt*. Barcelona: Fundació Mediterrànea.

Sánchez Vidal, Agustín (1984) *Luis Buñuel: Obra cinematográfica*. Madrid: Ediciones JC.

_____ (1987) *José Luis Borau: Una panorámica*. Teruel: Instituto de estudios turolenses.

_____ (1988) *El cine de Carlos Saura*. Zaragoza: Caja de Ahorros de la Inmaculada.

_____ (1990) *Borau*. Zaragoza: Caja de Ahorros de la Inmaculada.

_____ (1991) *El cine de Florián Rey*. Zaragoza: Caja de Ahorros de la Inmaculada.

_____ (1992) *El cine de Segundo de Chomón*. Zaragoza: Caja de Ahorros de la Inmaculada.

Smith, Paul Julian (2000) *Desire Unlimited*, 2nd edn. London: Verso.

Soria, Florentino, Domingo F. Barreira and Carlos Fernández Cuenca (1963) *Redescubrimiento de Florián Rey*. Madrid: Filmoteca Nacional de España.

Triana-Toribio, Nuria (2000) 'Ana Mariscal: Franco's disavowed star', in Ulrike Sieglohr (ed.) *Heroines Without Heroes: Reconstructing Female and National Identities in European Cinema, 1945–51*. London: Cassell, 185–95.

Vidal, Nuria (1988) *El cine de Pedro Almodóvar*. Madrid: Instituto de la Cinematografía y las Artes Visuales.

Willem, Linda (2003) *Carlos Saura Interviews*. Jackson: University Press of Mississippi.

Yarza, Alejandro (1999) *Un caníbal en Madrid. La sensibilidad camp y el reciclaje de la historia en el cine de Pedro Almodóvar*. Madrid: Libertarias.

INDEX